THE SPIRIT OF SOLZHENITSYN

The spirit of Solzhenitsyn

Olivier Clément

SEARCH PRESS · LONDON

BARNES & NOBLE BOOKS • NEW YORK

(a division of Harper & Row Publishers, Inc.)

Translated by Sarah Fawcett and Paul Burns

This book is published for the first time in
English translation in 1976 by Search Press
Limited, 2-10 Jerdan Place, London SW6 5PT
Great Britain
ISBN: 0 85532 372 8

Published in the USA 1977 by
Harper & Row Publishers, Inc
Barnes & Nobles Import Division
ISBN: 0 06 491212 4

Published originally in French under the title
L'esprit de Soljenitsyne by Editions Stock of
Paris (with the exception of Part six, which is
published here for the first time)
© 1974, Editions Stock
Part Six © 1976, Olivier Clément

Printed in Great Britain by Billing & Sons Ltd.
Guildford, London and Worcester

Contents

Prefatory note

Citations and references in this translation usually concern the standard English translations of Solzhenitsyn's works. Whenever the author wishes to make a point not brought out by the existing translation, the version is made from the original, and in that case the standard 'complete works' published by Possev of Frankfurt am Main (*Polnoe Sobranie Solshinenij*, six vols., 1969-70) and the Russian editions of *August 1914* and other works published by the YMCA Press of Paris, are relevant. Generally, however, the existing translations are referred to, and, to make reference easier for the majority of readers, they are cited in the paperback editions, for which page references are given throughout the text. That is not the case, as yet, for *Lenin in Zürich*, the cased edition of which is referred to here. The abbreviations used in references are as follows:

A14	*August 1914*	(Penguin Books, 1974)
CW	*Cancer Ward*	(Penguin Books, 1971)
CiW	*Candle in the Wind*	(Bodley Head, 1974)
FC	*First Circle*	(Collins/Fontana, 1970)
GA 1	*Gulag Archipelago* 1 (Parts I & II)	(Collins/Fontana, 1974)
GA 2	*Gulag Archipelago* 2 (Parts III & IV)	(Collins/Fontana, 1976)
LGI	*Love-Girl and the Innocent*	(Penguin Books, 1971)
LID	*One Day in the Life of Ivan Denisovich*	(Penguin Books, 1963)
LtP	*Letter to the Patriarch*	
LTS	*Letter to Three Students*	
LZ	*Lenin in Zürich*	(Bodley Head, 1976)
NPL	*Nobel Prize Lecture*	(Stenvalley Press, 1973; Bodley Head, 1973)

SPP   *Stories and Prose Poems*   (Penguin Books, 1973)
      (contains 'Matryona's House', 'For the Good of the
      Cause', 'An Incident at Krechetovka Station', and others)

All quotations from CiW, LtP and NPL are direct translations, and are not taken from the published editions given above.

The translators and publishers are grateful to Victor Gollancz Ltd, The Bodley Head Ltd and William Collins & Sons Ltd, for permission to quote from copyright translations.

Details of literary-critical, biographical and other commentaries on Solzhenitsyn's life and works referred to in the text are given at the point of first reference.

PART ONE

The closeness of death

1   The camp, war, cancer

The age of nihilism and the discipline of history

Solzhenitsyn speaks for every man; he speaks for *us*. The struggle he is involved in is not strictly speaking political: it is prophetic. It is a struggle about the restoration to a great nation − or rather to its citizens, to Russian men and women, because ultimately only persons exist − of their freedom to speak one word of truth to other men and women, and to hear the same from them. One word of *pravda* − an admirable term when divested, as it is by Solzhenitsyn, of all overtones of populist enthusiasm, and a comprehensive one signifying both justice and truth: not ideological or even conceptual truth, but the truth proper to living beings and to things, and the justice that respects all life in order that it may develop.

Solzhenitsyn is not content merely to claim this word for himself; he proclaims it, and for us all. Apropos of his short play, *Candle in the Wind*, he has said that he wanted to deal with the human problems of our industrial societies, regardless of whether they are capitalist or socialist and we hear in it too the particular 'sound of the jackboot' that is familiar enough to us on this side of the planet.

Solzhenitsyn's universality stems from his deep involvement in the contemporary history of his own country; of Eastern Europe, which, in our time, has experienced 'such profound upheavals', while Western Europe, since the end of the Second World War, has learnt the perils of stagnation − and to such an extent that a 'considerable part of her literature will not survive'.

After 1914, or rather after the cataclysmic trench warfare of 1916, Europe entered on a period of nihilism. Millions of men experienced in their flesh that death of God, that chilling of the heart of which isolated prophets, like Nietzsche, had a foreboding in the last century. The countless instances of physical death served to bring to light the spiritual suffocation that had hitherto passed unnoticed. Of course there were some contemplatives — read, for example, the letters Teilhard de Chardin wrote from the trenches — who recognised in the new Good Friday the impress of the risen Christ, who enters the hell created by his own absence in order to raise the dead there to life. Such men of vision, however, are few and far between.

Spiritual renaissances, precisely because they respect individual freedom, take time. Once the corpses on the banks of the Somme had become part of the geological strata, the majority fled like frightened animals from the nihilism which grew daily more apparent. Some, in the very history that was crushing them, searched for an absolute that would justify the holocaust. The old pagan divinities of the earth and of the race came back into vogue, along with the old biblical heresy of the liberating disaster which would assure the reign of the just for a thousand years. War became variously the ordeal of the race or the 'dawn' of the revolution. The search for the whole in the part produced totalitarianism. It was the age of ideologies. The Second World War witnessed the mutual destruction of the idols. In Western Europe, once Berlin, the focal point of that pseudo-integration, had been destroyed and divided (a destruction and division which powerfully expressed the destruction of meaning and the division of the soul), the masses veered towards the other form of nihilism: trying to forget it all by searching for happiness in the here and now, unconcerned for the meaning of life. That was rich soil for the flowers of rebellion and irony cultivated by intellectuals.

In Eastern Europe, on the other hand, after the Second World War there was a sudden upsurge of secular messianism, combined, during the last years of Stalin, with an extreme display of mass terror. Today, when industrial production and consumption are increasing in Russia, sporadic threats, to the extent even of very specific forms of 'psychiatric' treatment, are made in an attempt to reduce free spirits to silence. The historical experience of evil is still alive in that part of the world.

But that experience, destructive as it is for so many, has a terrible fecundity of its own in the case of the few. It is as though history were leading millions of men along a narrow route from which there is no escape: that of the most severe discipline. When men no longer offer sacrifice total wars break out. Wherever the monasteries disappear, there prison doors open to innocent people, and some of them become monks. If a civilization based on the pursuit of happiness knows no discipline but the dedication of sportsmen, weekend yogis and the devotees of the latest slimming craze, a tragic sequence of events imposes on the 'living dead' a new deprivation, fasting, continence and what is known in Orthodox spirituality as the *memento mori*. And yet, in the light of this spirituality, which has fashioned the hidden sensibility of the Russian, the *memento mori* can become a kind of resurrection.

Those who have passed through these 'disciplines of history' recognize one another by signs imperceptible to others: a word; a mere inflection of the voice; or even, in a moment of silence, a particular movement of the lips. These people would 'smile while others were serious or while others laughed' (*Cancer Ward*, p. 508): a reversal of the norm which points to an initiation. They have gone through the experience of *metanoia*: not in the sense of repentance (as it is so frequently translated), but of man's 'return' to his most profound inner depths. They can be said to have known the cross and bear the marks of 'Christ on their feet and palms' (*ibid.*, p. 508).

Henceforth 'all literary tragedies are just laughable compared with the ones [they] live through' (*ibid.*, p. 512) and when, like Solzhenitsyn, they themselves write, it is no longer literature, but a word sealed by silence and by death. 'The essential link between death and the word is obvious, but it is still unexpressed,' wrote Heidegger (*Unterwegs zur Sprache [On the Way to Language]*, 1959, p. 215). Heidegger probably means that everything that falls within the ambit of speech is doomed to die. But with Solzhenitsyn the relationship between the word and death is reversed: the word remains beyond death, it is a risen word.

As one who really knows, Solzhenitsyn is content to concentrate on one day or a very restricted number of days (the *triduum* of *The First Circle*). Those who know, know not scientifically or through gnosis — the science of the invisible — but through the delicate awareness and tenderness that are the characteristics of holiness. The writer speaks here of a 'symphonic novel' in the great Russian literary tradition, a symphony — not without its dissonances — of human existences brought together through the communication of their inner worlds or their juxtaposition as individuals. It is as if, passing from initiation to initiation, he had reached that Christian depth where no man is separated from another except of his own will; where, in the 'Homo maximus', to use the phrase of Nicholas of Cusa, there is truly only a single humanity — not of likeness but of identity — 'one man' in the irreducible variety of faces.

One day, or three days, then, on which one embarks knowing nothing, only to find oneself immediately in the familiar yet unfamiliar realm of persons, and in a world which, in order to exist in them and between them, becomes a genuine symbol. Thus *One Day in the Life of Ivan Denisovich* begins without any preamble to the sound of hammer blows against a rail in the camp, under the windows of the barrack hut. (*One Day in the Life of Ivan Denisovich*, p. 7). Everything is said accurately, concisely, and with a terrible truth. Sometimes there is a touch of irony which draws our attention to *dipsychia* as it is understood in terms of New Testament asceticism: the divided heart, in which unity has been destroyed by untruth. Irony emerges from the obvious contradiction between what is said and what is done. When in hospital, Rusanov declares in the course of a discussion with his fellow patients that 'people live by their ideological principles and by the interests of their society' (CW, p. 117); upon which, snatching the chicken leg that had just been passed to him 'he bit off the sweetest piece of gristle in the joint'. But ultimately everything is described with boundless compassion. At the end of the single day, as of the three, there is no conclusion, as there is with the other Russian novelists: good might still come of it all; and *The Gulag Archipelago* invites Russia — and the Socialist movement — to undergo a kind of collective *metanoia* which would enable them to create something truly living.

One theme of justice and compassion recalls the expression of Christ the Pantocrator as he is represented in the cupolas of Orthodox churches. The title Pantocrator indicates power to bestow both existence and meaning; but because the measure of the power was the Cross, this expression is the light by which man judges himself and achieves reconciliation; he achieves it in so far as he judges himself, acknowledging the hell for which he is responsible, and into which he has dragged others. The mercy of the Pantocrator comes by way of justice. Solzhenitsyn is merciless towards the executioners and their accomplices.

The camp

The crucial experience in the life of Alexander Solzhenitsyn was the labour camps. In his Nobel Prize address he presents himself as spokesman for all who died in those camps, supported perhaps, by their intercession: 'Accompanied as I am by the shadows of the fallen, bowing my head as I stand aside to let those other men who deserve this honour before me take their place on this platform' (*Nobel Prize Lecture*, p. 8). To go into 'an invisible country . . . not in the geography books . . . or the history books, this . . . famous country where ninety-nine men weep while one man laughs' (*The Love Girl and the Innocent*, p. 42), is simply to *descend into hell*. The idea reappears clearly in the very title of *The First Circle* with its reference to Dante and the first circle of hell. Only the first, because that centre for scientific research manned by detainees and ironically nicknamed by them 'the madhouse' (*sharashka*), contained in spite of its isolation an elementary degree of comfort, which was indispensable to the success of intellectual work. Ever downwards stretch other circles, prisons into which human beings are crammed at the point of suffocation, the labour camps of the North where the common laws reign supreme, and where inhuman regulations and starvation rations leave a man almost without defence against the rigours of the climate. Even more than of Dante, one finds oneself thinking of the definition of hell given by a monk in the Egyptian desert: 'There it is not possible to see anyone face to face' (Abbot Macarius, *Apophthegms*, p. 181). After his arrest, Innokenty Volodin comments that 'one prisoner must never be allowed to encounter another, never be allowed to draw comfort or support from the look in his eyes' (*The First Circle*, p. 659). Even in the *sharashka* 'people in one room knew nothing of those in the next, close neighbours were ignorant of each other' (*ibid*., p. 241). Arrest, interrogation, condemnation, the heavy tread of boots, the barking of ever-vigilant dogs, all help to make slavery second nature, until it seeps 'into the marrow of their bones' (*ibid*., p. 495). As long as a man remains alive 'there is always something which can be taken from him' (*ibid*., p. 661) – creating the endless spiral of fear 'which slowly destroys him as a human being' (*ibid*., p. 661).

Separation and anguish are two essentials of the human condition which prison and the labour camp bring out into the open. 'Tell me,' asks one of the prisoners, 'what is it that makes people in the camps so horrible? Were they different outside? Or were they just lying low?' (LGI, p. 57). To 'cover up' what is horrible is one of the aims, perhaps, of all civilization – what does the God of the ever-present Genesis do, after the first lie and the first crime, but shield us from the horror with the 'garments of hide' proper to maturity? But, illumined by a light that originates elsewhere, the horror can become resurrection. It forces a choice on one, the only choice that counts, laying bare death and freedom at once. To survive, man can become a beast, but an unnatural beast because he is without innocence, and therefore less than a beast. He is an object, in fact, which remains just about conscious. The Russian words for thing and for demon come from the same root.

But a man can choose to remain a man. That very determination, when he is deprived of everything, including perhaps life itself, bears witness to his transcendence. The choice is a clear one between what Gregory of Nyssa and Nicholas Berdyaev, meditating on the symbols of the Apocalypse, called 'the beast in man' and 'the divine in man'. Man is not neutral. He is an ever-moving point between the darkness of hell and the light which comes from 'something else even more brilliant' than the sun (FC, p. 313). Some 'becomes wolves'. But Ivan Denisovich and those like him are not wolves, even after eight years in the camp. Descending into hell, they remain in control. It can even become willed: as by Gleb Nerzhin who, ever since his adolescence, has burned with a passion for truth. He wants to understand his country, the age he lives in, the enigma of history, the mystery of man. Some instinct tells him that the principal witnesses are in the camps, which is why the *sharashka* is not enough for him. He rejects the possibility of staying there: 'I was given the chance, but somehow I've got used to the idea of leaving now. As the proverb says, "You won't drown in the sea — but you may drown in a puddle!" I want to try swimming in the sea for a bit' (*ibid.*, p. 683). He leaves for the uncharted forests and swamps where death is a continual threat, but where also are those who *know*.

This choice transforms the trial into a form of asceticism, in the strong sense of a struggle for the essential. Underneath it is a question not of death but of another life. It is the 'second wind' of the imprisoned Innokenty, 'just as an athlete's aching body revives to a new access of freshness and strength' (*ibid.*, p. 667). It is the fearlessness of men 'who have lost everything they ever had'. 'The prospects that awaited them were the taiga and the tundra . . . kicking and shoving, starvation rations . . . No fate on earth could possibly be worse. Yet they were at peace with themselves . . .' (*ibid.*, p. 699). Then the prisoner who has accepted the loss of everything, even his own life, can stand up to the powerful of the earth: 'When you've robbed a man of *everything* he's no longer in your power — he's free again' (*ibid.*, p. 107).

The death-resurrection cipher

Among men who have been renewed — even reborn — in this way there is a brotherhood of initiates, a bond of personal friendship between individuals, far stronger than the individual virtues of those whose remains hang from the barbed wire. Here Solzhenitsyn draws on the images of Europe's spiritual heritage. The ark first of all, to describe the *sharashka* on a Sunday evening, silent and cut off from everything. Those who prowl through the 'ark of the charachka' during these almost timeless moments '[are] detached and their thoughts can wander unfettered . . . A spirit of manly friendship and philosophy hovered over the sail-shaped vault of the ceiling' (*ibid.*, pp. 357-8). Moving over the waters of history, the ark is symbolic of an 'enclosed world' where each individual, from his awareness of the 'centre towards which all lines converge', finds peace and union with others. A mathematician of genius who has taken his place in the ark, can argue humorously that only a prisoner is capable of knowing his immortal soul. The free are tossed about too much by the waves, too wanting in the severity that comes with distance.

To this biblical image, Solzhenitsyn adds the great symbols of western occultism that were rediscovered during the Russian renaissance at the beginning of the century and invested with new meaning. During the first two decades of the twentieth century, in fact, before Marxism became – not with the Revolution, but with Lenin's New Economic Policy – an exclusive ideology, some extremely thorough research was carried out in Russia, and particularly in St Petersburg, into the Middle Ages in the West. Solzhenitsyn has that work in mind in *August 1914* as he shapes the personality of the brilliant and profound young historian, Andozevskaya, who speaks with such insight about mediaeval spirituality. In the same perspective, writers and philosophers of this period so rich in poetry and in spiritual discovery were glad to appeal from the West of technology and rationality (which degenerate so quickly into a scientifically based ideology) to the West of the spirit, to the imagery of light, the Quest of the Holy Grail, and the Rosicrucians – or rather, since that secret society, the objectives and achievements of which remained highly ambiguous, was not well-known, to the symbolism of the Rose and the Cross. The Rose which is born of the Cross in a transfiguring dawn seemed a happy corrective to the somewhat one-sided stress of Latin Catholicism on Good Friday and the Man of Sorrows. In 1913, after a visit to Brittany, Alexander Blok wrote his Celtic drama, *The Rose and the Cross*, and Nicholas Berdyaev, after travelling in Italy, particularly in Tuscany and Umbria, wrote his first major work, *The Meaning of the Creative Act*, which concludes: 'It is in the mystery of the Sacrifice that the Rose of universal life will flower again.' This throws light on the frequent references made by Solzhenitsyn in *The First Circle* to the Knights of the Grail and the Rosicrucians.

But it is the overall spiritual structures that have to be considered if one is to grasp the meaning of *The First Circle* as a great epic of captivity. At the heart of the *triduum* is Christmas Day on its western date of December 25th, and we are made aware of this in the third of eighty-seven chapters. The Orthodox Christmas — in Russia at least, where the Church, as if immobilized by the Revolution, has remained faithful to the Julian Calendar — is celebrated thirteen days later on January 7th. To clarify his narrative, Solzhenitsyn has chosen the western date of Christmas. He has selected the western symbols of the Grail and the Rose-Cross to describe the terrible initiation of the camps. He deliberately places Russia in the historical context of Europe. The agonized questioning within the Russian consciousness in the last century — Where do we belong? In Europe or Asia? — seemed settled by Stalinism in favour of Asia. Psychologically speaking, it was as if Russia had regressed to the Tartar period, retaining of its Byzantine heritage only the counterfeit traits of an East without transcendence, and attributing to Marx, that Prometheus among philosophers, 'a quality which linked him with the bearded genius who stood guard over the palaces of ancient Babylon' (Kostas Papaioannou, *Marx et les marxistes*, Paris 1972, p. 21). 'And we too are Asians,' Stalin had said to the Japanese plenipotentiary who had come to sign a non-aggression pact which, curiously enough, was respected until the last weeks of the war. Above all, the period of the action of *The First Circle* saw the victory of Communism in China, a victory impatiently observed and discussed by Lev Rubin, the only sincere Communist in the *sharashka*. In an interview in 1973, Solzhenitsyn stated unequivocally that 'the overall objective of the present suppression of thought in our country might well be described as a process of Sinization, the realization of the Chinese ideal — had that ideal not been manifested among us already during the Thirties' (*Le Monde*, 29.8.73, p. 4). He is not concerned here to pass a hasty judgment on the economic and social aspects of the Chinese experience, or to reject outright those Asian forms of spirituality in which he evinces the greatest interest. Sinization suggests to him a history in which the fundamental spirituality of the individual has not yet been revealed, because the dynamic power of the Cross and Resurrection has not yet broken into the closed circle of history (in the Marxist sense), or of an impersonal cosmos (as understood in the ancient traditions of the Far East). Yet precisely this cipher of death-resurrection is the clue to the meaning of the action of *The First Circle*. It takes place at Christmas time, and December 25th that year, 1949, falls on a Sunday. Now, to the Orthodox way of seeing things — an aspect Russian spirituality has stressed — the Nativity is first of all 'Kenosis' (*ekenosen*, says St Paul: God 'emptied himself' of his divine condition), as voluntary self-abasement, voluntary descent into the sin-bound abyss of human existence. 'You came down to earth to save Adam, and when you did not find him there, O Master, you went even into hell to seek him out,' says a liturgical text. The swaddling clothes of the divine Child presage the winding sheet in which the dead Man will be wrapped for three days while he descends willingly to the spiritual locus of ultimate separation. 'The light shines in the darkness' says the prologue to John's Gospel, and darkness signifies the hell in which humanity is capable of imprisoning itself.

Meanwhile Sunday, in the same tradition, is identified with Easter, as its Russian name makes clear: *voskressenie*, means resurrection. The linking of Christmas, understood as a voluntary descent into the hell of mankind, with Sunday, understood as Easter, produces the cipher 'death-resurrection'. The prisoners' dormitory has been set up in the former chapel of this manor house become prison – or more specifically in the dome which once hung over the altar, with a curve which leads the eye back to the now invisible centre where the death-resurrection of Christ used to be realized. The altar has disappeared now, just as the altar and church of St Nicetas the Martyr, on the hill where the rivers meet at the secret heart of Moscow, have been destroyed; and the chapters about this church, about its beauty and its spoliation, probably constitute for core of the 'initiation' theme in *The First Circle*. From now on the altar is invisible; it is the conscience of the individual: it is also the heavenly altar described in the Apocalypse, where by a strange paradox, the Lamb triumphs that was slain before the foundation of the world.

What is more, it is undoubtedly in a movement of death-resurrection that the two principal characters in the narrative are involved – Gleb Nerzhin and Innokenty Volodin. The former, having renewed his pledge of fidelity to his wife, whom he sees briefly at the heart of the absence, finds himself being more faithful than ever to his own vocation – to discover the truth of history, the truth about man, and the men of truth. He leaves the *sharashka* for a camp in the Great North Territory. Invested with the fearlessness of those who have lost everything, he descends, voluntarily, into the lower circles of hell. The other is a young diplomat with a brilliant career ahead of him; at liberty – unheard-of privilege for a Russian – to move about the world, refined and pleasure-loving in his life style, he runs the risk of arrest, of social and even physical annihilation, in order to save an elderly scientist, a man possessed not merely of knowledge, but of wisdom, who is threatened by a worse fate. He too goes down voluntarily into hell and

17

experiences the 'second wind'.

The name Innokenty speaks for itself. There is scarcely a work by Solzhenitsyn in which one does not find an 'innocent' whether in the sense of a very humble, good person who is accommodating like Matryona and gets pushed around; or of a man of integrity and righteous indignation, crushed by the machinery of 'this world', like Nemov, in the play with the doubly characteristic title, *The Love-Girl and the Innocent*; or else of the man who is carried away by his passion for justice and truth and who renounces everything for their sake, like Innokenty Volodin in *The First Circle*. Russian spirituality is obsessed by this theme of the innocent man who takes the 'folly of the Cross' and the topsy-turvy world of the Beatitudes so seriously that he seems dangerously mad to the Pharisees — the Church yesterday, the State today. As for Gleb Nerzhin, he is called after St Gleb, one of those who according to a characteristically Russian expression of holiness, 'voluntarily underwent passion'. At the time when Russia was ruled from Kiev, Prince Gleb was assassinated on the instructions of his elder brother. He died regretting the light of day and his fine young body, but forgiving his murderers, thus identifying himself with Christ who willingly bore his sufferings in order to set men free from the bondage of evil. Interpreted as the holiness of 'those who voluntarily suffer passion', this theme of the innocent reveals the presence of the Innocent One who submits to death so as to bring life to those who kill him.

War

Total war also constitutes a journey through hell, and was for Solzhenitsyn the fundamental experience that made it possible for him to brave the experience of the camps: '[children's voices] was a sound that soldiers and prisoners never heard' (FC, p. 241). Solzhenitsyn has given an incomparable description of the 'material war' which was started by the Germans in 1914 but would only reach its climax on the Russian front during the Second World War, so that it is legitimate to regard some of the descriptions in *August 1914* as taken from personal experience.

This war, from the time the bombardments with heavy artillery begin, assumes the proportions of a genuine cosmic disaster. Even during the daytime there is no sun, no morning, 'only black, smoking, reeking night'. 'The body of the earth', where the men seek refuge, as in a material womb, is 'disembowelled', violated (*August 1914*, pp. 254-5).

They 'key symbol' of *August 1914* is without doubt the wild billowing of flames, in contrast to the spiritual peace for which Solzhenitsyn uses the image of still waters. Two 'cinematographic poems' illumine this powerful historical novel with a sinister whirlwind of flame. The first (*ibid.*, pp. 257-8) describes how a windmill caught in the cross-fire, is completely engulfed in flames; although there is not a breath of wind, the burning sails begin to turn, moved by the warm currents of air: 'The ribs of the red-gold blades are turning mysteriously/LIKE A CATHERINE WHEEL,/And the wheel crashes/to the ground in a shower/of blazing fragments' (*ibid.*, pp. 257-8).

The other poem (*ibid.*, pp. 321-6) describes the wheel which in the midst of the confusion gets detached from a wagon and 'rolls on, lit up by fire . . . crushing everything' as it goes.

Spontaneously, and probably according to the laws of what, in contrast to the *imaginary*, subjective and unreal, is the imaginative — the profound inner truth of beings and things — Solzhenitsyn re-introduces here a number of ancient and universal symbols. He has known them by experience to the point of death: the eastern symbol of the 'fire sermon' which Buddha preached at Gayasisa, in a meaning-less circle men burn, they burn with the fire of desire, decline, suffering and death. 'The tongue (symbol of the aboriginal lie) is on fire', says Buddha, 'and life is the wheel of becoming'; and St James in his epistle (3.6) says almost the same thing: 'the tongue is a flame . . . it sets fire to the whole wheel of creation', the wheel whose turning is accelerated and rendered more apparent by war. One thinks too, this time in a purely biblical context, of the movement of the flaming sword which barred man's way at the entrance of paradise; and of the 'signs in heaven' of the *Book of Revelation*.

By the same token, war, like the camp, is a time of judgment, of winnowing the purification, 'gigantic flails were lashing up and down their ranks to thresh the souls out of their bodies like little grains' (A14, p. 256). Solzhenitsyn does not approve of war, he merely notes it as a fact. The central character of *August 14*, Colonel Vorotyntsev, considers Russia's entry into the war a mistake, although he is aware that the destiny of his country is at stake. Solzhenitsyn observes that war, like imprisonment or a serious illness, uproots a man from the coherent, familiar world of daily life, which is threatened by somno-lence, giving him the chance to be 'purified by the nearness of death' (FC, p. 351). The soldier, and not just the career officer, but the ad hoc leader too — some scenes in *August 1914*, when the organization of the encircles armies breaks down, remind one of guerrilla warfare —

discovers there a terrible responsibility, a moment of truth, this moment now, not later, for later is too late: 'Die Höchste Zeit' ('high time') mutters Vorotyntsev, mechanically repeating part of a poem by Goethe he had learnt at school (A14, p. 327). The young are matured by trials which brings into their faces prematurely the ruddiness of manhood (IKS, p. 101), for there exists a virginal (in the sense of complete all-embracing integrity) connivance between sacrifice and adolescence: 'He was suffused by that subline, youthful glow of virginal suffering' (A14, p. 359) writes Solzhenitsyn of a very young wounded sub-lieutenant. He also observes that there are warriors who are so by vocation, often enough career officers, and that they find in combat that 'lightness' which, in the symbolic world of Solzhenitsyn, comes to a man in a moment of surrender and self-transcendence. Vorotyntsev has left his headquarters in order to see the action for himself and to take part in it. Throughout his exhausting journey towards greater inner unity, when threatened by the worst, he 'feels stealing over him the happiness familiar to all who go to war'. 'The sleepless night caused [him] no distress at all, neither did the prospect of another long day's journey ahead of him . . . There was also the possibility of death . . . Not only was he not downcast! he felt an uplifting sense of buoyancy, and whether he slept or not, ate or not, was a matter of no significance to him' (*ibid*., p. 128).

Total war, and notably the First World War, has been emptied of any 'erotic' exultation by the sheer mass of techniques and the patience demanded of men. Brice Parain, who took part in it, has said that it demanded of the soldiers holiness rather than heroism. Or rather, a heroism which endures, and which is no longer carried along on a heady wave of enthusiasm, becomes a kind of holiness, and here the experience of the world wars in this century converges with that of the labour camps. The patient endurance, intensified by the unavoidable presence of death, so many men brought up against the *memento mori* of the ancient ascetics who contemplated the skull, which foretold their own future, this is what also made 'disinterested friendship' possible between one man and another: 'My friends, my comrades in arms, men of integrity . . .', dreams the author nostalgically, when, long afterwards in a forest where the front had become fixed forever, he comes across an old bucket which he describes tenderly. This bucket had ended up by serving as a stopper for the pipe of the little iron stove which heated the dugout: 'It had glowed hellishly hot, men had warmed their hands by it, you could light a cigarette on it and toast bread in front of it' (*Stories and Prose Poems*, p. 199). It was thus that 'in roadside ditches, waterlogged trenches, and amid the remains of burnt out houses men learned the meaning of true friendship' (FC, p. 351).

When, flattened against the side of the trench in the great din of the bombardment, the colonel-in-chief and the peasant mobilized the day before dare at last to open their eyes, it is as if 'they were the only two living creatures on earth', and the look they exchange, because it is perhaps the last, is transfigured by a radiant 'humanity' (A14, p. 255).

War can generate a compassion in which all self-complacency is destroyed. In *August 1914* the enigmatic nurse Tanya, picked out in the darkness of the hospital by the light from a flame that is at once internal and external, like someone in a painting by Georges de la Tour, suddenly sees the tragedy through which she matured — betrayal by the man she loved — as 'quite a minor affliction', in comparison with the overwhelming immensity of 'the pain of others' (*ibid.*, p. 546).

Cancer

The third experience which lends weight to what Solzhenitsyn has to say is cancer. Here there is no more east or west but simply the day-to-day life of our urban and industrial societies, but suddenly struck by disaster. Nearly everyone is afraid of cancer. It is one of the great terrors of our century, at least in the economically 'developed' societies. Even in the symbolism of its name it is like a modern form of demonic possession; a particularly eloquent expression of our mortal condition. In one of his short stories, Dürrenmatt has compared modern life to a well-oiled machine in which it takes a breakdown to produce anything out of the ordinary. Cancer is one of the most formidable breakdowns. Possibly, too, it owes something of its symbolic meaning (which is pointed up by its reality) to the fact that it consists in first the isolation and then the monstrous proliferation of one cell, which appears to reject the wisdom and order of being as inscribed in the human organism.

Here is the pattern that has by now become familiar: hell, death, ascetical process of detachment, signs of resurrection. Solzhenitsyn describes 'the sick who have become caught up in the infernal circle of cancer'. Rusanov, deprived by sickness of power and security, feels 'vulnerable and humbled in the dust' by the shooting pain caused by the tumour in his neck and even more by the lavatories which, in spite of their being cleaned frequently, always present 'fresh signs of vomit, blood and other filth' (CW, p. 215). Some patients, although remaining in a body that is still alive, give the impression that they have already crossed the threshold between life and death. 'Your blood still circulates and your stomach digests, while you yourself have gone through the whole psychological preparation for death — and lived through death itself. Everything around you, you see as if from the grave' (*ibid*., p. 41) — a condition, according to this patient, like that of trees and stones, in so far as they are grasped not in their beauty and inner exultation, but, after the manner of Sartre, as opaque 'en soi', in-themselves, closed in on their own nothingness. Each one is immured in his own private and essentially incommunicable world of suffering, or else in a state of inert detachment. And yet here too some kind of *metanoia* is called for. Suffering becomes judgment, and Rusanov, a member of the secret police whose every word, every gesture was a potential threat, a cause for fear, discovers himself before a tribunal of his own — there between his hair and his collar-bone. And before it he has no merits and no defence.

The sick person can then learn 'the wisdom of making sacrifices. The skill of shaking off inessentials' (*ibid*., p. 161). The first Christians thought that after death the soul, if it had not succeeded in finding detachment, integrity and peace here on earth, must go through a kind of spiritual customs, the last frontier where the forces of hatred and separation levy what is theirs, so that gradually stripped of its false identity, its dead skin, the soul becomes itself once more, rediscovers its original transparency. In reality, of course, the whole man crosses this frontier where the uncompromising customs officers await him. Sickness, in particular, while it can degrade a man, drive him mad, identify him with the suffering, disintegrating part of his organism, can also be a school of detachment. And the 'cipher' death-resurrection returns with all its force: quite clear if spiritually the cure is complete (whether or not the body is involved), ambiguous if it simply means a return to the life-cum-death we call 'life'. Resurrection of Christ or resurrection of Lazarus. In any case, a 'sign' in the Johannine sense: 'When I arrived I was a dead man. Now I'm alive' (*ibid*., p. 61).

2 Death and the meaning of life

What do men live by?

The threefold experience of war, imprisonment and cancer in the destiny of Solzhenitsyn radically calls in question the attitude of mind prevailing in the so-called 'developed' societies — though spiritually, perhaps, they are underdeveloped — which he sums up in two propositions: 'We only live once, we will never die.' In *Candle in the Wind*, which takes place in the West — a ' western representative of civilization on this planet' the latest wife of a celebrated musician, who, although elderly, is satisfied with life and rich in money and connections, is a young woman full of energy and passion, who, as she switches her attention from a passing affair to putting an article together in feverish haste for the 'cultural' pages of a national paper, exclaims to herself: 'I love life . . . I love it whatever it brings! After all, you only have one! One mustn't let anything pass one by.' In *Cancer Ward* the crucial question is there to confront both patients and nurses in the form of the title of a story by Tolstoy that is being passed round the hospital: 'What is it that makes men live?' The only person who, facing death and yet seeing beyond it, could have given the answer is a wise old Uzbek, but significantly he does not speak Russian: he stands apart in an 'east' which has as yet experienced neither the *angst* of the West nor the full Christian revelation of the person. Others give superficial answers, without ever thinking of death. 'What do men live on?' is how they understand it. Why, 'by their pay, that's what', suggests one. 'Their rations, uniform and supplies,' says another, who is almost cured (CW, p. 116). Dyoma, a studious youth, conditioned by his schooling with its moralizing approach and its confidence in the unlimited possibilities of science explains conscientiously that men need 'in the first place, air. Then — water. Then food' (*ibid*., p. 116).

Yefrem Podduyev, an unscrupulous man who for years relied heedlessly on his own powerful physique but who is forced now by a cancer of the throat to give some thought to ultimate realities — it is he who puts the question to the others — reminds himself that once upon a time he would have answered like Dyoma, only he would have said vodka instead of water. Everything had always been crystal clear for him (*ibid*., p. 162). A man is what he does, what he earns — or at least, that is true as long as he has not got cancer or some other fatal disease, as long as he does not know that he is going to die. Then, if he doesn't deceive himself, as most do, he discovers he has neglected 'something'. He asks *the* question.

The most thoughtful give as their answer the two great values on which Soviet morality, like other secular moral systems in the past, is based: work and the fatherland. As for Rusanov, an influential member of the 'new ruling class', busily muching a leg of chicken — a luxury food in the Soviet Union during the Fifties — he affirms that 'people live by their ideological principles and by the interests of their society' (*ibid.*, p. 117).

But work, the fatherland, the interests of society are all to do with 'the group', according to Kostoglotov, the principal character in the novel, a rough, detached man who has known war, the labour camps, the limbo of a life sentence, and is now coping honestly with his cancer. As he points out, work, the fatherland, an ideology, are all aspects of man's collective existence, this side of death: 'That's right. But only while he's alive. When the time comes to die we release him from the collective. He may be a member, but he has to die alone' (*ibid.*, p. 152). Death strips a man of everything that is less than himself. He is cast naked into the world and he goes naked into the hands of the undertaker. Job knew the truth of this.

Besides, how many really live according to an ideology? Once the first enthusiasm of the revolution is spent, once the war has been won, who would not prefer to throw in his lot with young Asya, who, when Dyoma asks her the inexorable question in her turn exclaims: 'What for? What do you mean? for love, of course . . . What is there in life except love?' (*ibid.*, p. 145) — and what she means is the sensual pleasure of young bodies. That is what the medical student, Zoya, and her friends think, 'that everything possible should be grabbed from life immediately and with both hands' (*ibid.*, p. 171), and they find it quite easy to play at love. After the dreadful massacres of the war what remains is the humble truth of human bodies, surrender to the dynamic life of the race, the 'little eternities of pleasure', as Kierkegaard called them, until it gradually becomes mechanical, and then there is encroaching boredom, secret panic at the thought of age and death, the aging aping the ways of the young, man sliding back into nothingness, man in a state of nothingness with the testicles of a monkey. In all this abandonment to the life force of the race, in which man is but the puppet of his own desires, the only specific sign of humanity is voluntary sterility: the successive abortions of the dynamic Dzhum's little friends in *Candle in the Wind* — and Maurice, as obliging as a father as he is as a husband, is always there to foot the bill; the systematic refusal of Innokenty Volodin and his wife to have a child while they lead the existence of young gods, wrapped up in their own passion in a world ravaged by war: 'You only live once' they tell each other, so let us grasp everything life has to offer, but not children, 'because children are tyrants — they feed on you, they suck you dry, without making any sacrifice in return . . .' (FC, p. 415).

Of course, really to love a child, or to try to do so, is to give of oneself without expecting anything in return but joy, as the Gospel says, that a man has been born into the world. No need to look for war, imprisonment, cancer. Right there is a kind of death to self in order than another might live. But why bother to pass life on if life has no meaning? When it is passed on on that basis, the child in effect becomes an idol. For his parents he becomes the be-all and the end-all of everything; as far as they are concerned he constitutes the meaning of life — a pathetic substitute for the absolute. And idolatry transforms the instinct for life into an ever-expanding void: either the idolized child is compelled to reject, 'kill' the parents who live off his life; or else the couple reject the child, slaughter the embryo, block off his chance of 'happiness' with the seal of sterility.

The most elementary experiences of 'the beast in man' are multiplied in a far more effective and general way than in the hell of the camps. Kostoglotov makes a bitter resumé of this 'philosophy of life': ' "Oh, life is so good! Life . . . I love you. Life is for happiness!" What profound sentiments. Any animal can say as much' (CW, p. 152). As far as he is concerned, death is a self-evident fact. But Rusanov, though fatally ill — and every man, after all, is born to die — cries: 'We mustn't talk about death! We mustn't even remind anyone of it' (ibid., p. 152).

A metaphysical neurosis

Our present civilization, which makes an absolute of this life mingled with death, this life on the near side of death, systematically conjures the latter away. Intellectuals like Innokenty Volodin, in the days before his awareness became conscious, are happy to quote Epicurus' dictum that death does not concern us: 'While we are here, death is absent, and when death comes we are gone' (FC, p. 599). But such a judgment is naive and over hasty: nothingness haunts us continually, it destroys the beloved faces around us, and even if science were to manage at some stage to confer on us a kind of 'a-mortality', death would still be there between us and within us as a state of isolation and failure — the failure to reach the true eternity. That is why 'developed' societies, in order to forget death, get the dead off their hands as quickly as possible. Everyone knows what happens in the United States — and is happening progressively in Scandinavia and Germany (possibly the Reformation encouraged the process by forbidding prayers for the dead). As soon as a man breathes his last, the corpse is removed, only to be glimpsed for one last time, in a brief, mundane — this-worldly — ceremony, once it has been carefully powdered and prepared so that one can forget it is a dead man. In the Soviet Union, too, the process is a rapid one — a simple lorry will do — and the desire to forget is manifest in the neglected condition of some cemeteries: 'Many of our cemeteries are shamefully neglected . . . There are no fences, the cattle wander over them, and pigs dig them up' (CW, p. 153). Often, too, 'they just roll them flat with bulldozers, to build sports-grounds and parks' (SPP, p. 205). In any case, Solzhenitsyn remarks, people no longer visit the cemeteries. When someone dies, they avoid writing or visiting the family: 'We do not know what to say about death' (*ibid*.). Marxism has nothing to say about death and Marx himself only mentioned it once — in the *Writings of 1844*, a youthful work — to recall the fact that a given individual is only a certain generic being, and as such mortal — a formula which gets rid of the person at little or no cost. But I cannot see that the younger generation in the West looks at it any differently. Perhaps we have simply adopted a compromise formula: in France we bring chrysanthemums to the dead once a year on the day dedicated to them — which demotes and assimilates the feast of All Saints the day before, which opens up a vista of hope. All Saints has become just another All Souls day, and the god who presides over these hopeless procedures, which the young openly resent, is a god, not of the living, but of the dead. As the 'old doctor' remarks, in *Cancer Ward*: 'Modern man is helpless when confronted with death, . . . he has no weapon to meet it with' (CW, p. 481).

Our age is familiar with every kind of excess and, with the desperate tenacity of the impotent, abuses the delicate machinery of the human body. The mass media have exposed the mysteries of the embryo, shown the moments of intercourse and birth in detail, less to give new cause for wonder than to provide the blasé with the cheap thrill of profanation. Obscenity is plastered over our screens not so much as a manifestation of irrepressible vitality à la Rabelais, but rather as the background to a despairing nihilism, in spite of the feeble excuse that it is social criticism — for it is always somebody else's fault. Some people, who experience their own skin as an unbearable limitation, something too specifically personal, try, through drug-induced ecstatic states, to prolong the striptease in a kind of intranudity, to lose themselves in an intracellular existence. In Stockholm, at the Museum of Modern Art, you can enter through the sex organs (called 'The Gate of Life') into a colossal Venus whose nakedness you are at leisure to contemplate from within; it is hollow. *Today only death is immodest, only death is obscene* – because we will never die.

To continue the striptease beyond the skin – the dream of sadists – is to discover the guts and finally the skeleton, symbol of the very death one is fleeing. Sickness, too, effects this terrible process of de-nudation. When Dontsova, the cancer specialist, is struck in her turn, abandoning all the familiar anatomical formulae, she comes to know her body as 'a helpless sack crammed with organs – organs which might at any moment be seized with pain and cry out' (CW, p. 478). The coherent, habitable area defined by men – we only live once, we will never die – is shattered by the appearance of some unexpected horror, and for the fastidious soul the horror is daily. Then everything familiar 'is turned inside out. Her body was, as before, composed of parts she knew well, but the whole was unknown and frightening' (*ibid.*, p. 478).

One might ask whether suppression of the mystery of death and hence of the mystery of meaning – which does not get rid of death, but rather encompasses it – does not produce in 'advanced' peoples a real *metaphysical neurosis* which, moreover, like the sadism of intra-nudity, in order to escape from death, multiplies it, concentrates on the skeleton, so that men will never be able to fall asleep entirely happy.

Formerly, as Solzhenitsyn recalls, the cemetery was 'venerated'. On Sunday people used to walk slowly up and down among the graves, and priests would swing their censers, as if to defy the corruption of the flesh, with this sacred sweet-smelling fire to bear witness. 'Loud and clear', priest and people would acclaim the victory that had been won forever over death, for all men and for each of us individually 'It set your heart at rest; it allayed the painful fears of inevitable death. It was almost as though the dead were smiling from under their grey mounds. "It's all right . . . Don't be afraid" ' (SPP, p. 205). Here one needs to think of the austere beauty of some of the Russian cemeteries: no grave-stones, none of the marble edifices which satisfy the family pride of the Latin races; just simple mounds, in fact, which grow green and put forth flowers in the spring because people have taken the trouble to sow them with seeds, and over each a wooden cross keeps guard, itself protected by a little pointed canopy. At Easter time especially people come to put coloured eggs among the new grown flowers as seeds of resurrection and to sing the hymn of victory: 'Christ is risen from the dead! By his death he has overcome death. To those who dwell in the place of darkness he has given life!' Thus the Cross took on its true meaning as the sign and presence of the Living One, the way to fulness: not our present life-in-death but eternal life. Frequently someone takes the trouble to put a little wooden bench by the grave, so that people can pause for a moment in silent communion. And the corpse itself is not hurried away: it is venerated as a relic, people keep vigil by it, singing psalms; it is brought to the church with the face uncovered so that they can kiss the cold lips, and finally it is committed to 'everlasting memory' of God who alone knows the true name of each man, and discloses the face that is the image of his own.

For Christians who appreciate the unique value of each person, the Office for the Dead underlines the unnatural character of death in order to move out with greater joy than ever in the hope of personal resurrection. For primitive peoples, susceptible to the mystery of the unknown, death is simply an absorption into the immensity of Being. This is true of some shamanist peoples of the Great North Territory known to Solzhenitsyn, as it is of the Russian peasants who live in contact with them and in whom Christian hope is combined with the almost vegetal peace of these Asiatics. On the banks of the Kama all submit to death *peacefully*. They prepare calmly for it in advance, 'deciding who should have the mare, who the foal, who the coat and who the boots. And they depart easily, as if they were just moving into a new house' (CW, p. 111). That is why the metaphysical neurosis which settles in the human organism through cancer is unknown to them: 'None of them got it' (*ibid*., p. 111).

A civilization that treats death as an obscenity and seeks at all costs to block this gateway to the transcendent seems to fall prey to every kind of cancer. One of the most pathetic characters in *Cancer Ward* is Shulubin. In order to survive and save his family, this intellectual stooped to anything during the Stalinist period; he lied, burned the books that revealed the truth to him, took part in cruel inquisitions; but he could not silence his conscience, and his long years of suffering, hideously incarnated now in a cancer of the rectum, at last give him the right to speak the truth again. Speaking to Kostoglotov, and quoting Francis Bacon, he mentions the 'idols of the market place': in the broad sense of a commerce that leads to alienation between men (*ibid.*,

p. 468). Cancer can be produced in society by ideological totalitarianism, in which case the camps would be the cancerous growth in the social body; or by the idolization of life — life on this side of death and therefore tormented by the presence of death — a form of idolatry which stimulates a 'monstrous commerce' in the proper sense of the word. And technological man, who seems unable to use his gifts for anything but increasing consumption, becomes the cancer which destroys the cosmic organism.

A closed world. 'circle of evil, circle of wickedness', present also in the outwardly brutal and stifling aspects of nature — what the religious philosopher Sergei Trubetskoy called its 'nocturnal' aspect: in the thick layer of frost on the window panes of the barrack hut where Ivan Denisovich and his companions sleep; in the thick gray mist into which the northern sun disappears prematurely during the prison winter, or else in the sullen grey sky above the *sharashka*, 'a dirty tarpaulin awning cast over the earth' which blocks all reaching for the heights, for immensity: 'It gave no impression of height' (FC, p. 562). For above all the idols, remarks Shulubin — and as a sign of the nothingness they represent — 'there is spread a low-hanging cloud of fear, covered with grey clouds' (CW, p. 468), in contrast to the open skies, to the atmosphere of the heights, to the furthest heavens through which the clouds pass like souls.

The first and last days of creation

Solzhenitsyn insists that the death he refers to, when he talks about death in war, in prison or in hospital, is a spiritual death. When a prisoner is released or a patient cured, however thrilling the experience might be, it is an unreliable sign, an invitation to avoid self-deception. If it fails to go deeper and establish itself through healing at the spiritual level, it remains arid and earthbound, like those rivers, in the central Asian steppes, that never reach the sea. In *The First Circle*, through the personality and destiny of Shchagov, Solzhenitsyn makes a dispassionate study of the 'adaptation' of a war veteran, and of how what was the ethic of the warrior deteriorates into nostalgia, a sentimental recollection of a moment of exaltation, like drinking a glass of wine: and even more is this true when the enthusiasm is expressed by former newspaper correspondents, historians of the conflict rather than active participants in it (FC, p. 453). Solzhenitsyn has also asked — and all the questioning of a Nerzhin or a Shulubin revolves round this point

— why a revolution which aimed to set men free, to alter the quality of life, in fact produced a tyranny. The answer is that such a revolution fails to gauge the extent either of man's depravity or of his nobility; it can neither control the one nor open up any reliable way to the other.

In this perspective, the final chapters of *Cancer Ward* constitute the shattering account of a downfall, of a growing inconsistency between the symbol and what it symbolizes, until the moment when a death-resurrection, freely internalized, destroys the gap. While convalescing (although he is enjoying no more than a remission), Kostoglotov has a direct apprehension of the original integrity of the world, of 'the first day of creation'. Celestial signs are given him: a rose-pink sky at dawn (rose-pink is almost always a dawn colour for Solzhenitsyn), soft clouds, tapering like the prow of a ship, 'the diving vessel of the moon' (CW, p. 536) — the luminous deeps of heaven (the primary meaning of the word God in the Indo-European languages), and the fluid movement of the moon which symbolizes the tranquil spirit. It is not simply the dawn of day, or even the springtime dawn of the year, which overwhelms covalescents, but the very 'dawn of creation' and all the joy of birth, or rebirth. 'It was the morning of creation. The world had been created anew for one reason only, to be given back the Oleg. "Go out and live!" it seemed to say' (*ibid*., p. 518).

Already some days before, watching the leafing trees, he had felt 'it was all so . . . good' (*ibid*., p. 461), as if the blessing of being that runs like a refrain through Genesis were resounding within him: 'And God saw that it was good.' All is miracle, Oleg knows that he will 'meet something unexpected at every step' (*ibid*., p. 529). The journey of this man reborn, like the long journey described in the Bible, goes from a garden to a city. From the park that surrounds the hospital, Oleg reaches the Uzbek city where men are living who seem set free from bad times and in tune with creation. At the centre of this eastern city, like the tree of life in the garden at the beginning or the city at the end, the magnificent apricot tree of Pamir is in flower and the world is flowering with it: 'Something pink and transparent. It looked like a puff-dandelion, only it was six metres in diameter, a rosy, weightless balloon' (*ibid*., p. 523). Here the earth grows lighter, fuller, penetrated and transfigured by light and air. Oleg 'gazed and gazed through this pink miracle' (*ibid*.). 'He'd planned on finding a miracle and he'd found one' (*ibid*., p. 524). Joy puts a rhythm into his steps as he moves into the European city. Joy awaits him; joy is his future. Standing in front of a shelf of medicinal herbs in a chemist's he marvels at the wisdom that bears the world; and in a photographer's window it is the faces that move him (*ibid*., p. 528).

But in order to preserve this joy intact a certain respect is needed; he would have to 'stop making mistakes' (*ibid*., p. 522). As it is the *shashlik* and wine bring contemplation down to the level of sensual possession. Then the department store turns out to be the 'cursed temple' of the 'idols of the market place' (*ibid*., p. 536). Narcissism and sexual acquisitiveness reign supreme there, masquerading as the refinements of civilization. The mirror of Narcissus and Don Juan has been set up, the mirror in which one only sees oneself — introversion, non-revelation. 'He should have been content to contemplate the flowering apricot tree', and to internalize the image of the soft sky, the true mirror where the reality of people and things is inscribed. The paradisal integrity has disappeared: 'This morning his soul had been all in one piece. Where had he broken it up?' (*ibid*., p. 537).

At first the zoo, 'a real child's kingdom' (*ibid*., p. 537), enables him to recapture the childlike vision. But it is a captive paradise, both contrived and degraded by man, so that in it the original, God-given beauty and the 'circle of wickedness' are inextricably mixed. The dignity of the goat, so immobile that he seems a prolongation of the rock, bear witness to the primeval age, as does the polychrome splendour of the pheasants, with its extraordinary synthesis of fire and water, of solar energy and the peace of the deeps. But the exasperated squirrel rotating in its wheel with no hope of reprieve but death prefigures, with its frenzied illusion, the great image of the wheel of fire in the cinematographic poems of *August 1914*. Under a roof which is too low and blots out the sky, the whiteheaded vultures open their wings in vain. The images of captivity multiply, bringing back the memories of prison which to some extent provoke them: the white owls 'do not do well in captivity'; the badger's striped snout is a reminder of prison uniform (A14, p. 540); the bear clinging to the bars of his cage is a picture of pure despair; the carnivores are identified with the 'common laws' who terrorized others in the camps (*ibid*., p. 540). The fall from 'paradise' to the concentration camp is a dizzy one. But then comes the final shock: the Macaque Rhesus is blind — a man blinded him. 'Another hurriedly scrawled announcement said: "The little monkey that used to live here was blinded because of the senseless cruelty of the visitors. An evil man threw tobacco into the Macaque-Rhesus's eyes" ' (CW, p. 541). The explanation of evil simply in terms of history falls short in face of such meaningless cruelty: 'This unknown man . . . was not described as "antihumanist", or "an agent of American imperialism"; all it said was that he was evil' (*ibid*., p. 542).

The apparent naiveté of the notice takes one back beyond ideological abstractions — and beyond our psychoanalytical explanations — to a 'hidden ontology', to the sombre liberty of the 'underground' man, in Dostoevsky's sense of the word. Once this was paradise and now the anguished cry rings through it: 'Adam, where are you?' (Gen. 3.9).

Then Oleg Kostoglotov falls back on the noble and pure love which for weeks has been growing within him. Back on the Vera Vega — the faith — the star which has brought him back the country of childhood; this woman, this doctor who, by establishing a relationship of mutuality with him persuaded him to accept the treatment that has almost cured him, though at the same time it has destroyed within him — for a long time? forever? — if not desire, at least his physical ability to satisfy it. She has brought him to see that man is more than his physical nature, more than the sexual satisfaction of his desire; moving via the realm of childhood, she has reopened for him the realm of faith. A personal love, with all the strange, savage purity of a child's love, has grown up between them. It is this love which now delivers Oleg from the nightmare of the corrupted garden by enabling him to discover, through the hidden presence of Vera, the 'miracle of spirituality' that is the antelope (CW, p. 543). But all this purity of childhood love, the nostalgia which is expressed with such freshness by his gift of violets to two Uzbek girls, is spoiled by the inexorable presence of the flesh. When Oleg goes to Vera's and finds her out, he notices spread out over the railing of the balcony the bed linen of the various occupants, including needless to say, Vera's. The forms of the flesh are everywhere: pillows with their corners hanging down like cow's udders, or sticking up like phallic obelisks (*ibid.*, p. 549). And what irony there is in the phallic quality of the bright red motor cycle which shoots out of the communal area ridden by a youth with a broad face and flattened nose — as if the motorcycle compensated for this lack of nose, enlarging it in the manner of Gogol. A moment later, pressed up against the body of a young girl in the crowded tram, Oleg experiences in a crucial way both desire and his impotence. There he realizes that it would be impossible for Vera and himself to be 'together, yet not together' (*ibid.*, p. 552). What he gave her would only be 'torture and deceit' (*ibid.*, p. 558). He forgets himself, sacrifices himself and by confirming Vera in her purity he liberates her future. 'You are right in everything', he begins, in his written note from the station. But he adds: 'You will bless this day, the day you did not commit yourself to share my life . . . you slaughtered the first half of your life like a lamb. Please spare the second half' (*ibid.*, p. 566). Only self-effacement and sacrifice — and the spiritual death experienced deep in the heart — open up for Oleg the way to an authentic cure and make is possible for him to leave: whether to a new life or to physical death it does not matter — not for nothing does the author leave us in doubt.

The man of desire

This is why it is not enough to cure individual and collective illness in order for man to know joy. Desire, even when it focuses on ordinary needs for a moment, at the risk of perverting them, points in fact to a yawning emptiness that far exceeds them. Man is insatiable; the Faustian achievements of science and technology aggravate his thirst without quenching it (FC, p. 47). At first Innokenty Volodin experiences the vertigo that turned him from a full, delicately Epicurean existence as a kind of disease: 'Innokenty experienced towards all the material fruits of the earth — all the things that you can smell, touch, eat, drink and handle — a sense of satiated, stale revulsion' (*ibid.*, p. 416). All of a sudden the way his wife — who is so beautiful and whom he loves so passionately — chews her food, strikes him as unrestrained: 'Had she only now developed . . . this way of chewing noisily, almost champing, especially when she was eating fruit?' (*ibid.*, p. 416) — a remark similar to the one made by Andrei Siniavsky about women stuffing themselves in a cake shop 'It is embarrassing to watch them eat; there is something unrestrained in the way they sit, in their gestures, and in the way they bite, avidly, like lovers kissing' (*Impromtus*). Woman is the magnified mirror image of man, more totally involved, perhaps, in the sensual manipulation as in the loving self-giving. And the man, because he has known the latter, above all, in the mother who protected his childhood, resents the former all the more strongly.

'He had everything, yet he lacked something' (FC, p. 416): thus Innokenty Volodin diagnoses his 'disease'. The fact is that *everything* is haunted by death, and yet man desires *everything*, that is, eternity: 'Everything in the universe is mortal, even the stars! And what is more we are forced to elaborate our philosophy in terms of death! In order to be ready for it!' (*Candle in the Wind*, p. 88). The present findings of ethologists suggest that man is alone among the animals in knowing that he will die. And alone, too, in knowing that he has a father; alone, as father, in knowing he has sons and daughters — something even the most highly-developed monkeys do not realize. The sense of fatherhood, the taboo on incest and the awareness of death are closely linked as so many signs of the Other. Otherwise, everything remains an impersonal toy in the ever-pregnant womb of nature: no more father with whom to identify in order to grow beyond one's present; and return to the womb as a way of making sure one will never die — symptoms of a 'regressive evolution' at the end of which man would be just one species of animal among others, and inferior even to the elephants who, though they do not realize they are going to die, can recognize a dead elephant, respect it and cover it with branches. But the goal is inaccessible, just as there is no cure for the double reminder of death and eternity (how should we be aware of death at all except in the light of eternity?). 'For me the essential question about life has always been the way', says one of the characters in *Candle in the Wind*, and in the *sharashka*, Gleb Nerzhin refuses the cultural 'distractions' offered him by a friend — though it was not easy to read Hemingway in a Soviet prison in 1949. But for Gleb it would be to 'shamble' along on the flat, 'in all directions at once' whereas he is interested now in one thing only, and feels that he has paid sufficient to be allowed to devote himself to it unconditionally: discovery of the meaning of life (FC, p. 28).

The parable of the rich man

The transformation of the question of death into a question of meaning is summed up for Solzhenitsyn in the parable of the rich man as recorded by Luke (13.16-21). Tolstoy's story, *What do men live by?*, which in *Cancer Ward* is a remorseless touchstone for the soul, is part of a collection in which the various texts are in many cases preceded by an injunction or saying of Jesus: 'Walk while you have the light'. 'He who sows the wind will reap the whirlwind'. The particular story in question simply illustrates, with the combined force of realism and fantasy, the parable of the rich man. In this case it is a nobleman who comes to order a pair of boots from the shoemaker; and if the shoemaker spoils the leather he'll pay for it out of his own pocket. The nobleman had 'a great snout, a neck like a bull's, his whole frame was as if of cast iron . . . Even death had no hold upon a clod like that' (CW, p. 113). Yefrem Podduyev, thinking over these lines, recalls all the 'noblemen' he has known and admits that he was well on the way to becoming one such himself — before he got cancer. Choosing words that refer to animals of prey — 'wolves', 'a healthy, overfed beast' (SPP, p. 156) — Solzhenitsyn evokes those men are above all 'flesh and blood', using the new testament expression which does not set the flesh up against the spirit – the spirit can be 'of the flesh' and the body can be spiritual – but denotes, rather the whole man in his rejection of the invisible, and hence in his opacity.

Now the cobbler has an assistant, a tramp whom he has taken in and instructed and who now surpasses him in the exercise of his craft. This man from elsewhere sees the invisible. He perceives something behind the gentleman. Quite calmly he makes a mere pair of slippers with the leather. 'This man,' he argues, 'is making provision for a whole year, and he doesn't even know whether he'll survive till this evening. Behind the nobleman he had seen death. The rich man does on the way home, and his wife orders the slippers for him to be buried in.'

If Tolstoy's story does no more than illustrate Luke's parable, the latter is quoted extensively in the pivotal scene 5 of *Candle in the Wind*. It shows the meeting between the elderly and celebrated musician, Maurice, who is dying, and his daughter Alda. He is intoxicated by intensity of life – creativity, adulation of his disciples and the public, money, by progressively younger women. She, abandoned by her father, whom she loved, for long unstable and tormented, has allowed herself to be treated by 'cybernetic neurostabilization' which has relieved her anxiety thus enabling her to 'profit from life' (it is almost science fiction). And suddenly, confronted by death and the revelation of their mutual feelings of tenderness, Maurice discovers the emptiness of his life, Alda is restored to her spiritual dimension: 'I have lived in the domain of happy men, and allowed myself to be consumed', says the old musician. What has he given his disciples? Many words, much knowledge perhaps, but not a grain of wisdom. He has been unable to pass anything on to the one being who is close to him, to Alda who 'carries music within her'. He snatched everything he could from life, in order to regret nothing, and now he regrets the transparency, the peace, the detachment that has nothing to do with the selfish accumulation of 'experiences' or with that frenetic energy and 'enrichment' against which Simone Weil set poor and humble purity. 'How should one live in order to die without regrets?' asks Maurice. 'What's the good of life for those who don't know how to live?' We *want* to live, *want* to have experiences, *want* to get rich. But the vision that sees beyond death comes as a result not of what we will but of what we are; and entry into the kingdom demands of each man the painfully purifying process of renunciation.

Maurice begs Alda to play *The Winter Journey* of which he murmurs a passage: 'As a stranger came I here/And as a stranger will depart', thus discovering for himself the immemorial wisdom of the 'old woman' who recalled after Matryona's funeral that: 'There are two great riddles in this world: How was I born? I don't remember. How shall I die? I don't know' (SPP, p. 42). And when Maurice is dead, and his relations, who are among those for whom 'We only have one life, we will never die', gather round in distress, another 'old woman' appears, Aunt Christine, whom the others previously ignored or poked fun at: she traces the sign of the cross on the dead man's forehead and reads the parable: 'And I will say to my God: My soul you have plenty of good things laid by for many years to come; take things easy, eat, drink and have a good time.' But God said to him, 'Fool! This very night the demand will be made for your soul; and this hoard of yours, whose will it be then?'

Next Aunt Christine reads the mysterious parable: 'See that the light which is in you is not darkness' (Mt 6.23), following the same sequence of texts as that found in the Tolstoy collection mentioned in *Cancer Ward*.

It is to the consolidation (through shadows clearly recognized as such) of this *light that is within us*, that Solzhenitsyn is dedicated.

PART TWO

Towards spiritual awareness

3 The dawning of awareness

An innate, inarticulate, rudimentary sensation

The light within us can be obscured. The Gospel says that it can appear
lost in the darkness. However, like yeast its activity never ceases,
and when it bursts forth from the night and man sees it, sharing for a
moment the inner joy it brings, it becomes more precious to him than
life and happiness.

Contemporary man, who speaks in terms of vital exaltation,
intensity, 'fulfilment' through experiences 'freely' multiplied, and who
wishes above all to 'live his life to the full', is at a loss for words to
describe this breakthrough. In *Candle in the Wind*, Philip who, like
Alex, has been unjustly imprisoned, has only one thing in mind: to fill
the breach that the unexpected has opened up for a moment in his life,
enjoy the heady wine of the successes and achievements of the so-called
'living'. Strong in the knowledge of his scientific and amorous successes,
he is preparing to rid himself of his sick wife by shutting her in a distant
clinic – the best equipped, of course; and it may also be that this lonely
suffering woman confronts him with the presence and the invitation of
another reality which he ignored because to listen would mean altering
the agreeable pattern of his life. Alex, on the other hand, makes a
different choice. He does not wish to forget the unexpected which also
brought initiation into the life of the Spirit. He remains faithful to a
deep-seated intuition he cannot define. And the woman who attracts
him is Alda, hesitant, awkward, not entirely of this world. When
Philip, sensing the unspoken reservations of his friend, sings the praises
of 'life' – 'We only have one life: this life here is the only one, and it
must be lived splendidly, to the full' – Alex stammers out that 'there is
something else we only receive once'. 'What's that?' 'An innate, in-
articulate, rudimentary sensation.'

One can reasonably suppose that Philip and Alex were sentenced to life imprisonment rather than to penal servitude. In the world of the camps, where death is a real threat, where horrors occur daily, awareness develops more quickly, especially when experience of the camp follows immediately on experience of war, as it did in the case of Solzhenitsyn himself — and as it did, in the case of Nemov in *The Love-Girl and the Innocent*. Talking to the 'love-girl', Lyuba, he asks *the* question: 'Are our lives so important? Are they the most valuable thing we have?' (LGI, p. 94). Philip, faced with Alex's similar question had retorted: 'What is then?' Lyuba, who is not on the defensive but pathetically receptive, asks: 'What else is there?' She senses, alongside this all too familiar world, of which the camp seems to be a sombre epitome, the emergence of a quite *other* reality. Nemov defends himself: 'It sounds funny talking about it here in the camp but maybe . . . conscience' (*ibid.*, p. 94). When conscience comes to the surface the relationship between a man and a woman is mysterious. To Lyuba, accustomed only to men's physical desire, to the instinctive gestures — always the same — of nature playing with nature, Nemov appears suddenly as *other*: as a person. The otherness of conscience lays the foundation for the otherness of the person. And, because Nemov loves her, Lyuba becomes aware of herself as a person, to the extent that she makes a most painful and ambiguous sacrifice, agreeing to live with one of the camp officers so that Nemov can be saved. Lyuba in Russian means 'love', in the sense of *agape*, the sacrificial love that comes from above, from the Other.

The story of Innokenty

This development of spiritual awareness is what the story of Innokenty Volodin is about in *The First Circle*, and it is all the more significant, to us who live after the totalitarian deluge, for the fact that prison, the camp, the threat of social and even physical annihilation do not enter into it — though they will be there as the risk to be run at the moment of choice.

At first the awakening feels like a strange 'malaise': staleness, and the growing emptiness of a full life. Gradually Innokenty discovers the inadequacy of the 'principle of pleasure' as interpreted for us by Freud, of whom the young diplomat is ignorant, in spite of being so widely travelled. Epicurus said belief in immortality was the result of misdirected cupidity — we would talk of an ineffectual, suppressed *libido* — in those who have made bad use of 'the time allotted to us by Nature', whereas the wise man knows how 'to encompass the whole gamut of pleasures' and his full life calls for nothing besides its own fulness. But Innokenty is tired of pleasure, of all particular pleasures, however much trouble or even art he might have put into refining them: 'He had had money, good clothes, success, women, wine, travel; but now he was prepared to consign all these joys to perdition in exchange for one thing — justice' (FC, p. 654). Justice and truth are expressed by a single word in Russian: *pravda*, which Solzhenitsyn uses in its most profound sense, understood in the light of the inidividual vocation and the demands of fellowship — a justice-and-truth 'which existed before us, without us and for its own sake' (A14, p. 430).

Pravda as a vision of persons in all their dignity becomes the authentic criterion of good and evil, replacing the principle of pleasure recommended by Epicurus. For him, in fact, good and evil could only be distinguished in terms of the well-being or discomfort experienced. Satisfaction signifies good, discomfort evil. 'In other words, only what I like is good, and what I do not like is evil.' As awareness grows this begins to seem no more than 'the philosophy of a savage'. Stalin takes pleasure in killing: but does that mean murder is good? To risk going to prison oneself in order to save another man is not a pleasurable experience: but does that mean it is wrong to save someone else? (FC, pp. 667-8.)

Innokenty Volodin clarified and deepened these intuitions in a kind of communion of saints; and here the mediating role of woman comes in again. Not Innokenty's wife. She, like him, is caught up in the round of pleasure and intrigue. They turned towards each other in a passionate, exclusive relationship which throughout the war made them indifferent to the unspeakable sufferings of their fellow men: 'Not a breath of the sorrow of the world fanned the cheeks of Innokenty and Datoma. After all, you only live once' (*ibid.*, p. 415). Now they are moving apart from one another because their passion is spent, and they seek pleasure in new adventures. It is Innokenty's growing awareness alone that enables him to rediscover his wife as another person with a kind of searing pity through which, humbler and purer now, the fervour of the first encounter returns. But here Innokenty is the mediator of light for Datoma, and not vice versa. True, he knows the clear gaze of his young sister in law, Clara, and her innocent questioning of suffering. But Clara is to be carried away by a great and as yet anonymous force: the life of the species.

The woman whose mediating action directs Innokenty towards the light is his mother: 'But towards his mother . . . he felt superior, as sons usually do, never suspecting that she had any life of her own, apart from himself, his childhood, his needs, never thinking about her being ill and in pain, or her dying at the age of forty-seven' (*ibid*., p. 417). And so it happens that, liberated by her early death from any 'functional' relationship with his mother, he finds her diaries and explores her library. And so he discovers the Russian renaissance of the first twenty years of this century, with its profusion of reviews and translations, of aesthetic and spiritual activity. At first he reacts like a young philistine to the words used and even to points of orthography: in these note-books God was spelt with a capital letter, something unheard of in the Soviet Union. Gradually, however, he 'poisons himself with . . . the air of his mother's private world', her spiritual quest for the true, the good and the beautiful, her discovery that evil is rooted in something deeper than history, her attempt to understand all created things as so many pointers to the reality beyond — or rather her particular way of looking at reality, which he had met in neither Marx nor Epicurus. Above all, he *meets* his mother, as a young girl filled with a disinterested love of art and enthusiasm for religious philosophy, who was suddenly plunged unprotected, into the maelstrom of revolution, and, half through fascination, half under constraint, like Russia itself, married a revolutionary clad in black leather — a reminder of those 'garments of hide' which according to the patristic interpretation of Genesis symbolize the extraversion and insensitivity of the powerful. Innokenty — like modern Russia — was born of this marriage between the religious soul of old Russia and the brute strength of the Revolution, which, because there was no love in it, was equivalent to rape. Orphaned of both parents, he first identified with his father, the *animus* in the Jungian sense, basing his life on a rationalism which seeks to explain and control everything, and which combines strangely with *eros* — producing a kind of erotic use of reason (which is one way of defining ideology). Now, through reflection on his mother and her world of Russian religious philosophy, the *anima* begins to awaken the spiritual soul, the central energies of his 'heart-mind'. What Innokenty, like so many of Solzhenitsyn's characters, then discovers, is that 'life' is in fact shot through with death, in league with death, overshadowed by loneliness and an inherent element of frustration, thwarted by a boundless injustice which should be checked but which cunningly shifts its ground and reappears somewhere else. 'Injustice is stronger than you are, it always was and it always will be, but let it not be committed through you' (*ibid*., p. 418), Innokenty's mother had written in her

'Ethical Considerations'. And Solzhenitsyn ends *August 1914* with an aphorism which he underlines: 'Untruth did not begin with us; nor will it end with us' (A14, p. 645).

This world of iniquity is the world of 'meat'. By using this raw, chill word Solzhenitsyn concretizes the biblical concept of the 'flesh': which is not the opposite of spirit, since the spirit can be 'carnal' and the flesh 'spiritual', but it connotes the creature rejecting the light, withdrawing into its own opacity and death. He often uses the image of the 'butcher' to describe the dominating and violent — those who thought of driving the prisoners through Moscow in trucks marked with the word 'meat' in several languages for the edification of foreign journalists (FC, p. 699). The generality of 'consumers' devour meat like animals, and the first shop to open in a new quarter is almost invariably the butcher's.

There is nothing complacent about this reference to 'cannibalism' (*ibid.*, p. 486), this 'necrophagia'. It is realistic in the same way that Soloviev was realistic when he used to say that we should not aim to transform society into a paradise, but struggle to ensure that it doesn't become a hell; or Berdyaev when he used to denounce 'the nightmare of the evil good', the totalitarian temptation to impose at all costs a good that is taken to be definitive. But above all it is made from a desperate desire to unearth, to disentangle from the heart of man that transparent core of innocence from which a light springs, transcending evil, preventing it spreading perhaps, and then beginning to heal it — avoiding in the process both a compromising *laissez faire* and a drestructive utopia, struggling against stupidity and hatred, like a transfigured Sisyphus. 'Let it not be committed through you' wrote Innokenty's mother about evil (*ibid.*, p. 418). The growth of awareness means the release of this transparent centre, one's own and that of others, and hence the discovery of the other beyond evil, however deeply enmeshed in it he might be. The eye that can perceive each unique other directly is the eye of pity: not in the frequently implied sense of supercilious condescension — a feeling 'shameful and degrading for the one who pities as for the one who is pitied' (*ibid.*, p. 418) — but in its true sense of *com*-passion, the capacity to break through exterior barriers in order to 'suffer with': 'Compassion is the spontaneous reaction of the virtuous heart', wrote Innokenty's mother (*ibid.*, p. 418). If science 'enlightens' the mind, only the spiritual values of awareness and compassion can lead to 'the mutual illumination of human souls' says Shulubin in *Cancer Ward* (CW, p. 408).

Thus awareness brings respect for the separateness of others, as is

well expressed in Innokenty's mother's 'Ethical Considerations':
'Never to be sure that you are more right than other people. Respect
their opinions even if they are opposed to yours' (FC, p. 418). This
would be untenable for anyone who sees truth as being contained
within a system of ideas. Innokenty's first reaction is: 'If my view of
the world is right, how can I respect those who disagree with me?'
(*ibid*.). But maybe — as women, except the few whose maternal instinct has been frustrated, know — it's a question of persons not
systems. In which case 'opinions' stop being weapons and begin to
define presences, offering an opportunity for insight into various
manifestations of being. Gradually they become part of communion.

These are the stages through which Innokenty passed on his journey
from the 'carnal', mortal life of the flesh to awareness. 'His philosophy
of life had been that we only live once. Now there had matured in him
the sense of another truth about himself and the world: that we only
have one conscience — and that a crippled conscience is as irretrievable
as a lost life' (*ibid*., p. 421).

When the moment of decision comes Innokenty is ready. In the
course of his work he discovers that an elderly professor of medicine
is to be tried, degraded and executed, as an example, if, as he has
promised, he gives the formulae of certain medicines he has discovered to his foreign colleagues. This man is no stranger to Innokenty:
he was his mother's doctor and looked after him during his childhood,
when he respected him as a 'great man' (*ibid*., p. 12).

Dr Dobroumov (his name is a combination of the word for good
and the word for spirit) stands for the true father. In the world of
'meat' fathers abandon their children or repress them, and the children
are driven to patricide. Where there is awareness, fathers 'edify' their
children in the true sense of the word, and children, because they
recognize this creative loyalty, respect their fathers. The world of
'meat' recognizes nothing but youth and imitation of youth, because
intensity of life is the only criterion it has. For those who are aware,
another light shines through as the body declines, and with age a man
can become a source of wisdom. In the Orthodox spiritual tradition a
great monk is referred to as 'an old man filled with beauty' — the
spiritual beauty that wells up from the heart at the end of a long life
spent in prayer and service of others. He is the *starets* for whom 'salvation' depends not on believing but on being healed: with Solzhenitsyn,
in *Cancer Ward* as in *The First Circle*, it is not for nothing that these
elders are physicians of the whole man, soul as well as body. Innokenty's steps to save the old man totally upset the biological logic of

the world of 'meat' where the utility and economic value of an old man carries little weight in comparison with that of a young one. Awareness comes with acceptance of death and respect for the older generation — two attitudes inknown to the animals, as we have seen.

So Innokenty rings Dubroumov to warn him, knowing full well that the doctor's place is bugged. We will never know whether or not his intervention did any good. What matters in the end is the decision, the risk, the freedom. 'So unused to carrying burdens', so 'solitary and frail' as he passes in front of the Greater Lubyanka Prison (*ibid*., pp. 12-13) Innokenty risks everything: 'If you always look over your shoulder, how can you still remain a human being?' (*ibid*., p. 14). Then a great peace comes over him, a peace not of this world, confirming him in his awareness. By sacrificing his physical liberty he discovers true liberty. In the same way, Nemov, in *The Love-Girl and the Innocent*, prefers to lose his place as head of production rather than deceive and corrupt others: 'I feel freer now I'm an ordinary black-faced working man'. To which Lyuba's answer comes back like a flash: 'There's only one thing wrong with being a black-faced worker — they die' (LGI, pp. 93-94). In the world of 'meat' what is called freedom is often no more than surrender to the principle of pleasure — a man becomes the slave, first of his passions, until he is crushed by their inevitable contradictions; and then, at a deeper level, of the determining forces of nature and society; and ultimately of death. As he grows in awareness, he sees more clearly the way to true liberty, both in nature and in history, through the attraction of what lies beyond both and transforms death into a mystery. What is more, this freedom does not consist in the mere fact of choice, but in adherence to truth and love, to the truth of love, so that, as Innokenty remarks, there is no other choice. This fidelity reveals the deepest set of a man's being, as is proved by that great peace in which man rediscovers his inner unity.

Responsibility

Awareness gives man both a sense of responsibility and the power to reach beyond himself.

Lying in agony in his hospital bed, Yefrem Podduyev submits to interrogation by Tolstoy, and indirectly by the Gospel: 'What do men live by? Fool, this very night they will demand your soul of you'. Reduced to the essential by the *memento mori* and the hidden influence of Christ, he suddenly appreciates the extent of what the old spiritual teachers would have called his 'dissemblance'. He discovers his culpability — so many women seduced with promises of marriage and quickly abandoned. Like everyone else he used to talk about the 'equality' of men and women, but 'deep down he never thought of women as fully fledged people' (CW, p. 115). He would promise personal fidelity and give nothing more than the ephemeral toy of pleasure, and quite without scruple, because a woman is not a complete being — her nature is so fascinating that she doesn't need to be a person: 'And he's have been amazed if some other fellow had seriously tried to tell him he treated women badly. But according to this curious book it turned out that Yefrem was the one to blame for everything' (*ibid*., p. 115).

Nor is that all. Yefrem played an active part in the exploitation of men and women during the Stalinist period. He was a foreman and the men of whom he had charge were convicts. One snowy day in November — it all comes back to him in sharp detail — he forced three exhausted men to dig a trench intended to take a gas pipe. Each time the starved, half-fainting wretches hoped they had finished he ordered them to dig deeper. The fact was he did not want to get into trouble himself, and what did they matter to him? 'Looking up at him, the three faces no longer seemed alive as the snow fell on them. The young chap forced his lips open and said, "All right chief. It'll be your turn to die one day." ' (*ibid*., p. 224.)

If he never forgot this curse, and that of one of his ephemeral mothers-in-law denouncing his lying tongue, it was because they had stirred his still dormant conscience. But the latter gnawed quietly away at him and maybe it was through the old woman's curse that his tongue was finally destroyed by cancer. Now he is spiritually aware and accepts the judgment, not in terms of a do and don't morality, but through the terrible confrontation with love. Yefrem, painfully enlightened — that evening, Solzhenistyn remarks, the lamp was lit earlier than usual — dies in a state of *metanoia*. But when the light of conscience manages, in spite of everything, to filter through to the opaque area created by the disease in Rusanov, who was not simply a puppet of the regime, but a member of the secret police, who abused power and denounced other people, all it can do is to bring him up against his own emptiness. His nightmare begins in the long concrete tunnel — like a pregnancy that cannot come to term. Man runs but is too heavy, not with the weight of the concrete, but with his own. He knows he must turn round (and this is the secret call to *metanoia* in the strict sense: a change of direction) because the path leads on into the darkness. And he does change direction; he comes out of the tunnel and recognizes at last what he has done in flashes of insight which comes 'not in a row, but all at once' (*ibid.*, p. 231). In front of him there is a drowned girl, with eyes like water, for whose death he is responsible — she killed herself because he threatened to bring her to court for making false statements; and an elderly couple for whom he obtained a permanent deportation order because the man was a nuisance professionally-speaking to one of Rusanov's friends, and whose daughter he had sent to an orphanage, having robbed her of everything, even her name. But when, arraigned before the Supreme Tribunal, he is confronted with his own moment of choice, he simply tries to justify himself by accusing others, finally reversing the roles and returning to his former one of accuser: 'We're going to purge the intelligentsia' (*ibid.*, p. 237). Then the dream becomes a nightmare again; Pavel Rusanov is all thirst, burning with thirst, and now he cannot even drink the water his victim drowned in, as he had intended earlier: 'He stretched out a hand to pour himself some water out of a carafe, but the carafe turned out to be empty. He nodded to his neighbour to ask him to pass a carafe from the other end of the table. It was passed to him, but that one was empty too' (*ibid.*).

Though Ivan Denisovich is not 'against God' (LID, p. 139), he refuses to believe in heaven and hell as objective places. They are within us. The difference between Yefrem Podduyev and Pavel is the difference between *metanoia* accepted and *metanoia* refused. The former becomes aware of the light and peace that are not of this world, the latter experiences the hell of everlastingly unappeased desire. The carafe was empty. Rusanov was empty, and because he was human he was filled with desire. Perhaps hell is no more than that: the confrontation between thirst and emptiness. Man drinks in his own emptiness and burns with increasing intensity: 'Love acts in two different ways: it becomes suffering in the reprobate and joy in the blessed' (St Isaac the Syrian, *Spiritual Homilies* II, p. 1).

Reaching beyond oneself

Even though awareness implies judgment, it takes man beyond himself, another aspect of the transcendence of the human person with respect to his biological, social and psychological nature. In *August 1914*, which vindicates the officer's calling, Solzhenitsyn has given a good deal of thought to 'men of duty'. His perspective is, of course, very different from that of Kant's categorical imperative which poisoned the moral systems of the west, secular and Christian, at the end of the nineteenth century. For Solzhenitsyn, and here again he simply repeats the Gospel, duty is one's capacity to 'lay down one's life for one's friends'. We 'whose daily life is always governed by considerations of self-preservation', remain within the limits of self-love and the love of those closest to us (A14, p. 403). Men guided by a sense of duty — professional soldiers or those engaged in the combat of life — 'cease to shun death', and 'will unflinchingly face a premature death, so fatal to the plans they have made for their lives' (*ibid.*). 'They had burned their boats. Others like them would retreat, return home; they owed such men nothing: they were not their relatives nor their brothers — yet they would stand and die so that they might live' (*ibid.*, p. 404). It is true that in many cases this is the result of a 'sound education', but others take up or discover such a course spontaneously, and it seems more honest to conclude that both 'draw on some unknown source of strength' (*ibid.*).

This 'unknown source of strength' triumphs over man's tendency to egoism, his individual or collective narcissism, his instinct for self-preservation, and the 'pleasure principle'. To point here, with Freud, to a kind of death instinct is to suggest that man can nail both love and death to the cross, but it says nothing about any possible resurrection. Yet this capacity to reach beyond themselves is what characterizes the higher beings, and it transforms humanity. So it is indeed an unknown source of strength that compels Innokenty Volodin to sacrifice his career, his well-being, the wife he loves and has just rediscovered, in order to save — maybe — an old friend and become, inevitably, one of 'the living dead'. The same strength leads Gerasimovich to opt for the labour camps of the Great North Territory in preference to the comfort of the *sharashka* and even to imminent release, rather than design the police gadgets he has been asked for: a camera that would work in the dark, and another so small that it would fit in a door-jam and snap automatically each time someone went through. Gerasimovich's wife breaks down, she can no longer bear the isolation that builds up increasingly round the wives of prisoners. He is aware of this, he has just seen her — yesterday their one annual meeting took place — and she begged him to invent something to secure his anticipated release: 'You're so clever, invent something for them. You must save me!' (FC, p. 276). With her cry ringing in his ears, he knows he could easily perfect this photographic equipment. But he also knows that science and technology are not neutral, and when the authorities in the *sharashka* try to make out that 'it's exactly in [his] line', he cries out shrilly: 'No, it's not my line! Putting people in prison is not my line! I'm not a fisher of men!' (*ibid.*, p. 607). In the camp described in *The Love-Girl and the Innocent* the same 'unknown source of strength' leads Grania to pass up the highly-coveted job of bread distributor. Acceptance would have meant food to satisfy her hunger, wamrth, survival: pushing a little cart with one wheel and two handles is not a very taxing occupation. But it would have involved taking from the rations of the prisoners in order to satisfy the powers that be who put her there and who assumed, moreover, that she would not go without herself. Whence Grania's refusal: 'What sort of a person cheats a drudge out of his bread ration even by a gramme? I made my decision — I'm not going to live like other people do in the camps. There's only one important thing — I won't see myself turned into a bastard. Live or die — what's the difference?' (LGI, p. 106).

For Solzhenitsyn this capacity for self-transcendence is not related to exceptional choices only, to such critical trials as war, imprisonment or cancer: in its modest way, daily life becomes ennobled. By humbly carrying out his duty, man fulfils himself through self-forgetfulness. But it is ennobled principally by two signs, privileged, but a feature nonetheless of daily life: the creativity of work or art, and patient fidelity, the touchstone and marvel of human love.

4 The act of creation

Marx's intuition and its limits

The one value of Soviet society which Solzhenitsyn has picked out in order to examine its spiritual significance is that of work. The ideology of the régime defines man first and foremost as a worker. By means of socialized labour, each man becomes involved in the common task, in the hope, or rather the certainty, that he is preparing a society where justice and prosperity will prevail, and where, no longer regarded as something that has to be endured, and rid of the tendency to specialize which leads to division, particularly between the manual and the intellectual, work will be truly an act of creation revealing each man to his fellows, and nature to mankind. In looking for the essence of man not in matter, but in the work through which man shapes matter and stamps it with his own image, Marx without realizing it puts the nail in the coffin of his own materialism. He identifies alienation with the objectification of the fruits of human creation by the cult of buying and selling. Socialism aims, therefore, to realize man's ability, in which he differs from the animals, to continue his work beyond what is necessary by pursuing consciously 'the laws of beauty' (*Writings of 1844*) – though Marx does not ask himself what is the origin of these laws, or the nature of man apart from matter, in order to ensure between matter and man the dimension of creative work.

Marx, in fact, ignores both the personal subject and transcendence. Work remains for him 'generic' and entirely immanent. By creating the world of things, man 'reveals himself beyond question as a generic being. What he produces is the sign of his creative life.' In the last analysis, humanity becomes the collective demiurge of the universe: through his productivity 'nature is seen as *his* work and *his* reality'. The final sentence indicates a strange narcissism in which the generic superman sets the seal on his own solitude: 'Man contemplates himself in a world which he himself has created.' (*ibid*.)

Without neglecting the positive aspects of Marx's thought, Solzhenitsyn places himself in a perspective that is less pretentious as well as more open; less pretentious because untouched by the titanism and the messianism of the early Marx. Contemporary utopias are only too glad to synthesize the Marx of the 'youthful writings', profoundly influenced as they are by the pantheistic mysticism of the German Romantics, and by Nietzsche as the poet of dance, laughter and play. In the new society, freed thanks to machines of all that is irksome and constraining about it, work will become pure creativity, and *homo sapiens* will find fulfilment as *homo ludens*. Solzhenitsyn is aware of the absurdity of such a distinction. He remains, however, profoundly akin to the unexpected Marx of the later years, who was to observe in *Capital*: 'The true reign of liberty can only flourish in so far as it is founded on the reign of necessity' (*Capital* III).

Solzhenitsyn's perspective is distinguished above all, however, by its opening premises: work is not the work of generic man, but of the individual person in communion with others. And the human person, at the deepest level of his being, is open to the realm of mystery. In the same way, the world is not created by man: it is offered to him in an incomplete state, not simply as matter to shape, but as meaning to decipher. Man does not contemplate himself in the world he creates: he harnesses the dynamism of being, unravels its wisdom, takes part in a manifold dialogue in which each one gives the world to others and seems to make with them a celebration. For Solzhenitsyn work (which he divorces neither from the humble tasks of every day nor from the most sublime artistic creation) requires and promotes a movement of self-transcendence in which spiritual awareness is established.

The first lesson that Solzhenitsyn draws from his long experience of the camps, his long association with the oppressed from every walk of life, is that political, economic, and social alienation does not fundamentally affect the nature of work. In the *sharashka* the prisoners 'were so wrapped up in their work, which brought them no return' (FC, p. 40). The most remarkable descriptions the author has given us of man at work refer to a prison camp in Kazakhstan, the camp of Ivan Denisovich. (*One Day in the Life of Ivan Denisovich* is nonetheless concerned with a good day in the life of a man accustomed to manual work. In many camps the work, exceeding a man's strength, would destroy him, and the prisoner could only respond with hatred, despair and duplicity.) Thus social exclusion and economic servitude in no way prejudice the ontological reality of work in so far as it is carried through by persons and is linked with the awakening of personal awareness; which is not the case when man 'becomes a beast', trampling mercilessly on others in order to survive. Solzhenitsyn has studied these different attitudes in *The Love-Girl and the Innocent* where it becomes clear that for him there is a real interdependence between work and awareness. In Matryona's case the alienation is not endured but transfigured: this sick and aging woman, exploited by all and sundry, 'loves her enemies', and transforming the importunacy of others into availability in herself, she finds joy in the work involved. What emerges most clearly from this is the profound nature of work. When Matryona is working she forgets that she is under compulsion, or has agreed to help, in order to become positively involved in what she is doing. 'Oh, she [an abusive neighbour's] got such large potatoes, Ignatich', she confided in her host. 'It was a pleasure to dig them up, honest' (SPP, p. 21).

Work, like the awareness it can express, is something more than the economic and social context in which it goes on. But what is it?

A calming discipline

Solzhenitsyn replies that work is first of all a purifying discipline, an approach to awareness by way of the body. In one respect this is the traditional Christian attitude: the Fathers of the Church in no way regarded work as a curse, but first and foremost as the 'absorber of iniquity', and ascetics know from experience how the most repetitive manual work can provide favourable conditions for concentration. When Innokenty Volodin finds himself alone in his cell, he tries to tidy up his clothes, which had been pulled about when he was being searched. He has to sew on a number of indispensable buttons, replace the lining of his uniform, and plump up the padding of his coat. He has never done any work like this before, or, apparently, any kind of manual work. So, while he is still suffering the first shock of his arrest, and stunned by the humiliations that followed it, he takes a humble lesson in concentration through activity. 'This absorbing, unhurried task . . . completely restored Innokenty's peace of mind. His anxiety subsided, his sense of fear and persecution ebbed away' (FC, p. 667). This reaction should not be attributed to Innokenty's lack of experience, to the novelty, for him, of manual work. Solzhenitsyn notes that when things are at their worst Matryona who, in the whole course of her life, has known no other form of occupation, regains 'her good humour through work'. Whenever something distressing happens in her private life, whenever she gets into difficulties with some distant bureaucrat or other (distant both in space and in the way they treat her), off she goes to dig potatoes, to look for peat or collect berries in the forest, and comes 'beaming back to her cottage, thoroughly delighted' (SPP, p. 18). It is neither the contact with nature (except perhaps because of the silence) nor the perhaps game-like aspect of berry-picking that have restored her peace, but the very fact of the effort, the struggle, the work accomplished with care, all of which Solzhenitsyn underlines when he observes that she returns, 'her back bending under the weight of her burden' (*ibid*., p. 17).

One of the reasons for the calming effect of work lies in the repeated gesture, in so far as it produces a rhythm which becomes one with the principal rhythms of the body, encouraging them and bringing them to the level of consciousness. Solzhenitsyn notes this process in connection with the handling of very simple tools, a broom for example, or a saw. Take Spiridon, the handyman at the *sharashka*. He has no more news of his family, especially of his daughter who works in a lumber camp, and his heart is heavy. Without enthusiasm he begins to clear away the snow in the courtyard. After the first fifty spadesful, however, the very regularity of his work turns constraint into good will. And each morning before settling down to their research, Nerzhin and Sologdin too make it their business to saw some wood, not indeed for any pleasure it gives them but in order to warm up more easily: 'The rhythmic strokes gave peace and a new direction to their thoughts' (*ibid*., p. 69).

Work, by the very fatigue it causes, activates, amplifies and enhances the breathing and deep-seated physical energies and draws attention to the healthy warmth of one's blood. The progressive onset of 'waves of heat' is particularly noticeable in very cold weather, as Solzhenitsyn remarks a propos of Ivan Denisovich and his companions: 'Thanks to the urgent work, the first wave of heat had come over them — when you feel wet under your coat . . . And after about an hour they had their second flush of heat, the one that dries up the sweat. Their feet didn't feel cold . . .' (LID, p. 82).

For most of our contemporaries in 'technopolis' these energies remain dormant; they are familiar with nervous exhaustion, not with the deep, healthy fatigue through which man restores his vitality. Now, the mobilization of these deep-seated physical energies is related to the search for what the ascetics of the Orthodox Church called 'the seat of the heart': when man enters into a dialogue with matter, whether directly, in nature, or in things made by others, the correlation between thought and gesture, the incarnation of thought in manual terms, awakens that centre of unity which the same tradition describes as the union of mind and heart. The man who has banished all extraneous thoughts from his mind is able to concentrate on a single idea (*ibid*., p. 52) and to *make* that idea, not by arbitrarily imposing it on matter, but by yielding to the latter in order to give expression to its structure and dynamism. So it is for Ivan Denisovich when, on a construction site, he works hard, to improvise a heating system, joining and bending the pipes that are to get rid of the smoke. The flow of associated thoughts impinging on the mind, time divided between nostalgic regret and worry about the future, and finally its absence, all this disappears when, in order to be realized in matter, an idea must recognize and take into account the possibilities of the latter, not just intellectually, but through the mediating incarnation of bodily gesture:

here it is a question of joining metal cylinders, the diameters of which are not exactly identical, of capturing and channeling the elusive movement of the smoke. There is the fact of the smoke, the recalcitrance of the ill-assorted pipes, and, the need for a smokeless heat which will make survival and work possible in spite of the severe cold of the steppe. This may be a point of detail, bit it requires the collaboration of several people in a vast dialogue between men, things and nature which, at the point where personal intelligence, the world and the body meet, facilitates the development of awareness.

Creating together

These characteristics are found and others emerge when the task in hand is truly the work of a team. Creative joy is born, not in spite of hardship and fatigue, nor by suppressing them, but through them, according to that pattern of self-emptying and self-transcendence which, in Solzhenitsyn, always accompanies a spiritual awakening. Once, Ivan Denisovich and his team-mates have organized a rudimentary stove near which the mortar can be prepared; they must set about constructing a wall out of stone blocks. The conditions of work themselves call for speed: the cold freezes the mortar within a few seconds, making it set too quickly, and if a block has not been put in the right place there is no time to try again or put it right, and the plumb is lost; if there is too much mortar the whole thing will begin to slip and will collapse when the thaw comes. To the need for speed is added the resistance, the hostility even, of the material and milieu: the cold bites and can even paralyze one, the blocks are sharp and one risks tearing one's mittens. What is more, the blocks are far from being uniform; they have 'chipped corners or broken edges or lumps on their sides' (*ibid.*, p. 81); the geometrical and industrially produced object thus rediscovers something of the character of its natural material — stone.

The work can only be carried out therefore through a synchronization of thought and action. There must be 'vision' which must in turn be translated almost immediately into action. Ivan 'sees', 'at first glance', the individual character of each block, its peculiar irregularity, and at the same time he 'sees' the place that corresponds to it in the wall. He takes the steaming mortar on his trowel, measuring the exact amount needed to fix the block horizontally, and to join two contiguous blocks, bearing in mind that this join will be supporting the middle of a block on the next row up. Next, before the mortar has a chance to freeze, but with sufficient care to protect his mitten, he grabs the chosen block, 'and without losing a moment he levels it, patting it with the side of the trowel', for 'the mortar is already freezing' (*ibid*., p. 81). The rigours of the climate and a hard-won expertise combine to produce a light, rhythmic, almost dance-like discipline, and man arranges matter according to the beautiful geometry it demands, in a play of alternating movements which conquers gravity by making use of it.

The rhythm is communicated to the whole team; as a result of the synchronized movements a wonderful relationship is established between the men, and finally between the stretches of wall that grow and connect with one another. Apart from brief appeals to the mortar-carriers, words are useless: everything goes so quickly that there is not even time to wipe one's nose. But there are signs of communication: Senka, who lays the blocks on one side, and Ivan, who lays them on the other, both on the same level, meet one another and begin to scoop mortar out of the same hod. The team, reflects Ivan Denisovich, is a family, and matter sets the seal on the brotherhood of the men in so far as the men seal the elements of matter together in some kind of order. Even with the team leader, whom he has learnt to respect, Ivan now feels on an equal footing: 'Now, after working like that, he felt equal to the team leader' (*ibid*., p. 91). In the same way, in the camp foundry, where the second scene of *The Love-Girl and the Innocent* takes place, the founders, as a team, 'work briskly and need no words to understand one another' (LGI, p. 22).

These examples show what manual work — which involves the whole man — means to Solzhenitsyn, and it is a far cry from the utopias of 'creativity' and play which would like to forget that the mastery of anything requires a hard apprenticeship and daily practice, and that exultation of the creative moment comes at the end of a long process of development. It is a far cry, too, from the piecemeal, totally un-stimulating work of so many modern factories where man is subjected to mechanical cadences which scarcely ever fall into a rhythm to synchronize with the rhythms of the body. The primitive equipment of the workers described by Solzhenitsyn, their need to get on with the job in spite of everything, paradoxically enough lends a freedom to their movements that many 'free' workers do not possess. Not that machinery as such is necessarily to blame, as the activities and initiatives of the foundry workers in *The Love-Girl and the Innocent* prove. What matters is that the worker should possess one or even several skills, and should feel sufficiently responsible as one of a team that is itself responsible. Some attempt is being made today in the industrialized countries, radically to modify conditions of work, and here Solzhenitsyn's concept of work as inseparable from spiritual awareness and the capacity to 'think with one's hands', as a dialogue with people and things through the medium of matter, could be very helpful — on condition that the primacy passes from the project of work to the man who works.

The teacher and the doctor

Work can also consist in direct service of others, and this is particularly true for the teacher and the doctor.

The true teacher, according to Solzhenitsyn — and it should not be forgotten that he himself was a teacher — commands respect by his sincerity, leading by example, like Lydia Georgievna, heroine of *For the Good of the Cause*, whom her pupils get to know when they go with her to do unpaid work on a building site. A teacher can 'look others in the eye' with a confident smile; he can give himself and yet hold back, in order to set the young on their way without beguiling them with his own personality. His aim is to enable them to live more deeply, to direct them 'towards what is good' (SPP, p. 56) knowing on occasion how to efface himself, when his role becomes superfluous. As for the authentic doctor, through a long discipline, in which science is never divorced from the capacity to accept others and to listen, he must become the kind of person to whom people 'can pour out the fears they have deeply concealed or even found shameful' (CW, p. 454). If he specializes in general medicine — a comprehensive approach much needed in current medical practice — 'he should have no more patients than his memory and personal knowledge can cover. Then he would be able to treat each patient as a subject on his own . . .' (*ibid.*, p. 456). In order to respect as a unity both the questioning adolescent and the patient for whom illness is not a chance occurrence but something that affects his future, one must learn to integrate onself, and to open oneself, too, with a true humility which leaves toom for reciprocity, so tht the adolescent, by identifying with his teacher can find his own way to self-mastery, and the invalid can become intelligently involved in the diagnostic investigations as well as in the successive stages of the treatment.

The awakening of conscience

Nothing fruitful can be achieved therefore in any domain whatsoever by someone who is not spiritually aware. If he wants to educate or heal others as whole beings he must strive first to unify himself; he must 'think with his hands' until he acquires that mastery which sets him free for laughter and from the weight of time. At the end of the day when Ivan Denisovich and the team leader share a good laugh, Ivan exclaims: 'Why do these rats make the work-day so short? We're just getting into our stride when they call it off' (LID, p. 91). If respect for man is one manifestation of spiritual awareness, so is respect for matter and the efforts of others. In Ivan's work teams that day they overestimate the quantity of mortar, and a boxful still remains when it is time to go. To leave it would simply be to waste both contents and container: 'Next morning they could throw the whole lot of it to hell — the mortar would have petrified, it wouldn't yield to a pick-axe' (ibid., p. 89). The team leader accepts the situation with reluctance — the more so because it would be dangerous to arrive late at the various control points separating the work yard from the camp. 'But Shukhov wasn't made that way: eight years in a camp couldn't change his nature. He worried about anything he could make use of, about every scrap of work he could do' (ibid., p. 91). In any case his energy and creative enthusiasm are such that he cannot simply shut off like a machine, so he stays there alone, at his own risk, to go one with the wall until the mortar is used up.

Scientific research can also become active contemplation, producing 'that mysterious state of mental exaltation for which physiologists have so far failed to account' (FC, p. 608). Indeed, apart from the fact that it is only too often used to satisfy a thirst for power or profit, scientific research 'is necessary not only for our minds but for our souls too. Awareness of the world and of other human beings can be as indispensible to us as . . . conscience itself' as a scientist haltingly explains in Candle in the Wind. As his questions grow in subtlety and respect, the scientist discovers that the world is intelligible, that a fundamental connexion exists between the order and beauty of the universe and man's spiritual awareness; the integrity and discipline involved in the research free the mind of prejudice, and make wonder possible.

The outward sign common to all these forms of self-mastery is beauty. There is beauty in the movements of Ivan Denisovich and his companions as they build a wall together; there is beauty in the silent, harmonious collaboration of the foundry workers. Lydia

Georgievna brings out in the faces of her pupils the beauty of trust and dawning awareness; the 'old doctor', whose shrewd gaze is tempered with self-discipline, makes available to his patients the peaceful beauty of his home and his welcome. The inspiration of this or that mathematician in the *sharashka* is not fundamentally different in kind from that of a Mozart. The intelligence which the scientist discovers behind the 'systems' that structure the world is inseparable from beauty. One thinks of those passages in the book of Proverbs where the wisdom of God is portrayed as creative intelligence, rejoicing in the superabundant divine energies, and as the Beauty enshrined in the work of the divine artist.

The mystery of beauty

Art is dedicated to this mystery of beauty, which does not try to reason, but takes hold of the whole man, and stirs him to the roots of his being. That is why 'the genuinely artistic work is utterly, irrefutably convincing' (NP, p. 6). If social and political programmes and philosophical systems clash with one another without convincing, art, like work — from which moreover it cannot be separated — stimulates spiritual awareness because 'even the resisting heat surrenders to it' (*ibid*.). In *The Love-Girl and the Innocent* an old writer of French origin who had come to Russia in the enthusiastic chaos of the revolution, when everything seemed possible, but who had subsequently and for no good reason been thrown into prison, tries, in spite of jeers, to share his sense of beauty with his companions, to show them 'that there is more to life than work parades, searches and prison soup' (LGI, p. 116). The indestructible nature of spiritual awareness as it transcends ideology to celebrate anguish and wonder, emerges most clearly in the highest realizations of art. Art cannot be reduced to a substitute, or a political stimulus, and Solzhenitsyn returns continually to the word 'mystery': this mysterious object — 'was it cast up by the ocean? Has it been long buried in the sand? Did it fall from the sky?' (NP, p. 3) — 'reflecting the light now dimly, now with flashing brilliance' (*ibid*.). Through the medium of art 'for an instant we glimpse the Inaccessible', we understand that 'some things lead us into a realm beyond words', the word of art moves beyond the human dimension, opening up, through splendour and horror, the mystery of existence; it reveals the silent places of the heart, and the infinite meaning in people's faces. Art is, in itself, victory over the forces of death, even and above all when it explores them, for the beauty it creates proves that the descent into hell cannot be the last stage: 'Art thaws even the frozen, darkened soul, opening it to lofty experience' (*ibid.*, p. 5). This phrase points unequivocally to the resurrectional power of art.

The word 'deed' or 'exploit' (*podvig*) has a very precise meaning in Russian ascetic literature: it refers to the death-resurrection of Christ, to his rising up here and now in combat against those 'monstrous sins', passive complicity and above all 'forgetfulness' or omission. Art is not identical with asceticism because it remains on the threshold of 'conversion' or 'aversion', but they have this in common, that art rescues man from the 'forgetfulness' of sleepwalking, it wakes him up, it nourishes within him, to borrow a term from the Pseudo-Dionysius Areopagite, the 'straining towards the highest life'. Art is 'awareness of awareness', but this heightened awareness does not rely on intelligence alone, but on intelligence united to the heart 'God was here and I did not know it!' exclaims Jacob on wakening from his visionary dream. But let us not love too quickly — art needs intermediaries, ambiguities even, and the biblical sense of overwhelming transcendence should be mitigated by the Greek sense of immanence. 'The gods are here too', Heraclitus would say to visitors surprised to find him at the baker's oven. The tree and the face are here, and I was unaware of it; art has revealed them to us and from now on we will always have the face of Samsonov lifted in prayer and agony towards the stars, in the nocturnal silence of the forest.

This link of art with what is original and unrepeatable, with existence and personality, explains the fact that one cannot speak of progress in this domain. Through the mud and the blood which form the raw material of history, art discerns the constellations formed by personal existences, and inscribes them in the heaven of the 'fixed' stars. 'That's just what I like about art — the fact that there can't be any "progress" in it . . . In the 17th century there was Rembrandt, and he's still with us today, and nobody can improve on him . . . or take the great inventions of the 1870s: we now think nothing at all of them, but has there been any advance on *Anna Karenina* which was written at the same time?' (FC, p. 397.)

Not that art is discarnate; but if it is 'true' in Solzhenitsyn's sense of the word, it achieves a degree of profundity which leads us to the heart of a universal communion — whence the possibility of the symphonic novel — and opens us to the light which comes to us from beyond ourselves. Thus 'true' art communicates both the full material reality of things, and the historical and cosmic weight of personal existences, together with what can be called their eternal dimension. In an interview given in 1967 to the Slovakian journalist Pavol Licko — almost a short autobiography — Solzhenitsyn said he thought that a writer should maintain the balance between present reality and eternity. A work which remains at the level of present reality 'will not be slow to perish'. A work that neglects the present, the tragedy and promise of history, will lack warmth and the power to persuade: 'The writer is always moving between Scylla and Charybdis. He must ignore neither'. The more 'incarnate' work is, the more chance there is of it reaching, in the very density of history — through persons and their relationships — history's meta-historical roots. The more it concentrates on the uniqueness of one person, the more, on the one hand, does it need to describe the human and cosmic whole which that person exemplifies, and on the other, to point to 'the centre towards which all lines converge'.

In the camp where the action of *The Love-Girl and the Innocent* takes place, some prisoners, in the course of an evening of so-called recreation, perform an utterly insipid patriotic play in which an old Russian peasant woman is heard to cry out in front of the Germans: 'Long live the collective farm! Long live our Soviet *kolkhozes*!' What is more, the insipid is mixed with untruth, for all are aware that one of the hopes of the Soviet peasants in the occupied zones was for the dissolution of the collective farms, which were being carefully maintained by the Nazis. The old writer, Gontoir, compares this ideological literature with the cosmic splendour of Essenin: 'We will bend the rainbow for you on the brows of our oxen'. There are, of course, many ways of evoking the Russian Revolution: it can be done at the slogan level — where it is objectified as violence and lies; but, like Essenin, one can also sense instinctively the meta-historical upheaval it produced in men's souls, the hope, inspired by the Gospel and by traditional peasant spirituality, of a cosmic transfiguration — 'We will make a harness of the Milky Way!' — before the revolutionaries, who are so impervious to the invisible, have a chance to triumph.

'True' art

The genuine work of art is neither an ideological drum nor the gold tracery that has nothing behind it. It is, Solzhenitsyn tells is, 'true', and the word needs to be examined. The truth of which Solzhenitsyn speaks, and which, as we shall see, is truth-justice, is radically different from ideology. It signifies the reality of people and things — their mystery, which can be reduced neither to conceptual form in a system nor to objective *praxis*. In *One Day in the Life of Ivan Denisovich* Tzezar Markovich, the film director agreeably relaxed, engages in a conversation on art with a prisoner, X123, who happens to pass through his office, and of whom we know nothing except that he is 'a stringy old man . . . serving a twenty year sentence' (LID, p. 70). A propos of the film *Ivan the Terrible* Tzezar praises the genius of Eisenstein. The old man's response is uncompromising. On the one hand, he says, 'it's all so arty there's no art left in it' — full of a self-conscious aestheticism, while true beauty is, to use Plato's phrase, nothing more or less than the 'splendour of truth'. Beauty is bread for the heart, but the aesthete forgets the bread of being and serves up nothing but a borrowed, violent beauty — 'spice and poppy-seed instead of everyday bread and butter' (*ibid*., p. 70). Beauty such as this is cut off from the true and the good; it can get on quite happily with ideological falsehood and political oppression. *Ivan the Terrible* attempts 'the justification of personal tyranny' (*ibid*., p. 70). Tzezar's answer to this is that art is not a question of content but of form, not of '*what* but *how*'. X123 explodes: 'To bloody hell with your "how" if it doesn't arouse any good feelings in me' (*ibid*.). It would be over-hasty and inexact to assume from this that the anonymous old man is one of the last surviving members of the sectarian and moralizing intelligentsia. He is a witness whom a tragic history has brought back to what is essential, to 'the one thing necessary'. By 'good feeling' he, like Solzhenitsyn himself, means that openness to being, that onto-logical goodness in which the person is fulfilled in the truth of love. The notion of goodness has great significance in countries that have been influenced by the 'spiritual sensitivity' of Orthodox Christianity. Firstly, because eastern Christianity remains, to some extent, an interiorized form of Hellenism, and has therefore inherited (although it transposes it by means of a different combination) the ancient equation of the *kalos k'agathos*, the beautiful and the good, in the sense of a craftsmanlike (and disciplined), heroic (and sanctifying) shaping of the whole man. Secondly, and above all, because man, according to the mystical theology of the eastern Church, is called to share in the 'divine energies' which are so many aspects of the Presence. Now, each 'virtue' signifies a share in one of the divine names — in a divine energy — and goodness manifests both ontological fulness and personal communion. It is inseparable from beauty, because the fulfilment of being in love allows the Light to shine forth. Authentic art — and this is surely true of Solzhenitsyn's — thus enables us to sense the holiness of being in the truth of persons.

A similar diagnosis of art is put forward by Matryona, a 'just' and humble heir — not without her own inner awareness — of the culture and faith of her peasant forebears. One day, on the radio, she hears Chaliapin singing Russian folk songs, but she refuses to recognize them and, questioned by the narrator, replies by making the same reproach of aestheticism: 'He plays tricks with his voice' — whereas, in the folk song, as in the liturgical chant, from which it is so often derived, voice and melody should serve the word, revealing its 'inner mystery' and transforming it into beauty which speaks to the heart. On another occasion there is a recital of Glinka's songs. 'Suddenly, after half a dozen of his concert arias, Matryona appeared excitedly from the kitchen, clutching her apron, with a film of tears misting her eyes. "Now that's . . . our sort of singing," she whispered' (SPP, p. 25). It is the spirit of a particular form of music that she recognizes: Chaliapin was giving a straight interpretation of folk-songs with which she could not identify, but she recognizes their profound sensibility in the transposition and harmonies of Glinka.

Just as the opinions of X123 cannot be equated with the moralizing attitude of the old *intelligentsia*, so Matryona's cannot simply be described as those of the so-called popular soul. Matryona is a latter-day representative of one of those Christian cultures that flourished in the Europe of the past and for which everything had a beauty of its own: sacred music and folk songs, clothes and houses, the objects of everyday life, the country-side of woods and fields, dotted with churches. Beauty was everywhere without one's having to look for it, a beauty nourishing like bread, which strengthened soul and body; and this was because everything was fully useful and yet 'salted' by prayer, taken up into the divine-human dimension so that heaven seemed to weigh upon the earth. The displacement of peoples from the land, and the eclipse of the human-divine shown forth in the Church, have made creations of this kind, in which an entire people expresses and ennobles itself, impossible today.

The collective creation of our age despises the mysterious and is unaware of the light that is in us. But the work of art as a personal creation can rediscover that same source of inspiration, in the measure that it has 'drawn on truth and presented it to us in live, concentrated form' (NPL, p. 6). Solzhenitsyn discovers spontaneously the correspondence established by the Pseudo-Dionysius between the negative (and therefore supra-conceptual) approach to the mystery and its celebration through symbols, through images as manifold as it is ineffable: 'Artificial, strained concepts', those that depend on systems and explanations, on the will to power and possessions, 'do not withstand the image test' and remain empty and unconvincing (*ibid.*). On the other hand, those that relate to 'the essential' become incarnate in 'tangible' forms, with a 'splendour' of their own.

A nuptial art

In *The First Circle* Kondrashov-Ivanov explains that the true painting can be neither a naturalistic copy nor a purely subjective play of images; instead, it is a nuptial encounter with the being which underlies all things and to which they open themselves; a quest for communion with the person one wishes to portray. All the analysis and labour involved are carried forward by an original perception in which man is caught up in the mystery of people and things, by an original truth whose 'emotional colouring' stirs him to the depths of his being (FC, p. 396). To paint a garden on a summer morning is not to take a photograph of it. One has to reach that spiritual place — common to the garden and oneself — where all perceptions are communicated, not just what is seen, but the song of the birds and the morning freshness as well, where sight, hearing and touch unite and transcend themselves in a unique celebration: 'and [one's] own feeling of somehow being cleansed by it all' (*ibid.*). It is the inner 'spirit' that the painter will attempt to convey in his own language of 'composition and colour' (*ibid.*, p. 395). In so far as the artist, through his work, penetrates to the original truth of the world, strange, awkward, unfamiliar aspects of nature come to his notice, which are missing from the hasty panoramic view or the rational exposition. Discontinuities appear, a vertical perspective, in accordance with the creative dynamism of being, and — like the idiosyncracies of individual speech — those 'words' which refer to the mystery, the *logoi* of the Logos which the Greek Fathers recognized as the foundation, form and living force of all created things. And it is in the depths of the cosmic Logos that the artist intues 'the ultimate unity of all things in nature . . . that gift of awareness, serenity and oneness' (*ibid.*, p. 310).

The need for communion is even more obvious in the case of a portrait. Resemblance is, of course, indispensable — 'the features, the shape of the eyes . . . and so forth' — but to reveal a presence not to indicate a frontier. One can only open onself to the 'spiritual reality' of another person by a revelation: one does not exhaust his secret by getting to know him; rather, it grows as more is revealed, and one would do better here to speak, with the spiritual writers, of an 'unknowing'. The genuine painter discovers in the face he scrutinizes hidden and unsuspected depths, not simply a distillation of the past but a future too, a world of possibilities, the magnetic attraction of an icon: 'If I look at the person whose portrait I am painting and discern potential qualities of mind and character which he hasn't so far shown in life, why shouldn't I depict them? What's wrong with helping a man to find his higher self?' (*ibid*., p. 395.) 'Self' refers here to the person in his highest vocation.

In his autobiographical notes Solzhenitsyn stresses that 'the writer's obligations to the individual person are no less than those he has towards society'. Or rather, it is when he starts from the person as a unique, irreducible expression of the biological and social whole that the writer can really understand and serve society. Only thus does he avoid the lies of the 'hirelings' and the temptation to retreat 'into worlds of his own creation or the wastes of subjective caprice' (NPL, p. 17); and so discover the seeds and roots of social phenomena, warding off or denouncing everything in these meta-historical depths that seems to him 'unhealthy and disturbing'. The great artist is a visionary, not in the romantic but in the prophetic sense of 'discerner of spirits'. Moreover, the artist, like the prophet, expresses far more through his art than he knows or imagines he is doing. For although his thoughts, more often than not, spring from his own inner world, his creative activity begins in that luminous darkness where he is separated from no one.

In this way the true creator senses in the 'heart' of man the orientations, attitudes and choices that will make the history of tomorrow. Dostoevsky, observes Solzhenitsyn (*ibid*., p. 19), brought to light the demonic forces that were to be unleashed in the nihilism of the twentieth century, and other examples come to mind: long before the First World War or the concentration camps, Kafka and Picasso described a world of suspicion and torture, the destruction of individuality, the 'death of man'. And yet, reading *The Brothers Karamazov*, Pasternak's *Doctor Zhivago*, or the novels of Solzhenitsyn, one becomes aware of the forces that are being mustered in secret by the powers of good and who tomorrow perhaps, a 'cloud of witnesses', will shine out in the history of our time.

5 Eros and love I

Conscious femininity

The encounter of man and woman, as described by Solzhenitsyn, takes place in a society in which the woman, legally and professionally emancipated and frequently engaged in the most laborious kinds of work, has had to assume responsibility for her own existence. All Solzhenitsyn's heroines work, including, if not the wives — whose problems with domestic help are very bourgeois — at least the daughters of the oligarchs of the regime. All of them hold down a job as well as meeting heavy demands at home. In the hospital where the 'cancer ward' is, most of the doctors are women. After she has fulfilled her responsibilities as head of department, Ludmila Dontsova queues up to buy supplies for her home. Zoya, who is twenty-three, does her job as a nurse at the hospital, her medical studies, and a few domestic chores that her grandmother, because of her age, cannot be sure of getting done. Zoya's parents are separated, her father has abandoned her and sends her nothing: in a society where family instability appears to be widespread, children must learn from an early age to cope with a tough world.

It is well known that in the Soviet Union, three-quarters of the members of the medical profession, as of the teaching profession and the textile industry, are women. However, either through persistence of the patriarchal tradition or through the unavailability of the women themselves, burdened as they are with their domestic duties, the posts of responsibility seem invariably to go to men, as in the hospital described in *Cancer Ward*, or in the technical college and town where the short story *For the Good of the Cause* takes place, although the heroine is in fact a teacher.

Just as a woman, while taking on the same professional tasks as a man, has besides these all her domestic cares which have been aggravated for some time now by 'communal' apartments and queues, so, in the concentration camp system, which is not content to crush both men and women, she has been cruelly prostituted. Solzhenitsyn returns more than once to the condition of women in the camps. It is one of the central themes of *The Love-Girl and the Innocent*, where a woman prisoner is heard singing with desperate irony:

> I loved a gang leader,
> The camp boss likes me best,
> I slept with the work clerk
> To feather my nest! (LGI, p. 12)

Kostoglotov, in *Cancer Ward*, says all there is to be said, a propos of the woman he loved, who, herself a deportee, has been separated from him by the ruthlessness of the camp system. There, he observes, women are violated by the 'common laws' to whom the authorities systematically give pre-eminence over the 'politicals' (CW, p. 185).

Thanks to the hard apprenticeship of the prison camp, of war — during which some were mobilized in fighting units — and of professional life, Soviet women have become tough and assertive, even where it entails reversing many traditional attitudes. Typical of this reversal is the *drame passionel* that took Grania to prison. It was war time. Her husband, an egyptologist and university professor, was not mobilized, but she, who had begun as a militant young Communist and then been taken as a volunteer in the Civil Defence Corps, was. Left behind in Moscow, he wrote her love-letters. She, a crack markswoman, quickly gained confidence, became head of her section and then sub-lieutenant. But one day she learned that her husband was having an affair with a singer from the operetta. She asked for leave, flew to Moscow, broke open the door, surprised the lovers in bed, and ended it all by firing her sub-machine gun at her husband (LGI, p. 36).

Lydia Georgievna notices, not without some concern, that the boys are spending more and more time on their appearance, and wearing more colourful clothes than the girls, 'as if it was not they who had to chase after the girls but the other way round; and more and more often it was not they who took girls by the arm, but the girls who took theirs' (SPP, p. 59). In *Cancer Ward* it is young archangelical Asya who takes the initiative with the timid Dyoma, who would contemplate her from afar in mute fascination: 'Why are you so shy? This is the second day you've been around. You haven't come up to me' (CW, p. 140). And Zoya, too, copes methodically with her young suitors: 'By her third year Zoya was well out of the "old maid" category' (*ibid.*, p. 171). Caught in the general shake-up after the war and worried because after so much carnage there were twenty million more women than men, she goes to find her partners at the House of Culture where the main activity is to organize dances in a pretty coarse atmosphere. As for Asya, she brings Dyoma quickly up to date on her own experience: 'Oh, me . . . since the ninth'. One of her companions in the eighth class got pregnant, and another 'was . . . for money'. Now it was more than half the girls. 'The earlier you start, the more exciting it is . . . Why wait? It's the atomic age!' (*ibid*., pp. 146-7.)

Equality of treatment, the somewhat dismal moral laxity, heavy professional and domestic duties can all be degrading for the woman; but they can also bring her to deeper, clearer appreciation of what femininity really is. What is more, it may be that the regime is less determined to condition the woman than it is the man, in that the themes of its propaganda, like all Marxist thought with its techno-logical titanism, are essentially virile. It may be, too, that the women's feeling for what is concrete, her interest in people and things rather than in ideas, have partially immunized her against the ideology. At the height of the Stalinist period, the 'free workers' employed in the *sharashka* do not take long to discover the true human worth of the prisoners who had been depicted for them as 'enemies of the people' and monsters. They have been trained as auxiliaries to the political police, but the youthful ardour that impels Clara towards Doronin, or the humble awkward, possessive feelings cherished by the un-fortunate Simochka for Gleb Nerzhin go far beyond any politics or police: 'In this way, the cunningly wrought chain broke at the link formed by a woman's heart' (FC, p. 42).

Obviously their many trials, their need to stand up for themselves and their desire to assert themselves after the long-dominant male pattern gave many women a virile quality. Middle-aged Russian women of the nineteen-forties appeared to Solzhenitsyn 'tough, weather-beaten . . . used to having things their own way at home and at work' (SPP, p. 144). Dontsova's brusqueness is very masculine, and yet she brings to the practice of her profession two qualities that would seem to be profoundly feminine. First there is her ability to synthesize, not where words are concerned, but in her appreciation and treatment of the invalid as a person. Dontsova has managed something that has become almost impossible in our specializing age — to acquire equal knowledge of radioscopy and radiotherapy. Secondly, and bearing witness to femininity at its source, there is the genuine spiritual 'maternity' she exercises towards her assistants, who respond to her with grateful trust and call her 'mother'. Dontsova is quite disinterested in her desire to pass on her experience to them; without any ulterior motive she expresses pleasure when one of them shows better judgment than herself. Vera Gangart, who has worked with her for eight years, since she finished her own studies, is aware that 'all the power to pull back from creeping death those who came and implored her to save them — every atom of it came from her contact with Ludmila Afanasyevna' (CW, p. 65).

If the older women, in spite of everything, have become slightly masculine, the younger ones try to recapture, within the framework of their dignity and freedom, a more complete femininity. Trained by Dontsova, Vera Gangart is a good example of womanly fulfilment in the exercise of responsibilities on a strict par with those of a man. In secondary school she wanted to become an engineer, but the tragic experience of a friend who was struck down by an incurable disease and suffered a long agony during which no one could relieve him, drew her towards medicine: to heal men rather than restrain matter — the choice is not insignificant. Time spared her nothing: her fiancé died in the war and she herself was suspect for a long time on account of her German name; but she has found inner stability and happiness in her profession. Having worked in radioscopy she is now concentrating on radiotherapy, gaining thus the all-round experience encouraged by 'Mother'. The patients 'had become *her* patients . . . her own permanent living charges who trusted her and waited on the encouragement of her voice and the comfort of her glance' (*ibid.*, p. 50). In fact her grave, gentle, profoundly feminine beauty helped her to encourage her patients 'with glances and smiles to make up for their finding themselves inside this notorious cancer circle' (*ibid.*, pp. 66-7). Her watchful brown eyes were indeed, for the patients, 'the eyes of a doctor', but they were also 'the eyes of a very old friend' (*ibid.*, p. 353) — a friend indicating a personal relationship that transcends the difference between the sexes. Her 'severity' is 'touched with softness', but 'not a dim, diffused softness'; instead, it is 'somehow melodic and based on harmony' (*ibid.*, p. 240). Her femininity is preserved intact yet 'methodically' integrated into a personal vocation and service.

Thus women — and particularly some women it would seem — inject into Soviet society a goodness and active love of which it stands in great need, and of which our civilization also stands in great need, relying as it does, in the West as in the East, on technology, ideology and drugs. But in Russia women have assumed a more specific role: they have passed on the faith.

Among the elderly it is a faith steeped in ritual, though now they are forced, by the persecutions and the breakdown of rural civilization, to be more scientific. Matryona does not go into the garden on St John's Day, otherwise there won't be a harvest next year, and when the east wind is up she believes someone has hung himself (though perhaps she prays secretly for his soul). She never makes the sign of the cross, as if, from the patrimony of traditional gestures, the choice between what is preserved and what disappears was made at random, super-stition proving more resistant than symbol. All the same, the narrator feels that she prays in secret, and he notices how she calls down God's blessing on her own work and that of others; in spite of the persecu-tions and the burning of statues, she has kept the icons in her house and lights the lamps in front of them on Sundays and feastdays; and above all she observes the evangelical command to love her neighbour, to love her enemies. Then there is Aunt Styofa, one of the patients in the 'cancer ward'. 'She [is] a mother and a grandmother already, and [has], like all grandmothers, wrinkles and an indulgent smile for human weakness' (*ibid.*, p. 135). She invites confidence, knowing how to accept and listen. Dyoma, an uncommunicative, silent adolescent whose idea of mothers, of women, was tragically distorted when his own mother prostituted herself in his presence, tells Aunt Styofa 'things about himself and even about his mother which he would never have revealed to anyone else' (*ibid.*). Aunt Styofa keeps up the traditional practices of religion and has a precise knowledge of the various 'meat' and fast days, though she explains fasting in a perspective that is more generally religious than specifically Christian: 'Because, Dyomusha, if you stuff your belly full it will pull you right down to the ground! You can't go on stuffing like that, you have to break sometimes' (*ibid.*, p. 138). And to Dyoma's intrigued question: 'What's a break for?' she has the decisive answer: 'Breaks are to clear your head' (*ibid.*). It is true that she does not say *who* is the source of this light or mention Christ's name, but she bears humble witness to his presence, not so much by words as by gestures and by her openness of manner — distributing the provisions brought her by her children among the women of the ward; recalling that life 'depends on God' and that he 'sees everything' (*ibid.*, p. 137). And her 'carefree smile' never left her' (*ibid.*, p. 138).

The recurrence of the kind of femininity that always sides with the underdog is more striking still, because apparently a *volte-face*, in the case of Agnia. This girl grew up, just before the revolution, in a family belonging to the intelligentsia and fiercely opposed to the established Church 'which had so easily come to terms with serfdom' (FC, p. 157). Agnia's mother and grandmother, with whom she lived, never set foot inside a church, ignored the prescribed fasts, despised the clergy and poked fun at the faith. They had 'their own staunch creed, which was always to side with the underdog, with anyone who was oppressed, persecuted or harried by the authorities (*ibid*., p. 157). But after the revolution it was the Church's turn to be persecuted. So Agnia turned to the Church, began to attend services, became interested and finally converted.

The faith is not merely passed on, but is also renewed in a 'crucified' Church. Solzhenitsyn describes an Easter procession which advances as an object of curiosity and derision through a crowd of young toughs. In it there are, as one would expect, some old women; but there are also a number of young girls, whose faces are stamped with 'determination and detachment' in their acceptance of the worst, and in contrast to the crowd which surrounds and insults them, the faces of the youngest shine with an inner purity.

The innocence of the flesh

Solzhenitsyn approaches the mystery of *eros* with a heart purified by the nearness of death. The old distinction between pure and impure, partly revived by Leviticus and then by the Church, has been swept away for good and all, along with the fascinated loathing for the flesh (which soon degenerated into mystical orgies) of the various gnoses and Manichaeisms (including the Christian Manichaeism of the monks) in the historical deluge from which he emerges. For Solzhenitsyn there remains the innocence of the flesh and the terrible freedom of the individual. He speaks tenderly and respectfully of the young, especially the girl who 'embodies some sort of enigma simply because she is young' (CW, p. 351). If young girls, like everyone else, are narcissistic, their narcissism cannot remain closed in on itself. They are vaguely conscious of celebrating a mystery: 'Every tone in the girl's voice was part of the enigma that surrounded her. She knew this, and when she spoke she seemed to be listening to her own voice' (*ibid*., pp. 351-2). It is enough for a real woman to turn up, one who is on the way to realizing her full personal vocation, for the girl's momentary fascination to fade: 'She was a girl like any other' (*ibid*., p. 355). It would be perfectly easy to run up a list of these young people, seeing in them nothing but puppets, all moved in the same way by the same impersonal power. Clara falls madly in love with one of the prisoners in the *sharashka* where she is employed as a free worker. But one evening at home, during a big reception, she accepts the attentions of a distinguished critic: 'It was not her fault that the time had come when she was compelled by nature's inexorable law to fall to the one who had caught her like a ripe September apple dropping from a tree' (FC, p. 457).

Personal awareness, however, is awakened too, and touches the soft impersonal flesh with regret, until a true love tries to reconcile them. When the critic, Lansky, kisses her hands and the embroidered cuffs of her long sleeves, Clara, as she lets herself go, 'feels a tightening in her throat'. It is not Lansky or Doronin that she loves, but love itself, life with all its mysterious contradictions: 'It was not her fault that the two of them — he and the other — were not one but two'. The intuitive perception of this difference catches at her throat, but it is still too soon. The idolization of being conflicts here with the uniqueness of the person. Each of us is inwardly aware of a pull, an impersonal *eros*, as in the ancient cults whose symbols are passed on by India even to this day — stylization of the sexual organs and their union, a divine interplay of the contrasting elements of the cosmos. Each is inwardly aware also of the Christian revelation of the person and of an unsatisfied longing for communion. If Solzhenitsyn roundly condemns all mechanical eroticism and the violence which prostitution does to women — 'Stuff it, there's no man who's sweet and kind. They're all the same, they're only after one thing . . .' (LGI, p. 35) — he speaks gratefully of the gift a woman can make of her body, in a brief encounter, to a man who has been crushed by life in the camps or by sickness. When Oleg Kostoglotov, barely convalescent, drifts into Tashkent and everything goes blurred for him, he finds himself pushed by the crowd in the tram right up against the body of a young girl who neither objects nor moves when some of the passengers get off, in spite of the rough, grotesque appearance of her neighbour. Oleg 'remembered gratefully the little curls on the blonde girl's neck. *Her face he hadn't even glimpsed*' (CW, p. 558, our italics) — she disappeared at one of the stops without turning round, having given the momentary contact with her body to this unknown man, like a gift of life. In *The First Circle*, Sologdin, who has the purity of the young hero, recalls 'with gratitude' the brief moment of carnal joy offered him by a nurse he met by chance in the camps. And after his initial automatic resistance — the woman's request seems as obscene to him as the use of foreign words in the Russian language! — he abandons himself to the caresses of the buxom Larissa, a 'free worker' disappointed in her husband, good, and humble as well, with something of the peasant about her. It is not a meeting of two people but a nourishing encounter with all the goodness of life, of the rivers, of mother earth, as in those old agrarian rites which persisted for so long in

Russia, and which Tarkovsky, in his *Andrei Rublev*, contrasts and unites, in a powerful counterpoint, to the ascetism of a monk-painter whose sensibilities, although sublimated, remain none the less vulnerable.

The encounter between Dyoma and Asya in *Cancer Ward* is a hymn to the innocence of the flesh.

To get the measure of this innocence one has to remember that the adolescent Dyoma has been scarred in the depths of his being by the most sordid experience to which our liberty — when it becomes fatality — can expose the flesh. His father died in the war when Dyoma was only two. His mother soon began to give herself to prostitution, and would bring men back to their only room: 'And it sickened Dyoma so much that the very thought of it, which his friends found so thrilling, seemed to him like so much pig-swill' (*ibid*., p. 136).

Then, in the hospital, where he has come to have his bad leg examined — and he has just been told it will have to be amputated — this adolescent, prematurely matured by the double wound in his soul and in his body, meets a young girl whose beauty, in — and in spite of — her 'hollywood' style, is almost unreal: she had 'yellow hair, the sort you never saw anywhere, with something light and rustling built up from it' (*ibid*., p. 139). Dyoma admires her from afar, until she comes up to him with slightly vulgar simplicity and tells him her name: Asya. Then she chatters away, trotting out all the platitudes of her time and milieu: she listens to music because 'silence always gets me down' (*ibid*., p. 141); it is dance music, and she is 'dancing in the mind'. Dyoma has to admit that he can neither dance nor sing nor play the accordion and that what is more he has got to have his leg off; to admit that he doesn't go in much for sport, doesn't earn much as a lathe operator and doesn't travel. whereas Asya belongs to a sports team and has visited lots of towns, even Leningrad. As for the meaning of life, for her there is nothing but pleasure, while Dyoma remains affected by Tolstoy's solemn question: 'What do men live by?' And when, put out by her companion's gravity, Asya exclaims: 'What a lot of Mummy's darlings you all are,' one only has to think of Dyoma's mother to realize how complete could be their misunderstanding.

But there is no misunderstanding. Asya talks as a bird sings. It is her way of being there. What matters to Dyoma is the fact that they have met and that he can look her in the face, discover her strange eyes with their touch of green — such honest eyes in her 'film star' get up — and suddenly he senses, through the open neck of the grey dressing gown she wears like the rest of the patients, the miracle of her young body: 'What had repelled him so much when his mother did it, now for the first time struck him as innocent before the whole world, unstained, capable of out-weighing all the evil on earth' (*ibid.*, p. 145). He realized that when Asya talked it was with all the naiveté of her young being, so that 'just as behind her dressing gown there was nothing but her nightdress, her breasts, her soul, so behind her words there was nothing hidden from him. She saw no reason to hide' (*ibid.*).

But it is a tenuous integrity: Asya obviously 'hadn't been through the disease at all; the pain, the suffering . . .' (*ibid.*, p. 145). When the testing time comes − although she has been expecting simple tests, she is told that her right breast must be operated on − she collapses completely and cries with all the despair of a child. Dyoma's soothing words, his timid declaration that he will always want her, none of it can touch this adolescent who cannor imagine how she can exist without a complete body. However, her tender feeling for the latter is transformed, through a spontaneous gesture, into tenderness for Dyoma. She brings he breast close to his lips, and he, awkwardly no doubt, 'like a suckling pig', but gratefully − how often Solzhenitsyn repeats this word − breathes in 'the warmth her body was offering him . . . Nothing more beautiful than this gentle curve could ever be painted or sculptured. Its beauty flooded him. Hurriedly his lips took in its even, shapely contour (*ibid.*, p. 425). Eroticism? No. Even if the personal encounter is merely touched upon between these two beings whom a shared suffering has brought together, two mysteries here penetrate the solar fervour of the flesh − 'It shone as though the sun had stepped straight into the room' (*ibid.*) − to give it an indescribable tenderness: of motherhood and of death.

'When she did not take it away, he returned to its rosy glow again and again, softly kissing the breast. He did what her future child would never be able to do' (*ibid.*). This tableau, rapidly sketched by Solzhenitsyn, lies somewhere between the ancient portrayals of Mother Earth and the nursing Madonna, that favourite subject of the Middle Ages, and it is not for nothing that Asya remains seated in a mother's position, rather than a lover's. She heals what a mother has destroyed. Instinctively she reconciles a man with motherhood, with woman, with life.

And the imminent operation which will deprive the girl of her breast is a reminder of the fact that even the most perfect forms must dissolve in death: 'He kissed and kissed the marvel hanging over him. Today it was a marvel. Tomorrow it would be in the bin' (*ibid.*, p. 425).

Here death provokes neither sexual paroxysm, as a way of forgetting, nor the disgust of false asceticism, but, instead, the most personal tenderness: 'You'll remember, won't you?' (*ibid*., p. 425). For there is no resurrection of the flesh except in the resurrection of persons.

6 Eros and love II

The ambiguity of eros

Absent for long periods from man's experience, able to come to him at the end of a life without problems — in his maturity or even his old age — giving him courage to ignore convention, *eros* is 'a benediction', an ardent passion (A14, p. 83); the blind benediction of fire. It can transcend itself and achieve fulfilment in the communion of persons; between a man and a woman it can become the language of immensity and silence, the power of mutual service. But by becoming objectified it can also drive them back into their respective solitudes, supplant the absolute, and then sink back, having reduced an hour, a month or a lifetime even to ashes.

The encounter of Oleg and Zoya in *Cancer Ward* expresses this ambivalence of passion and desire.

Zoya is well aware that her name means life. At twenty-three she grows, vigorous and strong, like a new bud, out of the bitter bark of the past. As a child, the war had tossed her about like the sea. She has lived through failure, exile, the panic-stricken evacuation of Smolensk, and those long hungry months when, far from looking after her, the adults would come and steal her rations. She has known the unedifying lives of her parents who practised a kind of mutual torture and, to crown all, abandoned her. Now, both medical student and nurse, she is confronted daily with the ravages of cancer, so much torment in which death almost always has the last word.

Her salvation lies in her own good health, her vital energy, her joy at feeling herself intact and healthy — from the roots of her being, through every cell in her body, to the very tips of her fingers. She is a matchless pearl in 'the salt sea of life' (CW, p. 172), so that it is no longer just an ocean of tears, but of universal fecundity. When Zoya runs she likes to feel the movement of her breasts — and their heaviness when she leans over a patient's bed. Any effort, by speeding up her breathing and her circulation, does her good — it never tires her but rather confirms her positive feelings about her own life. Just as she loves dancing because dancing is a formalized expression of desire, so, choosing, her partners to perfections, she enjoys the interplay of love because life becomes so intense in such moments, so intoxicating. And what is more, she does all this so simply, never allowing herself to become suppressed, adopting the approved 'masculine' attitude as is the right of every independent woman. When Kolya, who has taken her home from the dance, embraces her in the half-lit doorway, Zoya 'enjoys it', but remembering that she has to get up early in the morning she packs the poor chap off coolly enough — in any case his remarks had seemed a bit stupid (ibid., p. 171).

Even at play Zoya is a deeply serious person, a wise child. She manages her affairs with a great sense of responsibility, helping her grandmother in the house, bargaining 'like a fishwife' in the market whence she returns with abundant provisions (provision meaning foresight), and using her scant free time to make herself a blouse. Like a bee she is constantly at work.

In Zoya too, as in the bee, the life force is directed towards building the hive and continuing the species. She is aware of 'a certain balance and hermony in her body' (ibid., p. 173), and feels that passing love affairs merely serve to damage this innate tendency. The callow youths, to whom she is in every way superior, can never establish a balanced relationship with her — can never satisfy her yearnings: in the middle of a passionate embrace, she suddenly feels 'that it [is] a bit of a waste of time' (ibid., p. 171). The memory, and even the obstinate presence of death, war and cancer, do not produce in her — as yet — the feeling that she has to reach beyond herself, but rather that what she needs is a serene fulness: 'It all lacked that stable, deliberate continuity which gives stability to life, indeed gives life itself' (ibid., p. 171). The bee-like side of her only sees any point in strewing clothes round the room if it subsequently results in some kind of 'creative stability' (ibid., p. 263). Her grandmother has told her that it isn't a handsome suitor she wants, but a good one — that is, a man of integrity and courage. Zoya longs, with the whole of her being, for a man endowed with 'stability and strength', someone who, having undergone severe trials and come out on top, is worthy of her, the kind of person she would want as the father of her children. One day, Oleg points humorously to the connection between Zoya and the zoo — between life and animal life: 'What about the "zo-" in it? Don't you sometimes feel close to those zo-ological ancestors of ours?' (*ibid*., p. 188). Zoya acknowledges this continuity of the life of nature within herself: 'We're all like them. We provide food, feed our young . . . Is there anything wrong with that?' (*ibid*.). But where the human race is concerned, this wholesome animality calls not only for motherhood but fatherhood as well — which is something unknown among the animals. Zoya, by a deep-seated biological necessity, is a family creature. But virile flesh does not see beyond the present, and so passion and misunderstanding grow up between Oleg and Zoya.

For Oleg Kostoglotov, Zoya is a body, experienced simultaneously as mystery and as objective reality: the first female body he has been able to touch since the forced abstinence of war, imprisonment and sickness; the first he has been capable of desiring after the long, exhausting experience of cancer. Through the mediation of Zoya's body it is his own body, his own presence in the world that is given back to him: 'Now that his body was healing, the passions of life were returning to it. All of them!' (*ibid*., p. 188). Oleg sees Zoya from the legs to the lips; but not beyond them — that is to say that all he sees of her face is her mouth, focus and interpreter of her body, proclaiming her sexuality. Burning lips, 'neither pink nor painted' but 'the colour of pale flame' (*ibid*., p. 186). For Oleg Zoya is a 'top' and a 'buttercup'. A short, compact figure with strong, sturdy legs, and firm breasts 'which formed, as it were, a little shelf, almost horizontal' (*ibid*., p. 79). The top, with its rounded shape, is traditionally a symbol of fecundity, of the earth from which life can germinate; and the buttercup is a tiny vessel full of the golden luxuriance of spring. For Zoya, Oleg is the typical man forged by trial, possessed of real strength, physical and spiritual, 'something she had never met before in the boys she went with' (*ibid*., p. 186): 'She was pressed close to him, she could feel him with her womb, and was trying to guess, "Will it come from him? Is he really the one?" ' (*ibid*., p. 263). At one point Oleg tries to respond to this anticipation. He puts himself in Zoya's hands, entrusts his future to her, finishing his confidences with the plaintive cry: 'Who will share with me the wretched happiness of staying alive?' (*ibid*., p. 186). Later — though the words are more the reflection of a glowing present than a pledge for the future, he says: 'You will come to Ush-Terek, won't you? We'll get married, we'll build ourselves a little house' (*ibid*., p. 263). But the fact is that Zoya has not really understood Oleg. When he has finished his confidences she mimes for him the self-revelation of love, taking off her nurse's uniform with his help and parading before him in a dress that is not functional but beautiful — a buttercup yellow dress. But she confuses Oleg's strength with that of adventurers and vagabonds, and as she flits about she begins to sing a song from the film *The Tramp*: 'The Tramp's life was rather like yours' (*ibid*., p. 188). Oleg rebels: in the prison camps the tramps used to maltreat the 'politicals'; he himself stood up to them, clutching his knife — he did not come by the scar across his face by chance, but in the fight against injustice. Oleg's personal destiny, his burden of history, is lost on Zoya. Like so many women she does not need history because she has life — which is immemorial and has no memory. Virile strength is enough for her, *virtù* as the Italians of the Renaissance called it — but *virtù* does not reach good and evil.

There can only be a place, therefore, for desire, which gradually develops into passion. Their first kiss lacks the innocence of true love, it does not rise from the 'heart's fulness'. They exchange it with their eyes open, at Zoya's request, and there is something objective about the whole process: 'Close, unbelievably close, he saw two tawny eyes, almost predatory looking, and each of his eyes looked separately into hers. She was kissing with those confidently taut, experienced lips' (*ibid*., p. 262). At last he looks into Zoya's eyes, but they are 'predatory': he is their prey. His own vision is curiously out of focus: the unifying eye of the heart is missing. Neither lets go; already an expert, Zoya calls the tune, evaluating, no doubt, and making comparisons as she does so. This is why eroticism makes for such terrifying loneliness: here you have a language, and all the tools of that language, but no one to communicate: 'Their mouths joined again. They wanted to drain each other dry' (*ibid*., p. 262) — to get something and give nothing of themselves.

Soon, however, mechanical pleasure becomes habit, need, passion; and passion, because it fails to integrate a person's inner drives into a process of genuine exchange and mutual service, leads, paradoxically, to emptiness. Two isolated people, reaching out pathetically towards a form of satisfaction through which each merely consumes the other without bringing healing; two people who, precisely because of their isolation, are strangers to the suffering of others: passion might well be defined as the opposite of compassion. At this point the episode of the oxygen cylinder should be re-read.

When he comes across Zoya while she is on duty, Oleg's one concern is to find himself alone with her: 'He was thinking of this girl, this woman, this "bit of a skirt"', and how to persuade her to go off with him again that might' (*ibid.*, p. 265). From the girl to the woman to the 'bit of skirt', the transition from person to sex object gathers momentum as it goes. Oleg is like one possessed straining towards possession, where the word 'possession' includes the intrusion of the demonic. He follows Zoya 'like a chained man' (*ibid.*, p. 265). At one stage, Zoya has to take an oxygen cylinder to a dying man. They carry it together, and through it communicate to one another their trembling desire: 'All they did was give him the oxygen balloon and walk on. Those last four cubic centimetres of air in the doomed man's balloon had been no more than a pretext for going off into a corner together and getting to know each other's kisses' (*ibid.*, p. 265). Yet this man, trapped in his lonely suffering — his knees were raised 'as if they were a wall' (*ibid.*, p. 265) — would perhaps die that night with no one to relieve his last moments: 'Oleg's brother and neighbour, abandoned and hungry for sympathy' (*ibid.*, p. 265). Oleg had not given him a thought. Oleg wanted to forget death — that of others, and his own — 'He wasn't thinking of the doomed man he'd left. He's been one himself two weeks ago and in six months time he might be one again' (*ibid.*, p. 265). But can such an over-intense way of living really be called life, when it ignores death and denies a man the respect he deserves, just because he is going to die? The author's reply to this is contained in a few words, and it is terrible. He simply says of the dying man: 'He was still alive, but there were no living men around him' (*ibid.*, p. 265). Of course, that means that Oleg and Zoya had gone off. It also implies that at the height of their passion they ceased to be living men.

Passion is like a disease which is born, develops, dies, and is finally sloughed off like a dead skin. Oleg's passion for Zoya is no exception, and of course he discovers later, with Vera, quite another dimension of love. He undergoes a new form of treatment which leaves him in a debilitated state but his passion dies of itself while he is still carrying on his erotic games with Zoya, but has not really come to know Vera. When he first embraces Zoya, Oleg experiences the same feelings of distance and futility that Zoya had with Kolya, and he stops going to see her. Zoya meanwhile realizes that this desperately sick man is not the one who will give her the fruitful security she longs for. Their relationship is then reduced to the level of a game which has come to an end once all the possibilities have been exhausted. The last word relates back to the idea of nothingness and to the oxygen cylinder as a symbol not of compassion but of passion' 'Everything that had grown up between them, taut and strained like the oxygen balloon they had once carried together, had suddenly subsided little by little, until there was nothing' (*ibid.*, pp. 503-4).

All the same, Zoya makes Oleg a friendly offer of hospitality when he leaves hospital. Oleg, who knows what his position is and is taking stock of his loss of virility after a relentless course of treatment, refuses to dissemble, makes his act of renunciation and goes away. In the note he writes to Zoya from the station, he finally recognizes her true nature and wishes her 'honestly and sincerely . . . the happiest of marriages' (*ibid.*, p. 565). Then, leaving regret and bitterness behind him, he feels towards her nothing but 'gratitude', the fundamental attitude by which, in Solzhenitsyn's eyes, a man honours the transient gift — of beauty and presence — made him by a woman in a prison camp or a hospital. 'I'm so grateful to you', writes Oleg to Zoya, 'for allowing my lips to get a taste of genuine life . . . I will always remember everything about you with gratitude' (*ibid.*, pp. 564-5).

Beyond eros, love

Solzhenitsyn provides many examples to show that love is more than *eros*, and that the very distance that separates them points up the mystery of the human person and favours the awakening of spiritual awareness. Sometimes the woman is instrumental in such an awakening, sometimes the man, and at others the action is reciprocal. Agnia, in *The First Circle*, is in the great western-medieval tradition of the cult of the Lady, which appears again in Russia at the beginning of the twentieth century with the celebration of *La Belle Dame* by the Symbolists, and even slightly earlier in the mysterious visions of Wisdom which Soloviev describes in one of his poems:

> A stream of blue and gold,
> A strange flower in her hand,
> She was there smiling at me,

> And her smile was radiant
>
>   . . .
>
> And my soul drew away from the things of this world.

Agnia hardly belongs to this world at all — a statement which does not, of course refer to the world of God, and of men who pray, suffer and give themselves in humble service: she has, after all, rallied to the persecuted Church and loves to walk or sit quietly in the forest, the primordial temple, but only to the world of inertia, passion and the lust for power: 'Her step was so light that she seemed to walk without touching the ground at all' (FC, p. 154). There is something superior about her face: one does not notice her mouth but her quivering eyebrows and nostrils. Agnia's face, like Vera's, seems 'about to take wing'. She is moved by the sublime challenge of the Beatitudes; turning her back on the capable and the powerful, she loves those who are 'persecuted for justice's sake'. Her face passes constantly from shadow to light, from the darkness that wounds her to the light where she finds deliverance, but this is a change rather than a transfiguration: 'There was something childlike and innocent about her. The idea of making love frightened her' (ibid., p. 155). But this 'fear of life' for which her fiancé, an ambitious young engineer, reproached her, enabled her to penetrate more deeply into its meaning: her vocation is contemplative: ' "I'm sure you're going to be famous, successful and have all the things you want," she said sadly. "But will you be happy, Anton? . . . You must beware, too. If we get too interested in what's going on around us, we lose . . . we lose . . . how can I put it?" ' (ibid., p. 160).

With the faith of those to whom nothing is a matter of mere chance, she does accept the love of Anton Yakonov, but in her heart of hearts she wants to do without its physical expression. She feels she has something else to do for her fiancé — help him discover, through his experience of a pure love, the spiritual dimension of existence; and he, who is on the lookout for success and categorically rejects the invisible, who has already had his experience of women and likes them well-covered, is attracted to Agnia by something other than her body.

The day comes when she wants to introduce him to the other light. She takes him up to the little church of St Nicetas, high on a hill from which one can see the whole of Moscow — Moscow of the 'forty times forty' churches, which were to disappear in the turmoil of the Stalinist period. Agnia draws him to the spot with a promise of earthly beauty. But there is no discontinuity between earthly beauty and heavenly beauty, between created and divine wisdom. Inside the church the light becomes concentrated, the cupola captures it, and then reflects it back so that somehow it appears to come from the icons and from the great mosaic of the Risen Christ. Even Agnia, though she does not realize it, appears to Yakonov surrounded with light: 'Agnia placed a slender candle on a large brass stand and stood piously, unobtrusively . . . with a rapt expression. The diffused sunlight and the deep yellow steam of the candles restored life and warmth of Agnia's cheeks' (*ibid*., p. 161).

This girl opened up to the mystery an opaque soul, sated with its own vitality. Her prayer is identified with that of the Virgin Mother, which was able to open to the divine unknown a world under a curse. In the church to which Agnia has taken him they are preparing to celebrate a feast of the Virgin, and Yakonov is moved by the beauty of the hymn. He suddenly realizes that this beauty is transmuted and awakened 'not by a man's short-lived lust for a woman but by the rapture of sublime love' (*ibid*., p. 161).

Later on, however, Yakonov will 'renege'. He settles for untruth, and Agnia sends him back the ring he gave her. What has become of the girl in the tormenting process? Yakonov has his position of power, but he owes it to a ruthlessness that in the end will destroy him. On the fatal night when he learns of his unavoidable disgrace he returns instinctively to the hill, but the church, like his own life, is in ruins, and this man who once reproached Agnia for having too little taste for life now leans against the crumbling walls of the sanctuary 'wanting to die' (*ibid*., p. 162).

Just as the woman can mediate spiritual awareness to the man, so the man can do the same for the woman. Lyuba's parents were peasants who had the use of a family allotment. The entire family was deported when the land was collectivized and both father and mother died in the upheaval. In order to survive Lyuba took to prostitution, and in the camp where she has ended up she has become more of a 'love-girl' than ever. As far as she is concerned, men are 'only after one thing' (LGI, p. 35), so that she herself has been reduced to that one thing. Then a young officer, Nemov, who has been arrested for some unspecified reason, discovers her, and offers her tenderness and personal love. He does not ask for her body, but simply that she should be there because with her he feels good, free: 'It's as if you had released me, let me out into freedom (*ibid*., p. 118). And so for one week they live this true, liberating love at every level of their being, including the physical, and during that time he is rescued from the 'mist' in which he had been stumbling since his arrest, while she is set free from the objectivization of her own body. She thanks him humbly: 'I'll keep this last week as long as I live, hidden deep inside me' (*ibid.*, p. 126). Then she makes a terrible sacrifice: she agrees to go and live with the camp doctor, a sensual petty tyrant, knowing that in so doing she will be able to save Nemov. She gets his name stuck off a list of those to be transferred to a camp from which no one ever returns and cares for him after an accident. For him she is a lost woman in every sense of the term; he does not judge her, but his heart is chilled by what he cannot remedy. She, however, because he has made he aware of herself as a person, surrenders her life in order to save him. Her last words, spoken on the threshold of her place of humiliation are: 'He's alive' (*ibid.*, p. 139).

Solzhenitsyn has described the mutuality of a personal love capable of transcending *eros* in the story of Oleg and Vera which runs like a golden thread through the long narrative of *Cancer Ward*.

Vera means faith; but her secret name is Vega, the star, which conveys the inaccessible aspects of her personality in a light which can transfigure everything.

While Agnia is destined to live through a crucifying alternation of states, to know light, but a discarnate one (which is perhaps why Yakonov betrayed her), Vera's destiny seems to be transfiguration. Zoya's symbol is the 'top', the spherical form in which the here and nowness of life is affirmed; and Agnia's could be an inverted triangle, rooted in heaven with only one uncertain point in contact with the earth; but Vera's silhouette, her hieroglyph, is made up of two perfectly poised triangles, 'set apex to apex' (CW, p. 246), the one rooted in heaven, the other in this world. Zoya's element is the earth; Agnia's as her name suggests, is fire, the burnt offering; but Vera's is the air, vibrant and suffused with light, which unites heaven and earth: 'this gentle, ethereal creature' (*ibid.*, p. 354) has the slender legs of a gazelle, and so small a waist that it makes people want to pick her up and lift her into the air. She is neither fair nor dark: her eyes are the colour of *café au lait*, her hair chestnut — always the darkness is interspersed with light. But transfiguration is most obvious in her lips: they too were 'made for kissing' (*ibid.*, p. 79), which could not be said of Agnia's. The paradox is, though, that it is her lips which give Vera's face its miraculous delicacy — they are 'like little wings' (*ibid.*, p. 78); 'vital and separate' they seem about to flutter from her face like a lark into the sky (*ibid*., p. 79). They are full of life, but serve her mind and heart: 'Tiny movements of her mouth, quirks in the right-hand or left-hand corner, a slight pout or a slight twitch, emphasized each thought and illuminated it' (*ibid*., p. 357). Above all her lips radiate goodness: every time she smiled 'her goodness shone like a little sun' (*ibid*., p. 79) for 'her smile was kind, not so much her smile as her lips themselves' (*ibid*., p. 79).

Vera means faith, but it also means fidelity. Vera remains faithful to her fiancé who was killed in the war. He had been a childhood friend and gave her the nickname Vega. She is a doctor and familiar with the body and its laws, in a country where the official ideology is materialistic (though her situation would hardly be different in the west with its degenerate Freudianism). She is well aware that for the majority of her colleagues and contemporaries a young woman cannot find fulfilment, let alone exist, without an active sexual life. Chastity 'just wasn't possible. After all, the laws of tissues, the law of hormones and the laws of age were indisputable' (*ibid*., p. 371). Yet for Vera it is possible — the human person, and that person's fidelity to another, is able to transcend all forms of conditioning: 'What was the significance of the laws of cell-growth, reaction or secretion? What relevance did they have if there was no other man like him? And there wasn't' (*ibid*., p. 371). Not that Vera regards herself as eternally bound, but she knows that her dead friend needs her intercession if he is to get used to his new and mysterious existence in another dimension: she helps him by her faithful love, 'he is still present . . . he exists' (*ibid*., p. 371). She feels that only a relationship based on true love could put this earlier attachment in the right perspective; by a merely sensual affair she would risk breaking the chain of communion, the links of which, though invisible, are nonetheless real. True love is not something one finds simply by looking for it; it always comes as an unexpected grace. For the time being all her light is for her secret friend and her patients.

At first Vera and Oleg's relations are those of an attentive doctor and a difficult patient, who wants to know what is happening to him and what treatment he is receiving. Fairly soon, however, Oleg emerges from his 'utter alienation' (*ibid*., p. 74), sheds the characteristic mistrust of the prisoner, and begins to thaw under the influence of Vera's radiant gentleness; while she perceives the true quality of this unpolished, reserved man, realizing what he must have learned from his proximity to death and the fight against injustice. The relationship that grows up between them is very 'Pauline': a mutuality in which, however, the man ensures stability and protection. Oleg perceives that beneath her apparent severity there is 'something of the little girl' about Vera; and she, to cope with Oleg's inconsistencies — whether he is refusing to give blood or hanging on to his boots in spite of rules and an imminent inspection — talks to him quite spontaneously in a pleading way 'almost as if she was complaining to him' (*ibid*., p. 243). The tone she used with him wasn't even one of equality but almost deference. 'She was even surprised herself that it has arisen between them. She had never used it with any other patient' (*ibid*., p. 244).

The idea of having an affair never occurs to them — and in any case, for a long time Oleg thinks Vera is married, and she does not enlighten him. He simply wants to talk to her, 'not just for a moment but for a long, long time' (*ibid*., p. 79), and the world of childhood, with its games which are also perhaps rites, is open to them again.

Oleg has preserved in alcohol some rare roots which he dug up on the banks of a lake in central Asia: caught up in a dangerous kind of superstition, he wants to use it as a remedy and at this Vera, angry for once, confronts him with her sound common sense and her devotion: 'We're trying to save your *life*! She spelled it out with particular insistence, her eyes bright with faith' (*ibid*., p. 250). Then, after they had exchanged names — so that, like her dead fiancé, he knows that she is Vega — they go into the hospital grounds to carry out a symbolic act; at the feet of a solemn, silent Vera, Oleg makes a hole in the earth and pours the cloudy brown liquid into it; then he covers it with earth: 'There was something boyish in the way he poured the stuff away and put back the stone. It was boyish, but a bit like making a vow, too, or sharing a secret' (*ibid*., p. 254). Oleg gives up his earthy superstitions because life has become personal for him. He enters on the way of trust.

He becomes more firmly committed to it when he, who has never wanted to receive blood from others, allows Vera to give him a transfusion. For a moment he experiences the joy of allowing himself to trust. But only for a moment: he has been warned that the treatment he is undergoing will permanently affect his virility, and, all of a sudden he gives vent to his despair: 'Why bother to save such a life?' (*ibid*., p. 359).

For Vera everything is at stake: not just her reputation as a doctor — there is no other possible way of saving Oleg — but the very meaning of her life, that fidelity which implies the renunciation of *eros*. To Oleg's 'Why bother?' Vera replies: 'There must be some people who think differently! If everyone thought your way, who could we live with?' (*ibid.*, p. 360).

This cry rescues Oleg from his physical despair, awakens his awareness of himself as a person and gives him back not just the 'country' but the 'faith' of his childhood, when, as a precocious twelve-year-old, he rejected the materialism of the prevailing attitude to sex: statistics, percentages, degrees of pleasure, frigidity, and the physiological details which need to be taken into account, but which become terrifying when they seek to explain everything.

Then he receives a sign. In the peaceful silence of the room he notices on the ceiling a strange patch of sunlight with a kind of pulsating movement as if it were a luminous heart, or the mysterious cloud which, in the Bible, is a particular manifestation of spiritual Presence — the cloud, for example, which enveloped Jesus on the mountain of the Transfiguration. Oleg finally realizes that it is 'no more than the reflection of a puddle, a patch of ground by the fence tht hadn't dried up yet. The image of an ordinary puddle' (*ibid.*, p. 361). The transfiguration of something ordinary which to all appearances had been irretrievably wasted.

The transfiguration of the world begins with a relationship of truly personal love. Vera accepts the incompleteness of her life, Oleg that of his body. Their peaceful joy puts them in tune with the beauty of the world, and makes them especially attentive to those who are most deprived — because they too are persons. Vera sees the apricot tree in flower — 'you could always tell them by their airy pinkness' (*ibid.*, p. 363) — as she had never seen it before. For both of them their friendship was 'the only thing that stopped the cancer wing withering on the stem' (*ibid.*, p. 461).

For Oleg, 'there was a sort of bright, reflected light surrounding her and radiating from her figure' (*ibid.*, p. 500), where the rays of light are an iconographic feature. Vera transfigured joins Agnia: 'A stream of blue and gold . . ./She was there, smiling at me.'

True love is undivided. At the end of the transfusion Oleg wanted to kiss Vera's hand. In his farewell letter he says: 'I still wanted all the time, *all the time*, to pick you up and kiss you on the lips. So try and work that out' (*ibid.*, p. 566).

There is no contradiction. For a man and a woman *eros* is the natural language of 'spiritual communion' (*ibid.*, p. 559). If on leaving hospital Oleg had accepted Vera's invitation to share her place the unexpressed *eros* would have become *'this thing*, this sort of grey, decrepit, ever-growing serpent' (*ibid*., p. 566).

That is why the greatest thing Oleg can do to express his love for Vega is to disappear, to leave the future open for her by confirming her in her personal vocation. The overwhelming effect of a truly personal encounter can only achieve stability and fruitfulness through sacrifice — if the love cannot be given physical expression then separation must follow, as a blessing: 'You are right, right in everything, right in your past and in your present. Your future is the only thing you do not have the power to guess' (*ibid*., p. 566). And if the love can 'become flesh' there must be duration, serious mental commitment, and the no less sacrificial patience of a living loyalty.

7 Eros and love III

Separation and loyalty

The commitment of 'faith' between a man and a woman is affirmed beyond all carnal 'possession' as it is beyond all social conformity, in the fidelity of those who are separated. The extreme case, frequently evoked by Solzhenitsyn, is that of political prisoners and their wives. The latter, as accomplices of supposed 'enemies of the people', are subjected to a harassment which makes things very difficult for them in their university studies and in their professional work. The rare letters they receive from their husbands mark them out, as does the plain card with no envelope, which shows the date of their annual visit — all that is allowed to prisoners in the *sharashka*. This is why, to avoid being turned away again, Sologdin's wife 'lied to her employers, telling them she had no husband, and had stopped writing' (FC, p. 163), preferring brief verbal messages which one of her friends sometimes passed on to him. Nerzhin refuses to give his wife's address — a student's hostel where she simply says that her husband disappeared during the war.

In face of this social ostracization and of ever-increasing difficulty in communicating with the 'living dead', some try to forget, get divorced (not just for form's sake but really) and then remarry or 'live their own lives'. Others, lacking in strength of character, and childishly incapable of assuming responsibility alone for the material aspects of life, age prematurely and give in to despair, like Gerasimovich's wife, whose drawn face we glimpse for a moment and whose faint voice we hear, weighed down with intense suffering: 'I have no strength left to do anything. I really believe that if any man was kind enough to propose to me, no matter how old he was, I'd marry him' (*ibid.*, p. 260).

Many, however, remain faithful, with the humble fidelity of ordinary women who have less to lose and, more concerned than ever with health and nourishment, keep themselves busy making up parcels: 'They listed, in pounds and ounces, exactly what foods and how much of each they had brought . . .' (*ibid.*, p. 257); still steeped in their 'dogged wifely concern, that instinct . . . which keeps the human race going' *ibid.*, p. 257), yet dimly aware of sheer personal fidelity beyond it all. This fidelity is manifested in a less striking way in those — we do not know how many — who come through their trials to a full experience of communion. One of the most moving characters in *Cancer Ward* is the intelligent, bespectacled, formidably well-read woman who has become a hospital orderly and whose entire *raison d'être* is 'hanging on a single thread, a single thread of hope' for the hypothetical letter she will receive from her imprisoned husband (CW, p. 511). Hers is not that tense kind of expectation which would only drive her deeper into her distress, but an expectation full of faith which strengthens her inner resources and alerts her to the suffering of others. With quiet devotion to duty she 'crawls under the beds to wash the floor'; carries 'anything heavy, inconvenient or dirty' (*ibid.*, p. 508).

Sologdin's wife, whom he compares with Iseult, will live for months — years perhaps — on the brief message he sent her by word of mouth: 'He loves her, he believes in her, he hasn't lost hope' (FC, p. 175). According to St Paul these are the theological virtues — faith, hope and charity — but here they are reflected on the horizontal plane in the love of two human beings and therefore differently expressed. Love is fundamental — the pinciple, but also the goal; and it has been lived, as the Gospel puts it, 'in one flesh' wherever *eros* meets with tenderness, when its strength — source of all cosmic energy — is taken into the context of a human relationship, and the self-centredness characteristic of the flesh is transformed into that awareness of others characteristic of persons. Then, as in those stories where the couple are suddenly separated and have to undergo a long arduous process of initiation, distance intervenes, and makes all mutual help impossible. Only faith remains, trust and the commitment of one person to another, and faith opens up the future, introduces hope for a time when two human beings, profoundly transformed physically and morally, will still be able to recognize one another, will recognize in one another that eternal something which change cannot reach and which comes through unexpectedly in a look, in an inflection of the voice, in that unique way of maintaining the existence of a body and soul in a destiny ravaged with discontinuities: 'To *return* was impossible. After four years in the army and a ten-year prison sentence there would probably not be a single cell of his body which was the same' (*ibid*., p. 242). But in the stranger who returned, faith would be able to discern the familiar person, and the covenant sealed in the flesh could be renewed. Solzhenitsyn has observed that man escapes from seriality and social uniformity by reason both of his 'physiological' and 'spiritual' dimension. In the love of a man and a woman the two come together again.

Gleb and Nadya Nerzhin only lived together for a year, before the war broke out, in the whirl of their final exams. Then, during the war, taking advantage of a lull at the Dnieper front, Nadya managed, with the help of false papers, to join Gleb and 'they snatched back a few days of the happiness stolen from them ' (*ibid*., p. 244). But the fighting broke out again, Gleb disappeared, and from then on she would only see him in prison — brief, intense meetings, fairly frequent at first, when, in the relative disorder that followed the war, Gleb landed up in a small camp on the outskirts of the capital. Overcome with feelings of tenderness 'he kissed his wife's hand, and he watched for the light in her eyes' (*ibid*., p. 252), and then, as a supreme proof of the love that renounces all claim to possession, moral as well as physical, each gave the other freedom: 'Don't waste the best years of your life', Gleb tells Nadya. 'Leave me and marry someone else'. And she, who has seen women among the prisoners writes: 'I don't mind if you go with other women, if you're unfaithful to me . . . In fact I inists on it' (*ibid*., p. 253). It is precisely this respect for the other and that other's freedom which set the seal on their fidelity when Gleb left

Moscow for the north and they stopped seeing one another. Now he is back near the capital again, in the *sharashka*, but he can only see his wife once a year, and then for no more than half an hour, during which, according to a new regulation, he is not allowed to embrace her — experience of the desert where conjugal fidelity achieves full awareness. 'I thought I could stand anything . . .' says Gleb, 'but when they trample on the one live feeling that's left to me, my love for my wife . . .' (FC, p. 239); and Nadya recalls 'that timeless entity which was made up not just of him and of her, but of the two of them together, and which we usually call by that overworked word "love" ' (*ibid.*, p. 257). This frail woman is endowed with granite determination, and the political police officer in charge of the Mavrino who later meets her by chance in the metro is stunned by her intense, angry expression as she turns to speak to him: 'What power could make this woman cling so stubbornly, so desperately to a man she wouldn't see for years, and who was destroying her whole life?' (*ibid.*, p. 189).

The real obstacle between Gleb and Nadya, however, is not the fact of their separation, but the difference of degree in their spiritual maturity — expressed fairly accurately by Nietzsche's dictum that woman loves man but man loves God. Nadya's spiritual awareness is focused entirely on her fidelity. She does not yet exist of herself in a genuinely reciprocal relationship, but only through the mediation of Gleb. Her studies are in abeyance, her thesis on 'The Struggle Against Serfdom' has been rejected as a result of the authorities more rigid policy. She fails to make contact with the students whose room she shares; they interpret her enigmatic behaviour as that of a disillusioned 'old maid'. Gleb's fidelity, on the other hand, is born of a spiritual awareness that has long been vitalized by a passionate search for truth. It was this search, in part, which drew him to the world of the camps where he knew he would find the most reliable witnesses to the vicissitudes through which Russia had been living since 1917. Nadya is not involved in this search, which now turns inward as he looks for the spiritual roots of life. She was hurt because Gleb did not see her or hear her cries when for the first time he was marched in a column of prisoners, from the prison to the gate where she was watching for him: he was 'listening keenly and with evident approval to what his neighbour a tall, grey-bearded old man, was saying' (*ibid.*, p. 250). This difference of attitude explains also the fact that when they gave each other their liberty, Gleb said to Nadya: 'marry someone else' (*ibid.*, p. 252), while Nadya ended her letter with words that were subtly possessive: 'You'll come back to me, won't you?' (*ibid.*, p. 253).

The connection between love and awareness is manifested in a wide variety of ways. With Nadya love awakens awareness. With Innokenty Volodin and Gleb Nerzhin an already sensitive awareness is the basis of love. But that which carries love into a dimension beyond time, beyond the world, is what creates the risk that it will be lost in this world: Innokenty only discovers his wife as a person when he is about to lose her for having attempted to save his 'neighbour' from injustice; Gleb experiences the full force of his fidelity to Nadya just when he is about to descend, without hope of return, into the lower circles of hell, there to discover the truth about history and the meaning of life. Gerasimovich, another prisoner in the *sharashka*, rediscovers, in the course of her annual visit, all his feelings of tenderness for his wife. When he sees her, worn out, pathetic, and 'no longer very pretty' (*ibid.*, p. 272), he is shattered to realize that they have between them only one memory: 'No young girl, however pretty and fresh, but whose brief experience of life was a closed book to him, could ever mean more to him than his wife' (*ibid.*, p. 272). However, in spite of her despairing cry: 'You're so clever, invent something for them. You must save me!' (*ibid.*, p. 276), he refuses to perfect the police gadgets he has been asked for, and which would enable him to get an early release. He refuses to save his wife at the price of the suffering of a multitude of innocent people. True love only goes beyond *eros* to the extent that it does not become closed in on itself. Power gives it life even as it crushes it. Only a higher passion, which cannot exist without sacrifice, is able to encompass and go beyond erotic passion to make a genuine encounter possible. It is then that a true companionship of service begins, a common creativity; or else, if separation comes and continues, a common enrichment, attention to the same call, intuition of the same centre 'where all lines meet'.

The meeting between Gleb and Nadya in the Lefortovo Prison is, by its very reticence, one of the most intense love scenes in all literature. This single yearly visit — at least while Gleb is still at the *sharashka*, which cannot be for long — takes place in an interrogation room. Unlike the vision of Dante, which owes so little, fundamentally, to the Gospel, love is not a means of escape to the world above; like Christ and with Christ it goes down into hell. The meeting, in the presence of a guard, lasts half an hour. All they can do is to make allusions. *Eros* is not absent but even *eros* is there only by allusion, as the logical conclusion of their face to face encounter. The smile of welcome which Gleb reserves for Nadya makes her feel 'jubilant' (*ibid*., p. 262). She half unbuttons her coat and pulls it back to show him her new blouse — orange, as a reminder of the pact sealed in their bodies at a time when the sun shone on them: 'In the one long, roving glance, Nerzhin cast his eyes over his wife — her face, her neck, and the opening at her bosom' (*ibid*., p. 263). She draws her coat back a bit more, emphasizing the offering of her body, and her neck appears to Gleb 'finely moulded like a young girl's' (*ibid*, p. 264); and he visualizes the narrow shoulders 'which he had loved to fondle when he embraced her' (*ibid*.). Only her breasts, which he also visualizes under the folds of her blouse, have lost their fulness, symbolizing the aching barrenness of those lonely years: and Gleb understands that Nadya too has been crushed by history — 'It was borne in on him that her life, too, had been crushed under the wheels of the grey prison van' (*ibid*.). Their love has been crucified.

For what kind of resurrection? Their words, which come less easily than their gestures — the time is too short, the presence of the guard too inhibiting — are crucifying words at first. Nadya tells Gleb they should get divorced: she won't be able to survive otherwise; but as far as they are concerned it will only be a legal fiction. Gleb agrees but he is hurt; he then gives Nadya to understand that his detention may be a very lengthy one. She becomes desperate, and all the more so because she interprets her husband's strange detachment, and the quiet gravity he has acquired, as remoteness. 'It simply can't be!' she cries, when he brings up the idea of indefinite detention. 'Or did you think I would really leave you?' (*ibid*., p. 269). Her womanly, motherly intuition has registered the suffering, the call for help, the concealed weakness of this man who is apparently so steadfast and so detached. Then their conjugal faith is miraculously renewed — which is what resurrection is about in the first place: 'Her upper lip trembled, her face was contorted and her eyes were filled with utter devotion. "I believe you, Nadya!" he said in a changed voice . . .' (*ibid*., p. 269).

Gleb, who moves more quickly, has reached the point where his conjugal fidelity is rooted in his faith in God. Discreetly he tells Nadya about it: 'Don't tell me you've started believing in God? . . .'. He smiled: 'Like Pascal, Newton and Einstein' (*ibid*., p. 270) — Solzhenitsyn loves to emphasize the fact that the great scientists believe in God. Resurrection is this as well. In spite of the new regulation, they embrace one another: in the world of today, true love, like God himself, is against the rules. Gleb's voice 'quivers with tenderness' as he repeats his confidence in Nadya, whatever she does: 'Let's do what's best for you' (*ibid*.) The sign she makes to him then 'with the fingers of her ringless hand' is a definitive commitment which has no need of symbols: at this point, to quote Berdyaev, one passes 'from the symbol to the reality'.

This renewed fidelity is immediately put to the test and confirmed.

A few days before, Gleb struck up an ambiguous relationship with Simochka, a young free worker who works in the same laboratory as he does. She is a plain girl, small, with a long nose, and seems 'ridiculously weightless, like a bird' (*ibid*., p. 76). Most 'unexpectedly' − since she is there not simply to assist him but also to keep guard over him − she fell head over heels in love with Gleb: 'She had flung herself into his arms and clung to him, eager and frightened. Why should he hold back and deny her?' (*ibid*., p. 77). But there is a snag. Simochka is sincere, a little possessive, and has an eye on the future. In this post-war society, where the law of supply and demand is so heavily loaded against women, particularly the plain ones, she sees Nerzhin as a possible husband. She knows quite well that if he is married his wife by sheer force of circumstances will either have divorced him or been unfaithful. She on the other hand, will wait for him. Nerzhin plays somewhat cynically on her possessive sincerity: 'let her give herself to him and they will have a child'. So it is not just a brief encounter that he is proposing to her, but a future. Now, as far as he is concerned, there has never been any question about his fidelity to Nadya. He knows that he is soon going to leave the *sharashka*, and with a touch of irony, of tenderness even, he has pity on his own body, and on the rather pathetic body of this girl. But he does not love Simochka, he does not trust her; nor does he reveal to her the nature of his historical research − in his free time he is writing an account of Stalinism. The mistrust engendered by the realities of history remains with him: 'These trusting, loving eyes might very well be working for the Security Officer' (*ibid*., p. 78).

They have decided − he out of compassion for his body which for so many years has been deprived of all female closeness; she with her ideas of building a future − to meet on the Monday and secretly make love in the recording booth in the acoustics laboratory. Simochka gets ready with the seriousness appropriate to a wedding; she has a bath, puts on some scent, gets into her best dress: 'Yes she wanted to have his child and to look after it while Gleb was serving the rest of his sentence' (*ibid*., p. 620).

But on the Sunday Gleb saw Nadya. The confirmation of their conjugal fidelity then makes any kind of affair impossible in the future: this was not just a prohibition; he had received a new insight and could not preserve it in any other way: 'After his yesterday's meeting with her, his hands and lips were clean, and it seemed impossible to him now to go up to Simochka, draw her close to him and kiss her' (*ibid.*, p. 622). Instead he delivers himself, before the crumpled little bird, of some highminded reflections on conscience: 'What was wrong didn't seem wrong to me, but something normal, even praiseworthy. But the lower I sank in that inhumanly ruthless world, in some strange way the more I listened to those few who, even there, spoke to my conscience' (*ibid.*, p. 624). Simochka cannot weep any more; she makes no further attempt to defend herself; in the silence her eyes 'radiate suffering'. Then Nerzhin realizes that he is well on the way to becoming pharisaical about conscience: 'If you die knowing that you are not a swine, that's something, isn't it?' (*ibid.*, p. 624). He realizes that his words sound like an empty 'sermon'. His soliloquizing satisfies his own vanity but to Simochka he simply seems 'to be talking on and on about himself' (*ibid.*). Disconcerted, he switches on the radio: a programme of love songs evokes all the foolishness and the heartbreak of love, with a poignant beauty which touches their hearts and brings tears to their eyes. Gleb asks Simochka to forgive him.

Beauty, beyond an impossible moral demand, appeals to the mysterious. Gleb will remain faithful to Nadya. He will respect Simochka without despising her: the same love will begin to grow in her. He is no longer proudly alone with his conscience: 'It even seemed as though the decision had not been his own' (*ibid.*, p. 627) He presses his forehead against the window pane and looks out into the night. The lights cease to be those of the Moscow suburbs and become *the* light.

Returning to the students' hostel where she lives, for a while Nadya recalls nothing of her conversation with Gleb but the fateful announcement: he will not be freed for a long time, perhaps never. A terrible cold creeps into her soul. She would like to be alone, and she reacts mechanically to the superficiality and the petty worries of the girls around her. Then a friend of her own age turns up — his studies had been interrupted by the war. Like Gleb, Shchagov served in the army, but he is simpler, less intellectual, and his stability both attracts Nadya and calms her down. He would undoubtedly like to have an affair with her, since he is methodically pursuing his plan of contracting a rich marriage which will help him to achieve his ambitions. For a moment, Nadya allows herself to enjoy the consolation of male closeness, but she soon draws back, crying out that her husband is alive and in prison, and that she has just seen him. Shchagov leaves and Nadya is left alone, barely alive. In an adjoining room someone is playing one of Liszt's studies — marked *disperato*. She goes over to the window, reaching out to feel the cool panes against her palms, and stands there 'like someone crucified on the black cross of the window' (*ibid.*, p. 358). Then Shchagov, unsophisticated but loyal, comes back with a bottle of wine and two glasses: 'Well, soldier's wife! Don't lose heart! . . . Let's drink to the resurrection of the dead' (*ibid.*).

This is the mystery of conjugal fidelity. Nadya, who 'does not believe in God', has just participated in the death-recurrection of the unknown God who awaits us in the darkness even of hell. Two windows open on the same night. Between the separated couple there is only the night — a sign of crucifixion and resurrection.

Enduring love

Solzhenitsyn's works do not only describe separations. There is also the day-to-day experience of 'enduring love'. There is always the danger that the family may not be the outward expression of a marriage but its justification, so that two people who no longer love one another remain together in order to keep the human race going. The truly human family is born of a love that becomes and remains personal, thanks to — and in spite of — *eros*; thanks to — and in spite of — the children. Few writers have been able to evoke in quite the same way as Solzhenitsyn the humble tenderness involved in sleeping together, something unknown to the loose liver for whom a bed is simply a place of amorous adventures: 'She was sleeping on her side in a remarkably graceful position with her face against his shoulder, and her breast resting in the crook of his arm. They had been married for five years already, but even in his present half-conscious state, he felt a glow of tenderness because she was here beside him, and was sleeping in her own funny way, warming her small feet, which were always cold, between his legs' (*ibid.*, pp. 509-10). The author then evokes the slow dance of the sleeping couple. The wife, disturbed no doubt by a dream, mutters something without waking up, turns over, instinctively snuggling closer to her husband, to whom her back is now turned: 'he also turned over, curling round her. Gratefully she became still again. Their small son was sleeping very quietly in the dining room' (*ibid*., p. 512).

Nothing happens by chance with Solzhenitsyn: the man here is called Adam, which takes us back to the integrity of the beginning when *eros* was not an object; and the fact that this Adam Roitman is evidently of Jewish origin is a reminder of the tradition of the spirituality of the flesh, which was so strong in Judaism, as Rozanov has pointed out. In certain traditions of the Kabbalah it is said that the union of man and woman manifests the union of the earth and God; and St Justin Martyr, who records this idea, sees nothing in it contrary to the Christian revelation. St Paul himself placed human love within the context of the love of Christ and the Church, and what is the Church if not the world in the process of transfiguration? Yet for too long Christianity seems to have shrunk from the implications of this mystery. Jewish spirituality alone, in the biblical tradition, dares to affirm that the exile of the Shekinah (the bright cloud of God's presence) comes to an end every time a man and a woman truly love one another with all their strength, and remake from the earth of their bodies the Eden which receives life from the breath of Elohim.

In this enduring love the man does not play the superman: 'Hemingway's supermen were creatures who had not yet raised themselves to human level' (CW, p. 368); and the woman is not a Carmen, eager for pleasure for pleasure's sake, Carmen was 'a pseudo-woman, a man in woman's clothes' (*ibid*., p. 369), in the sense of the narcissistic virility of male-dominated societies. What a woman expects from a man, if love is to be an enduring love, is 'attention and tenderness and a sense of security when he [is] with her, a feeling that he [is] her shield and her shelter' (*ibid*., p. 369). So thinks Vera Gangart, who is socially independent and excels in her profession. This mutual exchange in which the man nevertheless plays a protective role cannot be explained in terms of sociology: it is in fact 'Oleg, a man without rights who had been deprived of all significance as a citizen, who for some reason made Vera feel protected' (*ibid*., pp. 368-9). At this point we are taken beyond all cultural contexts to the best of St Paul, to the mystery of being.

If everything is offered in the realm of love, nothing is guaranteed, 'there is nothing predictable' (FC, p. 492). Sometimes it seems as though things have reached an *impasse*. 'Everything that could be said has been said, all arguments have been exhausted' (*ibid*.). Words, quite as much as a hostile silence, can create a barrier. The mania for explanation and self-explanation which has overtaken the age we live in often leads one to diminish the other, to replace him by a verbal phantom, and the distance which he cannot but feel between himself and this phantom becomes his irremediable solitude. When the way becomes obscure it is far better 'to sit down and howl' (*ibid*.); then a minor miracle might bring down the barrier that each has created against the other: 'a chance meeting of the eyes', a tone of voice, might lead back to the mystery of the person. 'The blank wall may suddenly crumble away' like a mist of words when the heart's sun is risen, when the vision of the heart is reopened 'and where all was darkness there is light, and an easy path along which two people can walk again' (*ibid*., p. 492).

Sometimes, however, such measures are insufficient or impossible. The opportunities for mediation between two people do not arise. The bonds which united tenderness and *eros* are broken. Life together becomes a degrading burden.

Solzhenitsyn has ruthlessly analyzed this slow disintegration of love – true love and not mere passion – in *August 1914*. Georgii and Alina Vorotyntsev have been united in an enduring love. He, however, feels relieved and renewed as a result of the separation imposed on them by the war, and it seems to him that 'something had gone out of their life' (A14, p. 130). Their life together, like the bark of an aging tree, had become hard and rough-edged, and this 'hardened', 'shrivelled' life got in the way between two persons.

Admittedly they have not been united in genuine self-giving. They have no child and Alina has gradually grown tired of listening to Georgii telling her about his research and its problems – he and his friends have finally failed in their efforts to modernize the Russian army. In her disenchantment she saw her husband as from the outside – hardly capable of true concern for people, often cast down by depression, only interested in his work – and she began to erect the barrier of words, multiplying her repeated observations delivered in a cutting tone of voice, with the idea, of course, that he should change, mend his ways: 'Georgii promised to keep a check on himself. But after every one of their rows there was an aftermath of resentment and depression' (*ibid*., p. 132). Then the mediation of the flesh was reduced to the level of triviality. 'Even the ritual in bed became mechanical' (*ibid*., p. 131). After they had made love 'his wife would ask him to take his weight off her or would start talking in a workaday voice about domestic matters' (*ibid*.). From then on everything becomes mechanical and profane. There is no longer any mystery, only a ritual: the woman chatters during the act of love just as the priests might behind the iconostasis. Even clothing changes its meaning, becomes a barrier. Nadya's orange blouse is reversed in Alina's dreadful nightdress. 'She bought herself an ugly, thick flannel nightdress. "I don't like it". "Well, I don't care, it keeps me warm" '(*ibid*.). The less one gives of oneself, the more claims one lays on the other. ' "Every woman", thought Vorotyntsev sadly, "tends to lay too many claims on 'her' man" ' (*ibid*., p. 132).

The dream Vorotyntsev has not long afterwards is clear proof of his disaffection and unspoken yearning. He dreams of a woman whom he truly loves, with irresistible clarity: 'it was *she* – the one, the longed-for, the inexpressibly beloved woman, the loveliest . . . of all the women in creation' (*ibid*., p. 244). The image of Alina and of her nightdress – of finer material here, but inevitably a reminder of the thick flannel one – dissolve in this mutual 're-cognition'. His union with this unknown woman, whom he has somehow always known, is the celebration of a mystery: They are 'warmed by the boundless joy of the discovery that never, never again would they need to look for anyone or anything else . . .' (*ibid*., p. 245). There are echoes here of the Platonic myth of man's primordial unity; but whether it is a gnostic temptation or the maternal archetype is not important. What would human love be worth that had never been touched by this nostalgia, and how fruitful would that service be whose growth was never marked by these moments of reminiscence and appeal.

Vorotyntsev's dream is possibly a premonition: one day he will meet this woman and they will be united in an intense, serious and truly adult love. Solzhenitsyn, who is no youthful romantic, has exploded 'the myth that love comes only once' (FC, p. 350).

It is also possible that through the salutory experience of separation and war, Vorotyntsev comes to realize that this woman is his wife, and that the other woman is his wife as other, rediscovered in her separateness: 'It had all been some strange misunderstanding; somehow he had grown stale. When he came home from this war everything would fall into place again and their life would be as full of happiness as it had been . . .' (A14, pp. 535-6).

And so, at times, enduring love is achieved – not an imperative but a magnetic attraction; not constraint but appeal – and so enduring that in the end the couple come to resemble one another: 'They had the kind of happy affinity, both inwardly and outwardly, which makes a couple more than husband and wife' (FC, p. 274).

The children who are born of such a love are as it were illumined by it. Talking about a student who had come to Moscow and whom we see writing to her parents, as she often did, Solzhenitsyn says: 'Her father and mother still loved each other like two newly-weds' (*ibid.*, p. 323). Each morning when they parted, her father would keep turning round to wave to his wife, and 'their daughter loved them with equal devotion' (*ibid.*).

In the last analysis, Solzhenitsyn prefers the myth of Philemon and Baucis to that of Tristan and Iseult. The most 'successful' couple he describes is one whose love is enduring and indeed definitive since both have passed the age of sixty, and expect to die together. Nikolai and Elena Kadmin have been banished for life to a central Asian town where, each complementing the other, they practise medicine – which means that they have been banished to the permanence of their love. They met thirty years before, and 'this was not her first marriage' (CW, p. 290). The horrors of history may not have spared them, but they have merely served to confirm them. Ten years' detention in Siberia, far from one another, could not really separate them, and since they have been reunited their joy seems inexhaustible: 'If they managed to get hold of a loaf of white bread – how wonderful! . . . There was a good film on at the centre that day – marvellous! A dental technician had arrived to provide new dentures – excellent' (*ibid.*, p. 289). Their greatest joy was to walk out towards the Steppe to watch the sunset – he slight and mobile, but holding back, she plump, and grown heavy through ill health, and moving more slowly.

They bought a mud hut, 'their last haven' (*ibid.*, p. 289). A platform of dried bricks with a sack stuffed with straw on it became their 'conjugal bed'. Now they even have a round table and a glass kerosene lamp with a homemade shade – and the hut has been transformed into a living room in which to receive friends. Each stage of this adaptation was a source of wonder to them, and Solzhenitsyn observes that 'it is not our level of prosperity that makes for happiness, but the kinship of heart to heart' (*ibid.*, p. 290).

The mutual love of the Kadmins leaves them ready for anything. They radiate confidence and peace. Their patients, the townspeople, friends near or far, and even such humble creatures as their dogs benefited from their 'at-oneness'. One of the friends, Oleg Kostoglotov, writes to thank them, and asks for their blessing: 'Elena Alexandrovna says she has written ten letters in two evenings. It made me think what a wonderful thing it is – this sympathetic, steadfast consideration you have for people . . . So may you continue to flourish, my friends, and may your light shine (*ibid.*, p. 322).

Open to infinity, enduring love transforms a couple into a source of benediction.

PART THREE

Mystery

8 Being as sacrament

Rediscovered ascesis

War, imprisonment, sickness and the day-to-day 'feat' of fidelity and service can thus be internalized as a discipline through which spiritual awareness is released from its 'natural' associations and becomes capable of perceiving as mystery. Here the experience of some of those who survived the Nazi concentration camps links up with that of Solzhenitsyn who escaped with his life from their Stalinist counterparts. In November 1945 two French intellectuals, both former concentration camp internees, wishing to understand better the spiritual states they had experienced, came to consult Mircea Eliade, the great historian of religion. 'Both said that in prison they had been made aware of a new "human condition"; there they became convinced that man is something *other* than what they had until then thought him to be; that there is a spiritual reality . . .' (Mircea Eliade, *Fragments of a Diary*).

St John Climacus, one of the ascetical fathers who helped to form the Orthodox tradition, noted that man must learn to 'contain the incorporeal within the corporeal' by tearing himself away from the surface, where awareness 'prostitutes' itself, in order to recover a greater degree of transparency in the depths even of his body — and therefore of all the 'flesh' of the world, since the body is simply the world interiorized by the person.

Solzhenitsyn makes some sensitive and exact observations about the rhythm, the vigilance and the metamorphosis of *eros* — it is as if he had rediscovered, through his experience in the labour camps, the 'art of arts and science of sciences' familiar to the ascetics of the past. In the camp he learned to breathe, so that now, in the noisy waste land of the large town, it takes only a shower of spring rain on a tiny garden 'hemmed in by five-storey houses like cages in a zoo' and he is able to rediscover the power and the sheer joy of breathing. One must breathe as deeply as one can, resting the other senses — 'I breathe with my eyes open, I breathe with my eyes closed' (SPP, p. 193) — until one ceases to hear 'the motorcycles backfiring, the radios whining', and begins to drink in 'this air steeped in the fragrance of flowers, of moisture and freshness' (*ibid*.). Through this bodily respiration, and beyond it, respiration with another rhythm is set in motion: one 'breathes the Spirit' with a sense of 'plerophoria', as the eastern Christian spiritual writers say, of fulness at all levels of one's being. And if man is forced to keep vigil, or requires himself to do so, this rejection of a great natural rhythm affirms the transcendence of the person and enables him to penetrate with his conscious into the night of the unconscious (FC, p. 512); to discern, distinguish and rightly marry the as yet shadowly impulse of life and the 'transluminous' darkness of the spirit. At last *eros* can be transformed by continence, at least if the latter finds its place in the context of an all-embracing ascetism by which vital energies are transformed into 'sound thoughts' — and where the head and the flesh are in no way at war with one another, but where the entire being is unified in the heart.

Above all it is man's most fundamental link with the world — that concerned with his nourishment — that the long abstinence of the prison camp seems to modify (and that modification alone is what makes the sublimation of *eros* possible: to seek to reconcile celibacy and good living as do so many priests of the Latin Church, is a blatant mistake!). The prisoner learns to eat very little, sometimes to fast completely; he also learns that he must not simply bolt his food, while his mind is on other things and he is not concentrating on what he is doing; no, he must eat slowly and attentively. By over-indulgence the life force is prevented from passing from the world to man. Ivan Denisovich makes no bones about it: 'You had to eat with all your mind on the food — like now, nibbling the bread bit by bit, working the crumbs up into a paste with your tongue and sucking it into your cheeks. And how good it tasted, that soggy black bread!' (LID, p. 43). Awareness is born of this attention — an attention that leads in the end to gratitude: 'Remember that thin barley or oatmeal porridge without a single drop of milk . . .? You ate it slowly . . . and it spread through your body like nectar. You quivered from the exquisite feeling you got from those sodden little grains and the muddly slops in which they floated. And you went on living like that, with virtually nothing to sustain you, for six months, or for twelve. Can you compare that with

the way people wolf down steaks? Can you say you *ate* it? It was like
Holy Communion . . .' (FC, p. 48).

Two relationships with the world are placed in opposition to one
another here: either man identifies himself without more ado with the
universal pattern: one species devouring another — and the way he
consumes red meat makes one think of what the Indians call crude
corporeality, a simple clash of appearances where everything remains
exterior to everything else; or else man experiences the relationship
he necessarily establishes with the world through nourishment as a
communion. He is grateful because then the roughest bread smells
good to him, and a handful of badly cooked grains reveal their
'sweetness' — as if, and even above all, he was being nourished by the
sweetness of being itself. 'Every lamp is a plant, and its scent comes
from the light', wrote Victor Hugo.

Awareness distances itself from being, not to shun it, but to become
its secret transparency. In this way one achieves that peaceful concentration, that open recollection which Solzhenitsyn, having discovered
in it some very ancient symbols, describes through an imagery of deep
still waters in which the sky is reflected. While, as we have seen, the
destructive kind of agitation is expressed in terms of a wheel of fire,
loving concentration is a still lake (SPP, p. 194). In the *sharashka*
Kondrashov-Ivanov painted the cold, still water of an autumn stream
to express the 'sublime serenity' through which man experiences the
'ultimate unity of all things' (FC, p. 310). A lake, the basin where
the stream slows down is the place where the earth, which like us has
become opaque — because of us according to the Greek Fathers —
becomes fluid and transparent, like prime matter, the symbolic
'waters' over which the Spirit hovered. Water is ambivalent: for anyone who, like Solzhenitsyn, has lived in the desert, it is the great
bestower of life, the fundamental water of the forests and springs of
'true, legendary Russia' (SPP, p. 12), of the motherland; but grey,
turbulent water is a destructive maelstrom and symbolizes death. Jesus
Christ manifests this ambivalence on the cross: his baptism in the
Jordan pre-figures his death-resurrection. He makes his way along the
edge of the lake and over its waters, stills its tempests and appears on
its banks after his resurrection. Thus the waters of the beginning,
which became through the 'corruption' of man, waters of death, are
now baptismal, 'living water' matter of the resurrection. He who weeps
becomes the minister of his own baptism; the hardened earth of the
heart dissolves in the bitter waters of suffering, in the sunlit waters of
wonder, and the heart becomes the faithful mirror in which the truth

of men and things is henceforward reflected, because between the sky and the lake of the heart this mysterious exchange is taking place: 'The water looks up and the sky gazes down upon it' (*ibid.*, p. 194).

In *Cancer Ward*, the old doctor, who is both knowledgeable and wise, even holy perhaps, learns to remain frequently still and silent. For a long time all he needed, in order to achieve this peace, was the presence of his wife: the eyes of the person one loves contain the lake — are the lake — in which the truth about being is reflected. But after the death of his wife 'his body demanded this chance to recoup its strength, and with the same urgency his inner self demanded silent contemplation . . . free of everything that made him a doctor' (CW, p. 459). He seemed 'to crave a pure transparency. It was just this sort of silent immobility, without planned or even floating thoughts, that gave him a sense of purity and fulfilment' (*ibid.*, p. 460). The 'bare' state of the intellect which rests in the heart and protects from all 'thoughts' is a familiar one in the Christian asceticism of the east. Thus the heart becomes a faithful mirror. 'Limpidity and expansiveness are the language of water, of its full mirror', and the paragraph ends with an evocation of 'a silver moon in a calm, still pond' (*ibid.*). At such moments the old doctor sees people not as they appear in the intricacies of their social involvements, but as they are in their inner depths, according to the measure of their openness, or resistance, to the mystery.

From Mother Earth to the new earth

As awareness grows, being gradually yields up its meaning. The process of decoding moves from the still ambiguous uterine darkness of the earth to the gathering in of all things into the splendour of the end.

Those with cancer reach out nostalgically towards Mother Earth, towards the roots of trees or the unwonted excrescences on their trunks. These are secrets passed on in a jealously guarded whisper whether it is a question of the root growing on the banks of Lake Issyk-Kul, or of the *chaga*, a mushroom which thrives as a parasite on the birch trees in the forests of Russia. Each time it is sacred land, land at the heart of the country: the vast country of Asia, mother of all religions rising up to form a hollow round Lake Issyk-Kul; central Russia where, in the depths of the forest, the nation gathered its forces against the nomads of the Steppe. In both cases it is also the most feminine aspect of the earth: the root which assumes the form of a chthonic matrix, and the birch, most feminine of trees, and that pregnant look, paradoxical because foreign to vegetables life, that the *chaga* gives it. Kostoglotov is driven towards these forests by an animal instinct, like a sick dog which 'goes to search for some mysterious grass that will save him' (*ibid*., p. 161). He dreams of magic qualities of being, of plucking the fungus from the treetrunk, crumbling it and cooking it over the fire; then he would 'drink it and get well like an animal' (*ibid*.). Instinct steps outside the narrow confines of rationalism, recognizing the maternal, healing properties of being. As for the root he took from the lakeside, Kostoglotov has extracted a brown, earthy liquid from it, and the correspondence of *homo-humus* — man-earth — comes inevitably to mind, in the sense not of humility, which would be banal here, but of a possible regeneration. For if the earth absorbs whatever dies, it also gives life, and continues to give it, inexhaustibly. The brown liquid, like the earth, is ambivalent: it carries within it life and death. One must know this, and be prepared to take risks: 'There's something noble about treating oneself with a strong poison. Poison doesn't pretend to be a harmless medicine, it tells you straight out, "I'm poison! Watch out! Or else!" ' (*ibid*., p. 321). In India, the black goddess, who performs the dance of life and death, kills and devours. One has to know and recognize the roots and growths not in their physical appearance but in their subtle properties as these relate to the 'world soul', to a complete 'cosmopsychology' which alone can explain the pharmacopoeia of the old peasant societies. One of Solzhenitsyn's characters, a woman surgeon passionately involved in her work, recalls and appreciates what Tolstoy's old Cossack, Yeroshka, says about European doctors: 'All they can do is cut. Well! they're fools. But up in the mountains you get real doctors. They know about the herbs' (*ibid*., p. 121).

The earth, here, is endued with that all-pervading religious power, which was celebrated by the ancients and which the Russian peasants seem to have recognized for a long time. One thinks here of the paean of praise for 'the great, moist earth' sung by the mysterious lame woman in *The Devils*. 'O Great Mother, humid earth!' writes Sergei Bulgakov, taking up the popular insight revealed by Dostoevsky and giving it a more precise expression. 'You give us birth, and provide our nourishment, we feel you beneath our feet, and return to you at the last. Children of earth, love your mother; embrace her fervently, bathe her with your tears, water her with your blood, and satisfy her with your bones. Nothing perishes in her, because, as the world's mute mother, she preserves everything, because she gives life and fruitfulness.

The man who does not love the earth and has no sense of her maternity is a slave, an outcast: he rebels unhappily against his mother, and is of himself but a creature of nothingness' (*Unfailing Light*, Moscow).

However, it is not for nothing that Dostoevsky takes a crippled woman as the symbol of the mystery of the earth. The ambivalence is there: generation and decay, life and death follow one another unendingly, and when the jagged shadow cast by the mountain on the lake traces the outline of an island paradise, night falls and darkness triumphs: 'It is all so beautiful, and so sad', says the crippled woman.

In the presence and the destiny of animals we begin to perceive how the ambivalence might be healed. On several occasions Solzhenitsyn observes that animals have 'sad eyes': he evokes 'the large, sad, unblinking eyes' of the horses with their 'long, alert intelligent heads' (SPP, p. 158) and the 'permanently sad eyes' of Tobik, one of the dogs adopted by the Kadmins (CW, p. 296); and he gives this astonishing description of the Saint Bernard which haunts the old doctor's house: 'an intelligent, sad-eyed human being' with an expression of 'transcendental detachment' (*ibid*., p. 458). Vladimir Soloviev had already said: 'Never does one see on a human face that expression of profound and hopeless suffering which sometimes clouds the face of animals' (*The Justification of Good*). Animals seem to be affected by a mysteriours cosmic sorrow — the cosmos which St Paul says has been condemned to servitude and awaits redemption (Rom. 8,20-22). In the Book of Genesis, God commands man to 'name all living things', that is, to complete, through his attentive love, the 'intelligence' and 'reason' whose mark they bear, but which only the spiritual awareness of man can express. The animal has, so to speak, been created in the image of man, as in Adam, which is why an adamic face, veiled by an incompleteness now fixed in suffering, seeks expression in the dog's muzzle or the horse's nose. In fact, fallen Adam can drive the squirrel in the zoo to a madness that reflects his own madness, he can blind the captive monkey, ir in a fit of rationalist expurgation kill all the dogs in a village: 'The village council hired two hunters to roam the streets and shoot the dogs. They were walking down the streets, shooting' (CW, p. 442). When man becomes a beast himself — and it is no coincidence that Solzhenitsyn has called the security chief in Ivan Denisovich's camp Volkovoi (Wolfe) — he can, in his savage state, turn the dogs into wild beasts: 'One dog bared its fangs, as if laughing at the prisoners' (LID, p. 34).

On the other hand, if a man loves an animal, and gives it

a name, a kind of mutuality is established — to which he nonetheless gives meaning — and then the fundamental goodness of the creature is manifested. The Kadmins love their dogs 'not for their fur' — for the sensual contact or affective compensation they provide — 'but for themselves' (CW, p. 294): the animals find their own fulfilment in this friendship with man as a spiritual person, a being who stands erect and relates directly to heaven. The Kadmins' dogs come under the influence of a home — of a human relationship of love which acts as a lens in which light is concentrated: 'The animals absorbed their owners' aura of kindness instantly, without any training' (*ibid.*, p. 294). Which meant that one aminal, a kind of German sheep dog, which looked most fearsome, 'overflowed with the goodheartedness of most large powerful creatures' (*ibid.*, p. 296). The Kadmins' dogs 'knew unerringly, as if by telepathy' where their master was. One of them brought a note to Kostoglotov: 'Nobody had ever taught him, he wasn't trained to do it, but he understood instructions instantaneously, as if by thought waves, and carried them out' (*ibid.*, p. 295).

If man dictates the meaning, the animal bears direct witness to the mystery by his 'intelligence', his nostalgia, and that beauty in which the Pseudo-Dionysius and Nicholas Berdyaev have seen reflected the splendour of the angels — did not the ancient civilizations see in the constellations the heavenly animals, or even the heaven of the animals? The wall of fear disappears for the saints who live close to the wild beasts. In the desert, symbol of isolation, after he has triumphed over the 'Separator', Christ sees angels and wild beasts coming to his help, in the renewed unity of heaven and earth. The tree, too, is experienced not only as a matrix and a source of healing, but in its twofold enracination, heavenly and earthly. In *The First Circle* Agnia goes into the forests not to find a remedy, but to contemplate their mysteries.

This movement from the secret to the mystery, from ambivalence to the life-giving cross, allows the spiritually aware to discern the essence of things as a miracle and source of joy. The man who has been 'born again' is like a blind man whose eyes have been opened: he touches things, 'still afraid to believe . . . that these things really exist, that his eyes are beginning to see' (*ibid.*, p. 168). *The First Circle* contains some fine examples of the joy that comes when, having lost all his 'goods' and being stripped to the essential, a man forms a nuptial bond with existence, which, in its depths, is simply joy. This is the antithesis of Sartre's 'nausea', of the inverted ecstasy before the roots of the chestnut tree. Just as mere contact with an iron bar gave young Teilhard de Chardin an ecstatic experience of being, so contemplation of a bare ceiling with its peeling plaster can make a man 'tremble from the sheer joy of existence' (FC, p. 49). Ideology hardly counts here. It is in an area quite beyond his Communist fervour that Rubin experiences the full power of being. One winter night, at Christmas time, he goes out into the courtyard of the *sharashka* and feels 'the innocent, child-like touch of the cold snowflakes on his face'. He stops, closes his eyes, and is suddenly overcome 'by a delicious sense of peace': 'This powerful sense of being was all the keener for being so short-lived. What happiness it would be if he didn't have to go anywhere and beg for things, if he had no desires at all but could just stand here like this the whole night, as blissfully as the trees there, catching the snowflakes as they came down' (*ibid.*, p. 508). A conscious tree in the realm of being.

This joy is never far away, it is simply that we turn away from it. It only takes some trifling thing, almost a pretext, such as the Saturday evening respite in a hospital when the patients are temporarily spared examinations or painful treatment, to gladden 'some eternally childish part of the human make-up' (*ibid.*, p. 147).

So all is miracle, not in the sense of a transgression of the natural laws — going beyond the limits, that is, within which these laws apply — but because the eye of the heart, made clear by self-denial, perceives creation's openness to the mystery which communicates itself while remaining inaccessible, *nomen innominabile, nomen omninominabile* Meister Eckart called it. To celebrate the holiness of being, the word becomes poetry — there is the poem of the duckling: tiny, pitiful and weighing nothing, at the mercy of every outside force, he is, nonetheless, no mere assemblage that man could take apart and put together again, but rather a presence from elsewhere, fashioned by the mystery from the elusive 'dust of the earth'. Solzhenitsyn's brief prose poem evokes the duckling's little black eyes like beads and its 'sparrow's feet', and makes one think more tenderly, less critically of certain Japanese paintings, before which one can only utter an ecstatic, Ah!

Any humble object fashioned by man and marked with the impress of his imagination is likewise a poem. The old bucket, for example, abandoned in a forest where fighting took place during the war: at that time, it was used to stop up the pipe of a little iron stove, and the men would hold their pieces of bread close to its red hot surface till they became crisp and smelled good to eat (SPP, p. 199).

Existence thus revealed in all its transparency has something both eucharistic and ultimate about it.

Whatever a man experiences as a gift, as an undeserved miracle, awakens in him gratitude, the thanksgiving (*eucharisto*) of the convalescent wondering at his cure or even a mere remission: 'Even if there were never another spring, even if this were the last, nevertheless it was like a surprise gift, and he was grateful' (CW, p. 527). For the Kadmins, freed from captivity and no longer separated from one another, everything has become a cause for celebration. Flooded by a sense of peace and of the power of existence, Rubin 'scooped up a large handful of the gleaming white floss at his feet . . . and filled his mouth with it. He felt as though his soul had partaken of the freshness of the world' (FC, p. 509). In the same way, as we have seen, food is accepted with gratitude, as a communion: the body celebrates as it prepares to receive it, and takes it 'like the sacraments' (*ibid*., p. 48). All the time the final end is contained in the present, as in anticipation of the universal ingathering into the light. For Solzhenitsyn, the blue, boundless sky represents the opening out of existence to the Light. It is a transparent veil, woven by 'spindle-shaped, porous clouds, centuries of laborious workmanship' (CW, p. 518). In the first pages of *August 1914* we are present while the mountains are raised up towards heaven, and we feel that this alpha will be the omega of history, when the light will heal what is shattered: 'With every half hour [the mountain ridge] seemed to melt slightly at the base and detach itself from the earth, until it appeared to be no longer fixed but with its upper two-thirds hanging in the sky. It became shrouded in vapour, the gashes and ribs and mountainous features seemed blended into vast, cloud-like masses which were then riven into vaporous fragments indistinguishable from real clouds. After a while they too were wiped away and the range vanished as if it had been a celestial mirage' (A14, p. 7).

It is hardly surprising that the experience of being in its fulness and transparency is expressed for Solzhenitsyn in a colour: blue transfigured by gold. When the sun breaks into the room where Oleg Kostoglotov has just shared with Zoya his terrible secret 'the tablecloth burst into blue and Zoya's hair turned to gold' (CW, p. 185). The tablecloth is Uzbek work, and shortly afterwards the author evokes 'that inexhaustible Uzbek blue exploded in the sunlight' (*ibid*., p. 187). Finally in the virtually lost paradise of the zoological gardens, there is 'the indescribably turquoise neck of the peacock, the metre-wide spread of his tail, and its pink and gold fringe' (*ibid.*, p. 539). In most symbolic languages turquoise blue is a solar colour. When the convalescent Oleg watched 'the first day of creation' unfold before him, he was overcome by the all-pervading blue shot through with pink and gold from the sun which was rising.

Gold is the light of the spiritual sun, the glory which surrounds Woman-Wisdom — Agnia or Vera — and floods the church where Agnia takes her fiance, illuminating the icons (whose background, what is more, is called 'light') and the mosaic of Christ. Blue is the transparency of the air in which the mountains lose something of their mass; of water, when it is calm and looks upward towards heaven. It is the most profound colour and the eye is attracted to it 'from one beginning to another, through a sequence of endless beginnings', to use the words in which Saint Gregory of Nyssa evoked the flight of the soul through the heavens. For Kandinsky blue is 'a movement uniquely directed towards its own ever-unattained centre' but it never reaches it, which is why 'it draws man towards the infinite' (*The Spiritual in Art*). The incandescence of the gold dispels the coldness of the blue (in fact blue is the coldest colour, and in ancient Egypt was used as a symbol of death); and the blue, emanating in this way from the sun, is therefore the song of the risen life. In the mysticism of the eastern Church, above all in Avagrius, the mind at rest within is compared to a blue sky flooded with divine light.

For Solzhenitsyn, it seems that this colour is also a sound. For many spiritual people and poets (Rimbaud, for example), the transfiguration of existence produces a unified, comprehensive sensation, in which hearing is translated into vision and vice versa. In Old China the *Treatise of the Golden Flower* spoke of 'auditive light', and Saint Simeon the New Theologian, one of the greatest contemplatives of the Christian East stressed that in the 'unique experience' of God 'hearing becomes vision and vision hearing'. Kondrashov-Ivanov, one of the involuntary guests at the *sharashka*, where he plays the part of the court painter, thrives on these correspondences. For him 'C sharp major, for example, was dark blue and gold' (FC, p. 394) — C sharp major being a sound with a central position on the 'natural' scale.

Eastern cosmology and Christian spirituality

At first, this experience of existence might seem to be analogous with that of the non-Christian East or with the wisdom of ancient Hellenism, as these are interpreted today by thinkers like Heidegger. In *The First Circle*, Solzhenitsyn refers fairly frequently to the spirituality of the Tao and of India and particularly to concepts of the *Samkhya* and *yoga*. According to these, there are different 'states' of being which become available to man when he reaches the corresponding 'spiritual states'. Fallen man remains alien to his own body and to the world, he is only familiar with the purely phenomenal appearance of the 'body of flesh'. Through detachment and purification, he acquires an awareness of the 'subtle' mode of being which is itself rooted in and reabsorbed into a spiritual level of being. The 'subtile body' seems to be made of *prana*, the breath of life. The latter is nourished by a proper relationship with the universe which like the human organism is borne along by this life force. Man absorbs *prana* by eating and breathing in a particular way, which is why Nerzhin had given so much thought to the gruel which the prisoner learned to eat with concentration and gratitude: it was 'like the *prana* of the yogis' (*ibid*., p. 48).

References to the Stoic ideal of apathy or *ataraxia* are even more frequent, and the Indian ideal of the 'free living man' is outlined: 'There is only one way to become immune, and that is to kill all affection and give up all desires' (*ibid*., p. 239). The ironical beatitude that one reads in the faces of the Indian divinities, or of the yogi lost in meditation, has a certain analogy with the 'deconditioning' — also ironic — of the prisoner who baits the minister: everything has been taken from him, he is free (*ibid*., p. 107).

Elsewhere, man seems to lose himself in a sacred cosmos, in the violent cosmogony of the storm. In one of his prose poems the author celebrates the universe which rediscovers through the storm its original incandescence: set free from fear by the loss of its individuality, it is no more itself than a drop of water in the ocean, it is an insignificant particle of being, made fecund by the lightning (*SPP*, p. 202). In *Cancer Ward* Shulubin dies in the Plotinian hope that he will rejoin the universal spirit of which he is only 'a fragment' (CW, p. 517).

The men who are genuinely in tune with being are the Asiatics whom Solzhenitsyn was able to observe when he was sent to central Asia, and during his stay in Tashkent. In the eastern town described both in *Cancer Ward* and in a short story, *The Right Hand*, and which is probably Tashkent, the tea houses are significantly divided in two: on the European side people sat at tables, 'ate and drank quickly' and then left. In the Uzbek section they settled themselves on the ground 'on sackcloth mats beneath a rush awning', they knew how to find a comfortable position that allowed for immobility, and they would stay there for days on end in a lazy, almost contemplative present, free of the domination of a timetable (SPP, p. 124).

A more attentive reading will show that for Solzhenitsyn the individual is not absorbed into universal being nor being into an impersonal nothingness; on the contrary, for him existence finds meaning in the communion of persons; and the inexhaustible is not the undifferentiated, but the wonderful coincidence of unity and separateness.

It is the mutual love of the Kadmins, their availability to each person, whom they receive as unique (just as they really know how to read the letters people send them!) which frees the animals from their 'sadness' and turns the melancholy beauty of the sunset into a celebration. It is Oleg's love for Vera which enables him to give up his cosmic superstitions, and to see the antelope with its delicate legs and 'its big, trustful and . . . gentle, yes gentle eyes' (CW, p. 543) as 'a miracle of spirituality'. It is Matryona's link with the living God and with her neighbour that lies at the root of her attitude towards the fig plants, whose living silence she loves, the lame cat she adopted out of pity, the mice, which are providentially protected from the cat by an 'inner skin' of wallpaper that had become detached from the wall, and even the cockroaches ('and even the snakes' says Saint Isaac the Syrian') whose life moves on without falsehood or malice (SPP, p. 14). However great the mystery of nourishment might be, and the *prana* it can dispense, what matters still more is that it should be shared with a friend who knows how to smile. Matryona's smile, the goodness in 'her round face' made the daily diet of potatoes acceptable. It is Agnia's Christian faith which enables her to read 'the mysteries of the forest'.

The oriental experience is therefore absorbed, with radically modified results, into the Christian revelation of the person. In Solzhenitsyn the ontology of the mystery is an ontology of the person — although, while the Revelation is specifically Christian, it must be made clear that the reference is to eastern Christianity. The Orthodox tradition has consistently attached cosmic significance to the divino-humanity of Christ and his Body the Church. Everything is founded, built up, and given its direction by the 'reasons' of the Divine Reason and the 'Words' of the Word. Everything is vivified by the Spirit. Everything has been created in the Logos, through him and for him, and the meaning of existence has been fully revealed to us by the Son of God become Son of Earth: the First-born of God's creation (Apoc. III, 10), the Word, by his Incarnation, his life-giving death and his exaltation has become 'all in all' (Eph. 1.23) because he is the model of all things and they find their contemplation in him. As a eucharistic mystery, the Church gives us the key to a universe that was created to become eucharist: 'In all things give thanks' (I Thess. 5.18); and it is the metamorphosis, under the influence of the divine energies, of the whole of man's being, and through man of the whole creation. For the Greek Fathers *physike theoria*, spiritual contemplatation of nature, enables man to discern and grasp the *logoi* of things, by discovering that the world, under the ashes of sin, is a 'burning bush', the glorious body of the risen Christ. Russian religious philosophy in the twentieth century has insisted a good deal on this cosmic dimension of the Church, as much to draw attention to the significance and limitations of science and technology as to throw light on the poetic celebration of existence. This is not the place to analyse the stages and states of Russian 'sophiology' from Soloviev to Florenski and Bulgakov. The theological formulation occasionally leaves something to be desired, but the basic intuition, profoundly Orthodox, draws attention to the encounter in existence of the created and the divine wisdom, and to the fact that the transparent point at the heart of things, which we obscure by our resistance to openness, was definitively unveiled by Christ so that the divine energies might gush forth from it. *Sophia*, holy Wisdom points to the sacramentality of the earth, and to exist-ence as a sacrament, in Christ, in the mysteries of the Church. As Gabriel Matzneff, a French writer of Russian origin, has frequently shown, the old religions of the world take their own place in the context of a Christianity which is capable of transfiguring all things. Even earlier, Sergei Bulgakov wrote: '*Sophia* is revealed to the world as beauty, and this beauty is the sacramentality of the world . . . The spring flowers emerge from the sombre bed of Demeter; beautiful young Persephone, a creature of wisdom, makes her appearance in the world as she leaves the dark nothingness of the arms of Hades. For whom do they grow, these flowers, with a beauty which man, more often than not, never sees? Why have the birds . . . become like living flowers? . . . Why are the tiger and the leopard so beautiful in their awesome grace? . . . Why does the beauty of young girls blossom on earth? Is it not the radiance of *Sophia* illuminating the inert flesh of "matter" from within? And the erotic impulse of the creature drunk with beauty, how can we describe it otherwise than as a cosmic love? These wings of *eros* bear it to the foot of the altar of Wisdom . . .' (*The Light that never goes out*, Moscow, 1917).

Seen in that perspective, being is not the improbable and quickly reabsorbed flower of an impersonal non-being, of a Vedantan non-duality or the divine 'desert' of Plotinus. Being is openness to those divine energies whose source is the Father, which radiate from the face of the Risen Christ, and which the life-giving Breath of God communicates to us. Beyond existence there is not nothingness but the fulness of personal love, the origin of all existence in Communion. From God to man and from man to man, being is the gift, the dwelling place and the food of love. In the *Samkhya* the theory of the 'three bodies' indicates progressive reabsorption. As the Greek Fathers saw it, the psychic and the physical are inseparably united, mutually symbolic and together transfigured through the Spirit into the 'spiritual body' of Christ, who does not absorb them but completes them in the fulcrum of the divine energies.

The episode at St Nicetas' Church in Moscow, where Agnia takes her fiance, demonstrates admirably the articulation of created Wisdom and uncreated Wisdom (FC, p. 155). The place is a sanctuary in itself: at the centre of town and surrounded by rivers, the hill seems to emerge from the primordial waters and rise up towards heaven to gather up the rays of the setting sun. An old woman and a young girl are there — Wisdom is very ancient and ever new. The gold of the sunset, which is picked up by the already turning leaves and Agnia's yellow shawl, speak of this first, paradisal, marriage of heaven and earth.

Again one cannot help thinking of the sunsets described by the lame woman: (Dostoevsky, *The Devils* I, IV, 5). The East, and the island in the middle of the lake stand for the mystery of the beginning, the beauty of the cosmic Sophia, and then her sadness, her nostalgia, her disappearance into the night.

It is only in Christ that the sacramentality of being is restored. The rock supports a church and the tree leans towards it as in the Trinity of Rublev. The girl does not wait to look at the sun; she goes into the church, taking her companion with her. Inside they are just singing Vespers, which evoke creation and the darkness that came over it in order to celebrate the 'joyous light' of the Risen Christ. Through the mystery of the cross — the church is dedicated to a martyr — night is now no more than an empty tomb which becomes the marriage chamber of being; and while in Dostoevsky the sunset ends in night, here it is metamorphosed into glory: inside the church the last rays of the sun cast golden reflections on the icons and on the mosaic of the Saviour. With the glory of his transfigured face, the Pantocrator restores the primordial symbols, and delivering cosmic Wisdom from her sadness, leads her to the final splendour. It is the Vigil of the Assumption of the Virgin — which is also the assumption of the earth, because through the Virgin the earth has become Mother of God. In the Marian hymn by which, although he does not quote it, Solzhenitsyn says that she overwhelmed Yakonov, we read

> Rejoice, promised land.
> Rejoice, fruitful field, abundant harvest.
> Rejoice, for you flourish like a luxuriant meadow.

It was in a luxuriant meadow that Vorotyntsev, exhausted by the battle, fell asleep and awoke to wonder that 'untrodden, smooth, silky, the grass the was the source of the purity that was pouring into him' (A14, p. 466). It is the grass of his childhood, the grass over which the procession used to move on the feast of the Assumption, blessing the earth and its harvests.

Solzhenitsyn pronounces here his affirmation of the earth — not like Nietzsche or Marx, but like Dostoevsky who describes Alyosha kissing the earth in his certainty of resurrection; or like the Orthodox Church which sings to the Mother of God: 'By your dormition you sanctified the entire universe'.

Now, in many icons and consistently in all the mosaics in the vast Byzantine universe, from Torcello to the Cathedral of Sancta Sophia in Kiev, the Mother of God is swathed in a blue veil shot through with gold: the very colour which Solzhenitsyn associates with being in its transparent fulness, 'boundless blue, born of the sun'.

9 The irreducible person

Man reduced

The emergence of consciousness both discovers and proves the irreducible nature of the person.

Modern thought has tried to explain man solely in terms of nature and history. As the product of an evolution prey to chance and necessity, man is seen by some as a social being confronting nature through work, called to bring about a perfect society that will see the self-development of matter, through the vicissitudes of the class struggle and the final revolution, and in doing so create himself and his world; by others, as a being of genius made up of mineral and vegetable matter, on which he imposes his own laws, debunking the hypocrisy of the weak and affirming himself in the play of creativity that leads to the eternity of the moment; by others again, as the repressive or receptive cover for the *libido* whose waywardness explains his individual and collective destiny, with no principle beyond that of pleasure, the hapless victim of the struggle between *Eros* and *Thanatos*, love and death. The trauma of the 'death of God' has left the collective consciousness a helpless prey to these self-styled 'rational' explanations − rational in part, but whose quest for universality leads them unsuspectingly into realms of metaphysic and myth that make them gnostic rather than truly rational.

Marxism, for example, which is of particular concern to us here, implies a faith in matter as an unchangeable and indestructible metaphysical substance without beginning or end, basically good, ordered in time despite its eternity, matrix of all living and then thinking beings through a process of regular development in a history that is also basically good, at the end of which man will set every state of matter − inanimate, live and conscious − into a sort of mutual, universal clarity. It is thus a secularization, or parody − as Berdyaev has powerfully shown − of the Judaeo-Christian revelation, investing the dynamism of faith in pure immanence in matter.

In the nineteenth century, these attempts at 'reduction' were either kept in the speculative order of individual prophecy, totally committed politically, but operating on the fringes of society, or, while more widespread and effective, insinuated into a pluralist society. Our century has seen them claim universal dominion and become a central fact of history. Philosophies of life have provided the frame-work for nationalism and fascism; Marxism took over the Russian Revolution and pushed it into 'a-theocracy'; the pleasure principle of Freud joined with technological frenzy to produce a civilization of fanatical self-gratification in which the production-consumption cycle has no other end than its own acceleration.

Since the collapse of National Socialism, and in view of the fact that the pluralist societies of the West lay no claim to being unified communities, Marxism has emerged as the only one of these modern 'reductions' to sustain a real 'ideocracy', in Russia and China above all. Unlike Marxism in the Western countries, where it can often see itself as a philosophical position and hence an instrument of analysis and dialogue, Russian (and Chinese) Marxism claims to be *the* truth, at once scientific and all-embracing, pervading every detail of every-day life by means of a coherent system of social structures and cultural attitudes. There is a certain logic to this all-pervasiveness – the logic of weight and viscosity. It makes all dialogue impossible, knowing only unified community or excommunication.

For the excommunicated – the 'traitors' or 'enemies of the people' – the place is a camp where man finds his final 'reduction': to silence, despair, death – his only banner a number indelibly stamped on his clothes. 'Like something out of the Apocalypse', one of these prisoners mutters, thinking, no doubt, of the branding with the number of the name of the beast in Rev. 13.17 (FC, p. 16). Ideocracy regards itself as innocent and liberating, by definition. Evil, if it still exists, has pre-revolutionary social origins or is the product of anti-communist currents of contemporary thought, even defeated ones; 'political' prisoners, condemned on usually quite imaginary grounds (ideocracy needs its enemies, its 'demons'), and ex-prisoners of war sent straight to the camps on their return from Germany, are all 'Fascists' and as such handed over to the good offices of the common law criminals, who are held to be 'socially reclaimable'. Anyone who profits from the regime must do so because of his 'bourgeois social origin' (CW, p. 435). But Kostoglotov sees through this: 'It's human greed, that's what it is, not bourgeois mentality. There were greedy people *before* the bourgeoisie and there'll be greedy people *after* the bourgeoisie' (*ibid.*). Alla Rusanova, a young journalist who wants to launch herself into literature, declares that she is not going to waste her time describing each character as an individual: 'I'll go straight to the collective, I'll portray whole collectives, with broad strokes. After all, one's whole life is bound up with the collective, not with isolated personalities' (*ibid*., p. 306).

The endless advances of scientific progress in the fields of biology, neurology and psychology give the regime an excessive, almost fantastic, desire to condition men completely, through fear, conviction, or the promise of 'happiness'. Both *First Circle* and *Candle in the Wind* contain an element of science fiction. In the Soviet Union, this genre is used to express anxieties and spiritual quests, sometimes stretching the ambitions — and perhaps the fantasies — of the regime to extremes. Solzhenitsyn contents himself with a more general indication of the titanic nature of a power that looks to science, including para-psychology, for the ability to look into the soul and refashion the human psyche. This is the route taken by neo-Stalinism: it has abandoned the mass camps, but interns people discreetly in special 'psychiatric clinics'. This, says Solzhenitsyn, is 'spiritual assassination, a more ferocious version of the gas chamber; the victims suffer more cruelly and for longer' (*Open Letter*, 15.6.70). This attempt to re-mould the human psyche is the subject of a novel by Sinyavski, *Lyubimov, the Beloved City*, and the first imaginary account of a 'brave new world' of entirely conditioned human beings was not Huxley's, but was produced by a Russian writer of the twenties: Yevgeni Zamiatin's *We*. In *The First Circle*, one of the objectives of the research undertaken at the 'special prison' is, 'to find a way of identifying voices on the telephone, and to discover what it is that makes every human voice unique' (FC, p. 33). In *Candle in the Wind*, the originally intractable Alda, who ignores all frenzies of 'happiness', is persuaded to undergo a 'cybernetic neuro-stabilization' which cures her stutter and enables her to 'live her life' like everyone else. This is no longer the climate of ideocracy, but the science and happiness of the West; Alda is not forced, but persuaded, as though, once reduction through hell has failed, reduction through a paradise stripped of trans-cendence has to be attempted. The 'Munich spirit', which Solzhenitsyn sees as so often characterizing the West, is not only, and perhaps not primarily, political, but can equally, and perhaps primarily, be meta-physical. Will the West give way to its particular demons?

The apocalypse of the person

Solzhenitsyn's own example and the whole *corpus* of his work show that it is impossible to reduce man: the violence, brute or insidious, unleashed on him, brings his irreducibility into the open. Apocalypse means 'revelation', and the society of the concentration camps and that of the pursuit of happiness can both, paradoxically, give rise to an 'apocalypse' of the person. No-one, when his last moment comes, can escape the revelation of death: of love, of beauty and of death. Alda is snatched from her false tranquility by finding her dying father. Alex, Solzhenitsyn's own mouthpiece, it would seem, replies to Dr Sinbard, who explains everything human by hormones, with the two enigmas of beauty and death: 'Even Raphael and Chopin? Everything is mortal, even to the stars'. A simple peasant, like Spiridon, the almost blind orderly at the special prison, sandwiched between Nazism and Stalinism, can perceive what an intellectual like Sinbard tries to avoid: that there is a distinction between good and evil and that 'the wolf-hounds are right and the cannibals wrong' (FC, p. 486). In the camps, Ivan Denisovich and thousands like him do not 'become wolves'. Stricken with cancer, Kostoglotov refuses to be cured at any price, because, he says, 'There isn't anything in the world for which I'd agree to pay *any* price!' (CW, p. 81). Volodin, Gerasimovich and Grania are others who put truth and justice before everything else.

Man escapes from collectivity because he is rooted in heaven and earth, because he is a physiological and spiritual being before he is a member of society, and the life of society may not always accord with that of the individual. He escapes collectivity through his agony, not always suffered alone, but already wrapped in a sort of transcendence. It is when his tumour starts to send shooting pains through his whole body that Yefrem Podduyev feels something 'inside him' that must survive: 'It had started to throb evenly, in four-beat time, and each beat of the bar was hammering out: 'Yefrem — Podduyev — Dead — Full Stop. Yefrem — Podduyev — Dead — Full Stop.' The more he repeats the words to himself, the more remote he begins to feel from the Yefrem Podduyev who is condemned to die, who comes to seem a sort of neighbour to him: 'He was getting used to the idea of his own death, as one does to the death of a neighbour. But whatever it was inside him that thought of Yefrem Podduyev's death as of a neighbour's — this, it seemed, ought not to die' (*ibid.*, pp. 224-5).

Man, for Solzhenitsyn, is a complicated being. This complexity is not a mere puzzle, a tangle to be unravelled, but the 'bottomlessness' of his personality. 'Man is a complicated being, why should he be explainable by logic? Or for that matter by economics? Or physiology?' (*ibid.*, p. 87). We can never understand people right through:

this is the genius of Dostoevsky, to have shown the blinding light at the root of each person — and to have remained blinded by it: 'Stavrogin! Svidrigailov! Kirillov! . . . are as complex, as unpredictable as only people in real life can be . . . And literary critics think they can hold his characters up to the light and see through them. It's comic!' (FC, p. 461). Dostoevsky never ceased to oppose man's irrational freedom to the deceptive clarity of the 'crystal palace', freedom expressed either in the derisive insolence of the 'underground' or in supremely free faith, in the 'free love' that recognizes the Son of God in the 'man of sorrows' standing before Pilate — or before the Grand Inquisitor.

When we think we have understood a human being, 'Something unexpected always turns up' (*ibid*.) and calls everything into question again. Solzhenitsyn here paraphrases Kierkegaard's observation that the genius of the person holds to infinitely small grandeurs, at once unpredictable and essential. Like the God of negative theology, the person always escapes attempts at reconstruction. François Jacob, in his treatise on *La Logique du vivant*, reckons that one day we will reach the stage of being able to, 'reproduce human beings at will, in as many copies as required, exact copies of a politician, an artist, a beauty queen, an athlete, or what one will', once we know 'the genetic factors involved in complex qualities such as originality, beauty or physical stamina'. This is the tragedy of the wildest dreams of these demiurges: all they want to do is make copies. The whole idea of a copy is an immanent parody of the idea of image — man in the image of God — whose importance for Solzhenitsyn will be dealt with in the next chapter. A copy multiplies one thing; an image gives rise to another: the inexhaustibility of man reflects the inexhaustibility of God. A copy supposes an empty, spatialized time, in which everything can be repeated; an image supposes a living history in which nothing ever repeats itself. Originality is not a quality in series with others, but the unique mode of being of all qualities; the sum of the parts can never equal the infinite whole posited by the question: *who* is this politician, that beauty queen, or each of those men whom the camps have tried to reduce to copies of each other differing only in the number they bear . . .

Here one must go back to the dialogue between Nerzhin and Kondrashov-Ivanov in *The First Circle*, in which the painter puts his friend, who seems to be playing devil's advocate in order to be exorcised, to the test. Nerzhin begins by recalling that in the camps, 'they make us give up the last remnants of our conscience in exchange for

200 grams of black bread'. 'No prison camp should ever destroy a man's dignity', replies Kondrashov-Ivanov, to which Nerzhin replies with the Marxist tag: 'Environment determines consciousness, as we all know'. Then comes the painter's four-fold 'No!', and, 'that would mean utter degradation. What would be the point of living?'. If there is no life of the *person*, if life is determined by circumstances, by social determinisms, then there is no point to it. If this were so, why would lovers remain faithful to each other even after being parted? And why would people remain different from each other in the camps, where conditions are identical?

He uses a substantial vocabulary that has to be understood metaphorically: 'Man is invested from birth with a certain . . . essence. It is as it were the nucleus of his personality', but he then defines it: 'his ego' (FC, pp. 211-2). The ego is not some *thing*, essence or nucleus, but some *one*, who cannot be reified, grasped in a concept, summed up by a judge or held by a gaoler: the most that these can do is to destroy the empirical fragment of existence in which he happens to be expressing himself at that time. Whatever the original data of nature and the circumstances of history, the person shines though them as their only mode of being: he transcends them, qualifies them and thereby modifies them. The extreme example of this is a martyrdom freely undergone, in which annihilation is transmuted into witness: 'Every man who is deprived of earthly resources triumphs nonetheless by offering himself as a victim' (*Letter to the Patriarch*). The question that remains is that asked by Kondrashov-Ivanov: 'which determines which? Is man formed by life or does, he, if he has a strong enough personality, shape life around him?'.

If the person is a unique way of making the world exist, of giving it and receiving it, then any form of communion unravels and displays the true meaning of the world. The 'first day of creation' dawns anew in the noble, pure love of Oleg and Vera, just as their love gives them the courage to love and respect those who are suffering in the 'cancer ward'. For a real doctor, only the faces of the sick and their tragic destiny make sense of the 'objective' laws of the organism, the well-marked stages of illness: 'His case history . . . (has become a mass of) lines and figures entered in violet and blue ink. Behind this . . . both doctors saw a town-bred boy, sweating with pain, sitting doubled up on his bed' (CW, p. 69). This is what leads Dr Dontsova, without her realizing it, to re-enact the parable of the lost sheep: the extraordinary gentleness and humility of one patient, Sigbatov, have led her to change her scientific researches: 'She had become absorbed in the pathology of bones for one reason only – to save him. There might well be patients waiting with equally pressing claims, but even so she couldn't let go of Sigbatov' (*ibid*.).

Face and heart

The world's matter becomes most directly accessible to the person in the human face, in the eyes in particular. Looked at for a long time, 'The eyes seem to lose their protective coloured retina. The whole truth comes splashing out wordlessly, it cannot be contained' (*ibid*., p. 357). This is why a real portrait can never be merely a copy: it expresses a communion, and a loving knowledge of something that cannot be made into an object. A real portrait opens up the future of a person to the individual of the present: 'Who can perceive the spirit? But if I look at the person whose portrait I am painting and discern potential qualities of mind or character which he hasn't so far shown in life, why shouldn't I paint them?' (FC, p. 395). A photograph, on the other hand, merely blurs present immaturity: when Tveritinov shows his host the photo of his fourteen year-old daughter, with her long, slender neck and finely-drawn face, 'the picture gave the impression of something immature, of something that had been left unsaid: far from being cheerful, it was heart-rending' (SPP, p. 175). The sense of modesty concentrates attention on the face, on the person, that is. The nunnish uniforms worn by the Russian nurses in the First World War abolished the magic of their bodies, the impersonal femininity of their hair, so that their faces, closely framed, were left to show the breath of a spirit from elsewhere. These girls, 'impersonal and anonymous . . . education, social status and colour of hair unknown', suddenly become 'fresh, clean and severe' (A14, p. 154), so that their faces alone express their new personalities. For a long love, the face is all, the body in its beauty having no more effect than in its ageing. Nadia Nerzhin's neck may remain long and unblemished, but years of unhappiness have shrivelled her breasts, everything conspiring to compose her body like a face. Little by little, people battered by life, but with an inner light coming from trust and service, come to show another beauty, and there is no need of a veil to prove that it comes from elsewhere: 'people who are at ease with their consciences always look happy', Solzhenitsyn writes of Matryona (SPP, p. 33). An old face purified in this way loses nothing of the happy or tragic expressions of youth or maturity, but allows them to shine through, lights up a recapitulation of a whole life. When Matryona tells the narrator of how she wondered whether or not to marry another man when she thought her fiancé had been killed in the war, her face looks to him, 'as though all its wrinkles had been smoothed out . . . instead I saw the face of a young girl faced with a terrible choice' (*ibid*., p. 29).

When death comes, particularly to those who have found this final beauty, or are going to find it, their personality somehow rises to the surface of the matter they are about to abandon, and seals it, in a furtive anticipation, perhaps, of the final resurrection. This is why Matryona's face, dead, despite (or perhaps because of) her body being as mangled as her fate, looks calm and 'more alive than dead' (*ibid*., p. 40).

The personality is called to integrate the whole human being. Soul and body work on each other in a synthetic unity, but with a hierarchy that allows the consciousness to work on the body through the soul. This is why Kostoglotov, in his discussions with the other patients, insists on this role of consciousness and gives 'moral perfection' a biological effect (CW, p. 150). The studies he has undertaken to understand his own illness have shown him that specialists have documented cases of 'spontaneous cure', which they attribute to the little-understood relationship between the growth of malignant tumours and the activity of the central nervous system. Other specialists hold that there is 'some kind of blood and brain barrier' at the base of the skull, in which certain chemical substances sometimes predominate; their presence and balance depend, it would seem, 'on a man's attitude of mind' (*ibid*., p. 149). So Kostoglotov would not be surprised if, in a hundred years' time, they discovered, 'some kind of caesium salt (secreted by our organism) when our conscience is clear, but not when it's burdened, and that it depends on this caesium salt whether the cells grow into a tumour or whether the tumour resolves' (*ibid*., p. 150). In fact, the discoveries of the last fifteen years, defining life in terms of chemical agencies, have shown that these agencies act within cybernetic systems of incredible complexity. This is how the overall equilibrium of the organism — *homeostasis* — is assured by the 'messages' sent by chemical mediators from cell to cell. Such systems bear witness to an intelligence which it is difficult not to call spiritual, and which therefore has a likely correlation with the state of mind of man — individually or collectively, for how many innocents bear the cancers of a civilization in their flesh in this way! Western psychosomatic medicine has demonstrated that psychological factors affect either the onset of an illness or its cure, including certain types of cancer. If one replaces caesium by lithium in Kostoglotov's thesis, it is not so wide of the mark.

The personality integrates its nature in the 'heart', which thus becomes a sort of organ of knowledge of the whole being, inseparable from love. Solzhenitsyn here takes up the anthropology of the Bible as mediated by the spiritual school of the Christian East known as Hesychasm, from the Greek word meaning the silence and peace of union with God. It is a concept that has influenced Russian nineteenth and twentieth century philosophy of knowledge, which has developed a notion of integral knowledge whose organ is the 'heart-spirit', which gathers all the human faculties of the personality into communion, while being fundamentally united to both God and man. It is Solzhnitsyn's achievement to have re-discovered this anthropology of the personality and of love, doubtless both in the religious philosophers and in the spontaneous events of everyday life. He thereby bridges the gap which has opened, since the decline of the 'philokalic' movement of the late nineteenth century, between everyday life and traditional monastic ascesis, which has virtually disappeared from the Russia of today — to such an extent in fact, that when Lrasnov-Lecitin, one of the chief witnesses to the faith in Russia, was imprisoned with a group of young people in 1970, the only way he could find of explaining to thm what Orthodox monks were was, 'a kind of Russian yogi'. The quest for 'the seat of the heart' should not be understood simply as a technique of ascesis, but as the meaning of a whole destiny, so that it is our 'heart' that normally experiences those limit-situations, whether of joy or of sorrow, which in fact form the stages along which we travel on our way to the final concentration and expansion of our beng in love. 'What name can one give it? Frustration? Depression? When melancholy sets in, a kind of invisible but thick and heavy fog invades the heart, envelops the body, constricting *its very core*' (*ibid.*, p. 65). The image of fog recalls the 'inner heavens of the heart', which is a frequent image in the ascetics of Eastern Christendom.

Oleg, once he has begun to love Vera with a friendship beyond *eros*, experiences a veritable awakening of the heart that opens him to the mystery of beings and things, and makes him susceptible to their sufferings. It is completely different from what he had experienced in his earlier love for Zoya, which 'had not been in his chest': 'An inner tension had built up inside him — . . . He could even feel the exact place where it was: in the front of his chest, under the bones' (*ibid.*, p. 460). This is the seat of the 'spiritual heart' which corresponds to the physical one by a symbolical relationship in the Hesychast tradition, but does not coincide with it. It is striking that Solzhenitsyn's description of this awakening of the heart is almost word for word the same as that found in many pages of the *Philokalia* or the *Tales of a Russian Pilgrim*: 'The tension was pressing lightly on him like warm air . . . producing a sort of pleasant ache. It was somehow even audible too, except that its sound was not of this earth, not the sort of sound that is heard by ears' (*ibid.*). Oleg remembers that he had known this sort of tension as a young man, but then forgotten it. This 'feeling in his chest' produces both fulness and openness. It bridges not only the gap between our daily life in the world and an ascetic tradition, but also that between the monastic condition and true matrimony. Solovyev and Berdyaev had foreshadowed it, but in a gnostic way, in the perspective of a disincarnate love, while the love of Oleg for Vera, though it goes beyond *eros*, needs it to tell itself. And this is why Oleg effaces himself and leaves, since this incarnation is impossible. After knowing the return to Paradise, the fall and the saving cross, he leaves the town, perhaps life, and something decisive happens to him, 'in his heart, or his soul, somewhere in his chest, in the deepest seat of his emotion' (*ibid.*, p. 569).

To end these reflections on the person, let us hang up the icon of human dignity painted by Solzhenitsyn in *One Day in the Life of Ivan Denisovich*, in his description of the old man, Y 81, sitting at the refectory table in the camp. He no longer has a name; he has not even, in the usual sense, had a life: he has been in the camps 'for an eternity'; he no longer has any hope on earth, because he knows that, ten-year term after ten-year term, his sentence will go on being renewed. He has lost all his hair and teeth; his hands are cracked and blackened, proving he has never done any cushy jobs. He looks as though he has been carved out of dark stone. In the midst of the noise and hustle of the other prisoners, his silent serenity is all the more striking. 'He held himself straight . . . and looked as if he'd put something extra on the bench to sit on'; instead of crouching over his food like the others, 'he raised the spoon high to his lips'. Upright man, different from the animals, close to heaven . . . A final touch, briefly sketched, but the most striking: '*He* wasn't going to put his three hundred grammes [of bread] on the dirty, bespattered table — he put it on a well-washed bit of rag' (LID, p. i 23). Out of respect for himself, no doubt, but also out of respect for the bread: a priest at the altar.

10 Conscience in the image of God

The living God

What, then, is the source of this 'unknown strength' that allows man to surpass himself, of this light that will make our being 'shine forth'? Why did life appear on this 'small and insignificant planet' (A14, p. 212), and of what does it consist? There is no simple answer, for, 'just as the essence of food cannot be expressed in terms of calories, so the essence of life is not to be conveyed by a formula, however brilliant' (FC, p. 420). Matter reposes in being, and being is an open fulness, but open to what? In our person, 'deep calls to deep', but which? 'You see,' says Varsonofiev, 'the more important something is to us, the more impenetrable it seems. Only simpletons find things absolutely clear' (A14, p. 423). Faced with death, man's meditation concentrates on 'something different, something pure and unshakeable' (CW, p. 441), but without necessarily knowing where to find it. We wait in darkness, before 'that impenetrable yet yielding wall behind which there seems to be nothing' (*ibid*., p. 157). And when the dying man — who is all of us, in a sense — torments himself with wondering how to accept death, he cannot work it out, 'and there is no one to tell him' (*ibid*., p. 111). Yet even in our everyday life where there is no place for mystery, there is a Mysterious — a loving, free presence — that, 'suddenly flashes at us, "Don't forget me! I'm here!" ' (*ibid*., p. 157), I have not forgotten you.

There is no one to tell him the answer, but the Answer gives itself, *reveals* itself as the ultimate Name, God. This can mean a simple *reveals* itself as the ultimate Name, God. This can mean a simple designation of the full depth of human experience in a writer using the cultural heritage he knows, but in this case we must go deeper: no longer man but the One who responds to man: 'Don't forget me! I'm here!' And the name we must give this Presence, with a conscious capital letter, is the Name that is above all Names: God.

The God of forests, of the vast forest of Grunfliess in *August 1914*, which belongs neither to Russian nor German, where the wind gently stirs the trees, and all creatures can find shelter, the shelter God offers his creatures.

The God of the scientists, of Newton, who 'believed in God, like every other scientist' (FC, p. 58). To the fury of the warder, Gleb Nerzhin mentions the names of 'Pascal, Newton, Einstein' (*ibid.*, p. 270), in order to persuade his wife that he has met God. *Candle in the Wind* is a meditation on science amongst other things. Its conclusion is that, though distorted by the will to power, science is man's conscious assumption and offering-up of the world. Science reveals the Wisdom that carries the world: 'You imposed the limits they [the waters] must never cross again, or they would once more flood the land' (Ps. 104.9). Science shows these insubstantial 'limits' that structure the world to exist in the order of Intelligence, perhaps of Love. 'Beyond its visible aims, those everyone can see, science has others that remain hidden. Just like art . . .' (CiW), since the order of the world is also its beauty, and science is a way to grasp its wonder. 'We need science not only for our reason, but also for our soul. Being conscious of the world and being conscious of humanity are perhaps as necessary to us as . . . being conscious' (*ibid.*).

The God of those who create beauty, the 'divine fire' that one day, for the young peasant Yesenin, scorched the horizons of that 'deepest Russia' in such a way that we can see them now etched in his verse as sharply as Cézanne's mountains of Provence etched live in the naked flesh of light. The Creator hurled his fire on matter and 'into the heart of that quick-tempered country boy'. Fire joined to fire, and 'the shock of it opened his eyes to so much beauty — by the stove, in the pig-sty, on the threshing-floor, in the fields' (SPP, p. 201). 'The very irrationality of art, its wonderful ways, the overwhelming influence it has on human beings, all this is too prodigious to be attributed simply to the ideology of the artist, to his plans and labours, or the application of his unworthy fingers' (NPL, p. 103).

And, above all, the personal God of people, he who comes to us as a friend, as '*Someone*'. Solzhenitsyn concludes his meditation on art by saying, 'We have received this gift from the hands of *Someone*' (NPL, p. 103). And Nerzhin, when he decides to remain faithful to his wife, despite the separation, and not lie to Simochka, feels that, 'the decision had not been his own' (FC, p. 627).

There can be no doubt that for Alexander Solzhenitsyn this God is the Living and Life-giving God of the gospels, who has revealed his love to us 'in Christ the Lord'. The very imagery of totalitarianism has disqualified human language from coping with the mystery of omni-potence and omni-presence through its analogous references to the 'Father of peoples' and his police. In the mock political trial mounted by the prisoners in the *charachka* one of them intones Psalm 139: 'Even were I to rise up to heaven, Thou art there' in order to exalt the power of the judge (*ibid*., p. 365). And what can be meant by the old symbol of the 'all-seeing eye' applied to the man thrown into a cell, who feels a 'fanatical, unwinking eye' gazing at him through the peep-hole, 'that disembodied eye, an eye without a face — an eye that alone expresses all that is behind it — that eye watching a man's death!' (*ibid*., p. 637)? From now on, the revelation of the Living can only be in the form of Christ: the Innocent, the Witness to the paradoxical Beatitudes in the face of all social evils. The One from elsewhere, who comes not to judge but to be judged, not to exclude but to be excluded, not to imprison, torture and crucify, but to become the prisoner, to be tortured and crucified in the omnipotence of his love — so that every horror may be consumed like a derisory drop of hatred in the vastness of his love, and crucified mankind find in him the strength of the resurrection.

The whole of Solzhenitsyn's work proclaims that fact that his God is the liberating Father who raises the Crucified — and all those cruci-fied in history with him — from the dead, by his Spirit of life, love and beauty. His incomparable achievement is to have shown the presence of God crucified and risen in the hollowest as well as the most meaningful junctures of our existence, in our anguish as well as in our wonder. His whole work shows love to be stronger than death; in the truthfulness of people, in their free responsibility, in their deep joy at being, in their very being. Throughout his work it is the sense of the presence of Christ that brings his openness to the ultimate reality, his tenderness devoid of sentimentality, his infinite compassion. The flavour left by his work is one of a sanctity at once loving and just: every man judges himself, or will judge himself, in the light of love.

Sometimes, a simple allusion to the life and passion of Christ is used to illumine human existence. The anguished wait of the transferees at the end of *The First Circle* is compared to Christ in the Garden of Gethsemane, continuing to hope and pray (*ibid.*, p. 691). Freed from the camp, Kostoglotov hears the command of Christ to the paralytic echoing in his ears: 'Take up thy bed and walk!' (CW, p. 283). Nadya Nerzhin, returning overcome with despair from her annual visit to her prisoner husband, is told to 'drink to the resurrection of the dead' (FC, p. 355). The theme of the innocent, the just person unrecognized by the world but without whom the world 'cannot stand', weaves through the fates of Innokenty Volodin, Nemov, Alyosha, Matryona. *The First Circle* describes two voluntary descents into hell, not without hints of a resurrection to follow. *Cancer Ward* brings us up against the parable of the rich man. The fate of Kostoglotov retraces that of Adam: paradise, fall, sacrifice in the glowing shadow of the second Adam, Christ.

And throughout, as refreshment after the disqualification of the 'virile' and 'inquisitorial' images of God, there is the presence of woman, making itself felt sometimes as a simple servant of life, sometimes as dispenser of Wisdom. Agnia and Vera have some of the characteristics and light of the Virgin Mother and the woman crowned with the sun in the Apocalypse. Lyuba, the 'love-girl', is the harlot forgiven by Christ because she had loved much. The communion of people become one body in the living Christ shows the paschal structure of being, the eucharistic basis of the world.

Prayer

Man meets the Living God in prayer. 'He prayed silently for her. (He had learned to pray in the camps)' (FC, p. 575). At the gates of death itself, we are bound together in God and prayer becomes the essential expression of love. Prayer is this openness of man in which God reveals himself. In prayer, we discover God as, 'the One with whom living becomes easy', the One, 'in whom it is easy to put our trust', the One who opens up a way in the midst of our deepest distress, and makes a future possible in the very light of his appearing: 'When my thoughts falter, assailed by doubt, when my spirit weakens . . . Then, Lord, you send me this luminous certainty: you exist and you will see that not all roads to the good are barred!' (*Prayer*, p. 100).

In *August 1914*, Samsonov's prayer is related with such precision and truth that it must express something that Solzhenitsyn himself experienced. At the outset, there is the quest for a state of silent recollection similar to that practised by the 'old doctor': Christian prayer takes on the universal experience of concentration, not as a fusion of all beings, but in a relationship that is inexhaustible because it is personal. The image used is that of a liquid that needs to stand for a while in order to settle, like a jar of oil shaken until it is cloudy, if it is to regain its 'sunny, transparent colour' (A14, p. 329). The prayer that both allows and surpasses this concentration is not like the morning and evening prayers, 'over-familiar and mumbled in haste', so quickly that they bring no state of prayer and 'thoughts race ahead to cope with more mundane matters' (*ibid*.). These prayers are like 'washing one's hands fully dressed, a mite of cleanliness so small as to be almost imperceptible' (*ibid*.). The prayer the soul needs in order to gain the 'peace and quiet' in which God speaks beyond words, is 'concentrated, dedicated prayer, prayer . . . like a hunger that must be satisfied and for which there is no substitute' (*ibid*.). Water, here, is more than an outer cleansing; it is the 'living water', the very life that alone can satisfy our desires, the water we must drink and make our own if we are to live. Beyond all passions and partial longings, man then understands that he is the 'man of longing' of the Apocalypse, the man with only one longing, for God: 'Let all who are thirsty come: all who want it may have the water of life, and have it free' (Rev. 22.17). 'That kind of prayer', notes Solzhenitsyn in the person of Samsonov, 'always transformed and fortified him'.

This is not to say that liturgical prayers are vain: even though they are not enough, they are a sure 'support' — 'at first he recited in full two or three familiar prayers' — and make the movement of the lips reach the heart. And even when prayer has become a mental state, or rather a dynamic flow of one's whole being, reaching beyond language to the Spirit that proceeds from the Word, it 'occasionally leans on the support of certain powerful, memorable phrases' (A14, p. 330) and flourishes in short phrases from the pure adoration of the Church. The essential prayer, however, is that which 'forms itself unconsciously' (unconsciously, because it shares in the inaccessible transcendence) and 'without spoken words'. 'It is well to be absolutely silent at the coming of the Holy Spirit', said St Seraphim of Sarofsky; yet the light of the Spirit sometimes flashes from the face of the Risen Christ, so loving words may be used from time to time to remind us of this meeting: 'Thy most radiant countenance, O Giver of Life!' (*ibid*., p. 330). This brings about the spiritualization of the whole being in its very earthliness, as though this were no longer turned toward the centre of the earth, but toward God. Kneeling upon 'aching knees (although he was now oblivious of the pain)', Samsonov abandons himself to 'silent devotion'. Then, 'the burden of his body seemed to lighten, and light filled his mind' (*ibid*.). The inner strength held down and distorted by passion is set free, regained in its first spring, offered as though eucharistically to the divine fire. This changes it into active love; man in prayer rises to the surface, to the Christic limit of the divine and the human, rising from the bloody waters of his history, 'to float into union with the powers above and to give himself up to their will' (*ibid*.).

Once it has been opened to the Spirit by these forces of personal openness, liturgical prayer can then bless the land, put off death. In it, man becomes a liturgical being, a being who gives praise. After the disaster of August 15th, Vorotyntsev comes to in a field by a small chapel, which reminds him of childhood processions on the Feast of the Assumption, 'a date probably chosen because it marked the end of the harvest in the Kostroma region' (*ibid*., p. 467): the Mother of God becomes the Earth Mother. Later, the dead colonel is buried in the forest: 'And soaring higher than the sun, higher than the sky, directly to the throne of the All-High, from fourteen men's voices the familiar chant arose . . . "To Thee, O Lord . . ." ' (*ibid*., p. 512).

The Castle of the Holy Grail

Within this perspective, Solzhenitsyn rounds off his portrait of personal consciousness as the image of the living God. Now we can understand why the person is irreducible, why he cannot be fully explained in terms of his nature and history: the person is rooted in transcendence. The fact that man cannot be reduced to his nature is a fragment of transcendence, and on this our freedom is founded. If God does not exist, man is a derisory fragment of society and of the universe, and his thirst for freedom an aimless longing to be crushed against the battlements of death. A scientific 'a-mortality' would merely make death no longer a battlement, but an atmosphere which would poison this blind longing without our realizing it, by satisfying it, by becoming an infinite Absence that one could no longer even name.

Only the Living God — because he alone is the Living — can open a breach in all determinisms, change Absence into Love. Far from constraining man, he is the Spirit that inspires him, the infinite space of his freedom.

Solzhenitsyn here again recalls the great Patristic theology of the person as image of God, though his words are sometimes new: 'Sometimes I feel quite distinctly that what is inside me is not all of me. There's something else, sublime, quite indestructible, some tiny fragment of the universal Spirit' (CW, p. 517). Shulubin's imagery, while it could be Plotinian, is no less appropriate, if taken in a Christian sense, than Gregory of Nazianzen's celebration of the 'fountain of divinity' in man.

The 'old doctor', when his 'inner consciousness' achieves a 'silent immobility' which gives him a 'sense of purity', sees the meaning of existence not in people's 'work or activity', 'which they believed was central to their lives and by which they were known to others', but in preserving, 'untarnished, undisturbed and undistorted the image of eternity which each person is born with' (ibid., p. 460).

The wild painter at Mavrino, Kondrashov-Ivanov, holds that man is irreducible because 'he has something against which to measure himself' (FC, p. 312), something which transcends nature and history: 'Because he can look at an image of perfection, which at rare moments manifests itself to his inward ego' (ibid.).

In Solzhenitsyn, as in the Fathers, this image is removed from any substantialist conception. It is not something dropped into us like a lump of matter, nor is it part of our being. When he says that we 'have' this something, the verb is used metaphorically. The whole of man is created 'in the image'. It forms the basis of his nature and his moving force, moving him to adore, and the basis of his personal transcendence and freedom. Only this freedom can make the image 'like'; it can also bury it with the world around him, peopled by blind monkeys and butchers, in a tragic 'unlikeness'. For the image can either be withered, blurred, disfigured, or shine forth in a dynamic clarity ever more like its Archetype. The Incarnation is based on this mystery of the image, and thereby restores it, since man, according to the Fathers, has been created in the image of Christ. The Cross cannot be separated from man's deification, that is, the transfigured fulness of man in God. This is why Solzhenitsyn, in his survey of the human countenance, finds both bestiality and the divinity of Christ and man in his image.

Invitation to this inalienable and also faithful image is expressed in terms of the hero's vision of the castle of the Holy Grail, at the end of his fateful quest. This is the vision of which Kondrashov-Ivanov shows Nerzhin a sort of reflection, after telling him of the image of perfection each man carries within himself. The Grail, we have seen, was a common image in Russian symbolist poetry and religious philosophy at the beginning of this century. Serge Bulgakov sees it as not only the eucharist, but also the symbol of the restoration of our nature and of the entire cosmos through the divine-human blood bathing the earth at Golgotha and transforming it.[1] Myrrha Lot-Borodin has studied the influence of Oriental Christianity, and particularly of its liturgical rites, on this great symbol of Western spirituality.[2]

So Kondrashov-Ivanov produces a small, secret canvas, which has been hidden in a corner, and brings it over to Nerzhin as though initiating him into a rite. 'In shape the picture was twice as high as it was long': it's movement is one of ascension. It shows 'the moment when Parsifal first sees the castle . . . of the Holy . . . Grail!' The foreground is a 'wedge-shaped ravine dividing two mountain crags', symbolizing the mortal fissure, the mortal fission of being. Its 'menacing, prehensile thickets' are rebel nature after the Fall and the crown of thorns. But beyond them 'vaguely discernible in all its unearthly perfection, enveloped in a shining and lilac-coloured aureole – stood the castle of the Holy Grail' (*ibid.*, p. 313). Above it, the 'upper reaches of the sky [are] suffused with an orange-gold radiance' which is the dawn following the dark night of West and East, the dawn of which Solzhenitsyn is a witness.

An ethics of collaboration with God

'These laws of a long humanity, born in the timeless depths of the centuries, which will last till the sun no longer shines' (Address to the Secretariat of the Writers' Union, 22.9.1967), have been worked out to mark the passage from 'image' to 'portrayal'. In *Candle in the Wind*, Alex tells Sinbard, who holds morality to be always relative: 'There's something wrong with your theory of relative morality! You could use it to justify any sort of crime!', and he follows this with examples of violence done to the person, in which, as Dostoevsky observed, a desire to profane plays its part. This fascination with profanation proves that it is not a question of moralism, but of the holiness of creation and the person, of the divine requirement of justice. So it is always wrong to rape a girl, in any civilization; and to beat a child, or drive a mother from her home. Truth is the next requirement, no less divine, so calumny, going back on one's word, and abusing trust placed in one are equally wrong. Sinbard replies by quoting the contradictory diversity of custom in different cultures: 'Is it always wrong to kill one's parents when they're old? In some tribes it's the right thing to do!' Then Terbolm, for whom science must go hand-in-hand with conscience, interrupts: 'Perhaps the law exists but it takes us thousands of years to see it? Perhaps it also has to be worked out in different ways in different cultures?' If God is the *ethos* — the dwelling-place — of man, as Heraclitus said, then one would expect ethics to be refined with the development of revelation. There are the various 'covenants' of the Old Testament, for example: the covenant with Noah, kept with a certain amount of degeneration by primitive traditions, in which law is respect for universal rhythms, the unity between social order and cosmic order. Then, with the covenant with Abraham, the father of all who believe in a personal God, law becomes submission and obedience, but without love — as in Islam today. The covenant with Moses introduces love between God and his people, but the very choice of a people restricts its universality. All these are taken up, purified and universalized in Christ's commandments of love of God and of one's neighbour, which repeat the covenants with Abraham and Moses, in the eucharistic transfiguration of being which repeats the covenants with Adam and Noah, completed in the new revelation of the person in communion. From then on, human history unfolds within the context of Christian revelation, even when denying it.

This is why real justice 'is not in the least relative', and 'one can't just understand as one pleases' (*Letter to Three Students*). 'It exists outside us and in itself' (*ibid.*) and we have to seek it out, guess at it, making ourselves receptive to the 'heavenly forces' by 'perfecting the development' of our own souls (A14, p. 428).

In this way, man comes to collaborate with God, no longer proclaiming himself the centre of the universe, setting himself up as demiurge. He knows that, 'it was not he who made this world, not he who gave it its meaning and direction' (NPL). He comes to recognize himself as 'tributary of a power that is greater than he', and so to work, 'as a humble apprentice under God's heaven, with a far sharper sense of his responsibility' (*ibid.*).

Solzhenitsyn sums up his feelings on man's relationship with God in the hymn of gratitude and trust he composed either while he was still enjoying the official favours of the Soviet Union, or after he had been awarded the Nobel prize:

From the heights of earthly fame I look back in wonder at the way without hope that brought me here;
In this way even I have been able to spread the glow of your glory

far among men!
> For as long as necessary, You will give me the means to do so,
> And when I no longer can, You will entrust this task to others'
> *(Prayer)*

NOTES

1   'Le Saint Graal', *Put* 32 (Paris, 1932) — in Russian.
2.   *Romania* (1951), pp. 202 ff., 'Lumière du Graal', in *Cahiers du Sud* (1951), pp. 151 ff.

11 From evangelism to Orthodoxy

The Baptist influence

The dominant Christian sensibility in *One Day in the Life of Ivan Denisovich* and *Cancer Ward* is one of primitive evangelism, marked by Baptist fervour and Tolstoyism: in the first, the Baptist Alyosha is the great Christian figure, and the second is illuminated by a parable from Tolstoy. The feature common to both is direct experience of the Gospel. Like most Russians who look for the meaning of life, Solzhenitsyn, after years of atheism, came upon Christianity *from outside*. In Russia today, the evangelical sects, with the Baptists foremost among them, are the only missionary force capable of bringing the overwhelming testimony of the Gospel to secularized men incapable of complex meditations on faith. The wonderful liturgical riches of the Orthodox Church, which impregnated the life of the peasants, is alien to the rigid rationalism of industrial man. While its original inspiration was no doubt scriptural, its development came to a halt at the end of its first thousand years, so that now it stands in need of interpretation and the naked Gospel makes a completely different sort of impact. Its liturgy uses an archaic language, familiar enough under the old regime, but far removed from contemporary usage. Its Sunday readings stress the miracles of Christ at the expense of his teaching, which must be the best way of alienating any Soviet listener, however well-disposed.

The Baptists, on the other hand, stress Jesus' teaching, present it in everyday language, and set it like leaven in the dough of everyday life. The effect is that Christian life seems to operate *within* the Gospels and the Acts of the Apostles.

In the camp where Ivan Denisovich is sent, Alyosha the Baptist has made a notebook 'in which he'd copied out half the New Testament' (LID, p. 24). 'Clean and tidy', he reads it each morning, 'under his breath', keeping it hidden in a chink in the wall, where 'it had survived every search' (*ibid*., p. 25). The reading, Ivan thinks, 'is perhaps especially for him — those fellows were fond of recruiting' (*ibid*.). He overhears a paraphrase of the Gospel in a passage that emphasizes the redemptive suffering of the Christian: 'If you suffer, it must not be for murder . . . if anyone suffers as a Christian, he should feel it no disgrace, but confess that name to the honour of God' (*ibid*.). And at the end of the day, when Alyosha hears Ivan automatically praise God: 'Glory be to thee, O Lord. Another day over' (*ibid*., p. 137), he turns to him and goes straight to the point: 'There you are, Ivan Denisovich, your soul is begging to pray. Why, then, don't you give it its freedom?' (*ibid*., p. 138). They have a long discussion on prayer, in which Alyosha gradually points out the correct interpretation of prayers of intercession: 'We must pray about things of the Spirit — that the Lord Jesus should remove the scum of anger from our hearts' (*ibid*., p. 139), and shows how faith can transmute the sufferings of their 'stretch' into spiritual growth. He spontaneously brings in an allusion to the parable of the Sower: 'In freedom your last grain of faith will be choked with weeds' (*ibid*., p. 140), and a quotation from St Paul: 'For my part I am ready not merely to be bound but even to die for the name of the Lord Jesus' (*ibid*.).

This meeting with Jesus and reflection on his teaching provide the basis for an ethical code. And nothing, it would seem, is of greater concern to today's Soviet Russians, lost as they are between the collapse of the patriarchal order, the exhaustion of revolutionary fervour and the exciting but inhuman progress of their technological culture. For any thinking man, the great problem must be to discover whether a criterion of good and evil exists, and if so, whether one can order one's life according to a code of ethics. The Baptist faith seeks to answer this question by rigorous and clearly formulated demands, based on the Decalogue and the 'commandments of Christ'. While it is good to suffer as a Christian, you must not suffer, according to Alyosha's notebook, 'for murder, theft or sorcery, nor for infringing the rights of others' (*ibid.*, p. 25). Alyosha himself sets an example of how to live by his creed: he is content with his ration, refuses to take part in any deceit, is open to his neighbour, and helpful and modest in the team building work, the sort of work that the Soviet authorities regard as being of the highest importance. Furthermore, his ethic is not simple moralism; it is inspired by the joy that comes from the presence of the living Christ. It is this joy, rather than any 'recruiting' that raises questions. 'Alyosha . . . looked happy, a smile on his lips. What had he to be happy about? His cheeks were sunken, he lived stictly on his rations, he earned nothing' (*ibid.*, p. 39).

The Baptists' strength lies, basically, in the fact that they organize themselves in small community groups around their pastors, who have nothing of the cleric about them but work like everyone else. In these communities the terribly alone man of industrial society, prey to obsessive propaganda, can find real experience of mutual help and brotherhood. These groups are lightly structured, and can be formed anywhere, in the camps, even. Ivan knows that Alyosha, 'spent all his Sundays muttering with the other Baptists. They shed the hardships of camp life like water off a duck's back' (*ibid.*, pp. 39-40).

The ways to Orthodoxy

Nevertheless, from *The First Circle* to *August 1914*, there is a strong thread of Orthodoxy running through Solzhenitsyn's published work. For him, as for many others of his generation (though in no way for the young people of today), Orthodoxy is primarily a sweetness and light felt during his childhood, when the meaning of words was less important than 'heaven on earth', the great feast of beauty, the clouds of incense, the lights, the chants, the feeling of an inaccessible mystery combined with an almost carnal blessing on the fruits of the earth, on foreheads signed with the oil of jubilation. It is in these terms that Solzhenitsyn, in his *Letter to the Patriarch*, evokes, 'my tenderest childhood, spent in the detail of liturgical service, with those wonderful feelings of indelible freshness and purity that no mature disillusion, no failing ideology, have ever been able to wither or delete'. *Cancer Ward* hints at, if not a conversion, at least a sudden experience of the faith and purity of childhood. Oleg Kostoglotov, who at the beginning of the story did not count himself a Christian, 'indeed the very opposite sometimes' (CW, p. 41), finds himself 'surrendering joyfully to his former faith' (*ibid*., p. 362), through the mystery of his love for Vera, when the blood transfusion becomes a soul transfusion too. Could this be a transposition of an experience in Solzhenitsyn's own life? He seems to have found two main ways, closely linked, back to the Orthodox Church: the first, his identification with Russian history; the second, his desire to relate to the main stream of Russian thought of the nineteenth and early twentieth centuries — until 1922, when the burgeoning ideocracy reduced it to silence.

Russian history is rooted in Orthodox Christianity, which in Russia arrived in a cultural vacuum, not in the middle of a humanist culture as in Byzantium or the West, with the result that the greatest achievements of Russian culture — such as the ordered beauty of everyday life — have necessarily been 'orthodox'. At the worst moments of a stangely dislocated history, such as the Tartar period of the 'time of the troubles', the Church has always suffered with the people, comforted them, given them the strength to collect themselves once more (as it tried to do during an even more 'troubled' period: the Second World War). Solzhenitsyn's short story *Zakhar-the-Pouch* recalls this gathering together of the different regions of Russia, a process favoured by the Orthodox Church and the work of the great prince John-the-Pouch amongst others, symbolized above all in the battle of Kulikovo in 1380, when a prince of Moscow, blessed by St Sergei, dared to take on the Mongols — and beat them.

The story makes reference to a poem by Alexander Blok, 'On Kulikovo battlefield', published in 1909, which is symptomatic of Solzhenitsyn's desire to re-establish the continuity of Russian thought — a continuity broken by the regime, which seeks to ban the reading of the religious philosophers of the nineteenth and twentieth centuries, and throws their books out of the libraries. These men, who were often prophetic, tried to awaken Orthodoxy, to drag it out of its ritualism, put its intuition of the Spirit to work in order to enlighten and enliven all aspects of contemporary civilization. In *August 1914*, Solzhenitsyn mentions the collection of essays, *Signposts*, published in Moscow in 1909, by a group of religious philosophers including Berdyaev and Bulgakov, with the aim of exorcising the temptation to secular messianism among the *intelligentsia* and recalling it to a sense of creative spirituality combined with a realistic approach to politics. In *August 1914*, two characters, Varsonofiev and Andozerskaya, expound the principal theories of these philosophers. The speech for the Nobel Prize affirms Solzhenitsyn's adherence to this line of thought by quoting the two writers of the last century — Dostoevsky and Soloviev — who inspired the religious writers of this. Soloviev is also quoted, for his economic and social teaching, in *Cancer Ward*. It is his spiritual intuitions and moral requirements, rather than his system — or rather systems — that interest Solzhenitsyn. These aspects of his work are worth a moment's study: for him, the time had come when Christian truth had to free itself from all superstition and find its valid expression in turning modern rationalism into what might be termed a 'monstration' of the Absolute, a conception dear to Solzhenitsyn, for whom, as we have seen, 'the great scientists believe in God'. The full synthesis of human and divine in Christ sums up natural evolution as well as human history. In the non-Christian East, the divine diminishes or absorbs the human; in the rationalistic West, on the other hand, man seeks to deify himself through his own efforts. Only the fulness of Christ can make sense of modern anthropocentrism, not by rejecting it, but by opening it to the Spirit: a vision of profound relevance to contemporary Russia, with its acceleration and extreme adoption of Western technology, taking it in half a century from the divine claiming to absorb the human to the other extreme.

The essential point Solzhenitsyn takes from Soloviev's 'sophiology' is the theme of *Sophia* — wisdom — as the all-presence of God, the secret heart of matter, its transfiguring, feminine aspect, shining with tenderness and purity. This feminine and cosmic side of divinity brought out by Soloviev was bound to appeal to Solzhenitsyn, since Stalinism had disqualified the image of the 'strong' ruler so often applied to God in the Bible.

He also absorbs Soloviev's central concern: to define the relationship between Christianity and history in a manner free from all the evasions of pietism. 'Christianity', he wrote, 'is not a rule of everyday life, but the motive force of the whole future of mankind'. The type of Christian ideocracy he at first envisaged would not appeal to Solzhenitsyn, who rejects any form of ideocracy. But Soloviev's politico-religious hopes collapsed in the last decade of the nineteenth century, and he came to see history as a tragedy with no solution, in which man must constantly struggle in his personal and social ethics, in love of his fellows and in an art that can 'enlighten and transform' the world. He wonders whether the growth of 'progress' will not lead to unprecedented barbarism. He reflects on the absolutes that no human progress can overwhelm: beauty, love and death, the ultimate defences against the anti-Christ whose advent he prophesied. Solzhenitsyn says the same, but after, not before, one of the manifestations of the anti-Christ.

If Soloviev's feeling for the reciprocity between spirituality, aesthetics and ethics seems to have a direct influence on Solzhenitsyn, his relationship with Dostoevsky is more complex. He quotes him often, as the one who showed the irreducible nature of freedom, the one who 'was granted to see clearly into the depths of things and to be dazzled by them' (NPA). His relationship to Dostoevsky contains a sort of reversal: Dostoevsky was writing in a relatively stable Russia, in which the monarchy and the Church seemed secure, and the patriarchal and communitarian culture of the peasants who made up nine tenths of the population was still virtually intact. The abysses were still hidden; the Western trauma of the 'death of God' was being proclaimed by only a few isolated prophets. The convulsions that were to shake society in the twentieth century were only a few far-off rumbles. Dostoevsky's genius was to plunge into the abysses, to espouse the causes of revolt and destruction against a slumbering Christianity, to push dissociation and absence to their extremes, to the final choice between God-made-man and man-made-god, to Christ more deeply present in hell than any of the damned.

For Solzhenitsyn, the hurricane foreseen by Dostoevsky has been unleashed, the abyss has become history. It is no longer a question of looking for the forces of destruction beneath a surface stability, but of hunting among the ruins for the foundations of a possible way of life. Dostoevsky's approach was designed to combat the morality of his time; Solzhenitsyn is looking for an ethical base in his. One denounced false securities, shook foundations; the other denounces hell in history, builds on foundations. Both find Christ in hell, but one at the end of a process of destruction, the other at the beginning of a period of construction: Solzhenitsyn's work is 'edifying' in the full sense of the word; it triumphs over the nihilism that Russia produces in her history, not in her literature. But his ethic is forged in hell, on the edge of death; it is an *ethic of resurrection*, and this is the spiritual bond between him and Dostoevsky.

The Soviet critic Yuri Kariakin, writing before Solzhenitsyn became a forbidden subject, compared the conversation between Ivan and Alyosha, in *One Day in the Life of Ivan Denisovich* with that between another Ivan and another Alyosha, in the chapter 'Pro et Contra' in

The Brothers Karamazov. In both, the subject is God, and Alyosha the novice and Alyosha the Baptist are both witnesses to him. But Ivan Karamazov, while accepting the existence of God, *metaphysically* rejects a creation in which innocent children can be tortured, whereas Ivan Denisovich, while also accepting the existence of God, rejects a particular *history*. Captured by the Germans in one of those pincer-movements that nearly cut off the ill-prepared Red army, he was sent to a prison camp as a 'traitor' after his release. This is why he can say to Alyosha: 'Jesus Christ wanted you to sit in prison and so you are — sitting there for His sake. But for whose sake am *I* here? Because we weren't ready for war in '41? For that?' (LID, p. 140). It is not a metaphysical, but an ethical objection. If Ivan Denisovich is not interested in heaven and hell, it is because he already knows hell too well — the hell of history. Dostoevsky could shrug off historical problems in myths — such as that of the 'God-bearing' people — but Solzhenitsyn can no longer do this: history, in the twentieth century, *has itself become metaphysical.*

Towards an integration of evangelism and Orthodoxy

It was just the problems of the meaning of history and of existence that led Solzhenitsyn away from evangelism, or rather drew him to broaden it into a fully 'orthodox' vision. Baptist spirituality, despite its concern for everyday life, is 'vertical', narrow, a-historical. Alyosha can find nothing to say to Ivan about the camps, beyond that one must praise God for being there because they give one plenty of time to think about one's soul. The criticism of evangelism is overt in *August 1914*, with a brief but pertinent attack on Tolstoy. The young Sanya, who tries to be a perfect Tolstoyan, but feels reservations growing in himself, goes in search of his 'prophet'. He finds him and questions him, and is answered — with the fatigue of the man of letters who has said all he has to say — in a series of stereotypes. Sanya timidly articulates his reservations: the doctrine of love alone might be fruitless or very premature? 'Only through love! Nothing else', is the reply, and with that, 'he seemed to have said his say' (A14, p. 23). Sanya makes bold to admit he writes poetry, and the master replies with total lack of sensitivity: 'How can you enjoy lining up words in ranks like soldiers according to their sounds? Childish nonsense! It's unnatural. The job of words is to express *thoughts*, and you don't find much thought in poetry, do you?' (*ibid*.). Sanya is disappointed; despite

Tolstoy and his puritanical condemnation, 'he still remained secretly attached to composing verses'.

Tolstoy did in fact show a strange dissociation between the quasi-sacramental feeling for beings and things that inspires his great novels, and the evangelical rationalism of his later works. The conventional nature of society and culture distressed him early on − perhaps it always had − but his reaction was to look beyond this to the good life, to the power and gentleness of nature, which he found in fruitful love, birth, work, death, the immensities of earth and sky. But this does not constitute a Christian mystery; it is rather the impersonal fulness of the old paganisms. Even history only demonstrates this impersonal nature, and Tolstoy has nothing but contempt for those so-called leaders who claim to be able to influence the immense flow of life: a point on which Solzhenitsyn frankly disagrees with him − for example, *August 1914* chapter 13. And when Tolstoy turned in anguish to the Gospel, his moralizing and rationalistic Christianity rejected the revelation of God made man, which makes sense of the mystery of existence and the whole of human history. His evangelism despised understanding, art, law, social structures, and even the humble joy of living in the companionship of friends and familiar objects. His mystery is not Christian, and his Christianity is without mystery; he moves from a sacral but pagan ontology to a fideist existentialism in an empty world. From this point of view, Solzhenitsyn can be seen as a unified Tolstoy, illuminating history and existence with the Cross of Christ. Even *Cancer Ward*, in which a short story by Tolstoy plays such an important part (but mainly because it illustrates and presents a gospel parable), the evangelical sensitivity is always diffused through the great 'Orthodox' tradition.

Through Dostoevsky and Soloviev, Solzhenitsyn rediscovers what might be called the 'philokalic' genius of Orthodoxy. *Philokalia* means 'love of beauty', and is a term used strictly to designate those collections of spiritual writings that help man in his quest for the supreme beauty: union with the Lord of Beauty. Beauty expresses the mutual integration of the being and the person in a light of trans-figuration: that of the icon. 'The classical triad of the Good, the True an the Beautiful', to which Solzhenitsyn refers in his speech for the Nobel Prize, is not only a Platonic concept, but was taken up by Soloviev as an approach to the Trinity, in which the Absolute 'brings about the Good through Truth in Beauty'. It is Solzhenitsyn's achievement to have rediscovered this identity of being and beauty − identity of love and beauty − in absolute intersubjectivity, steering a course between a Christianity that had degenerated into moralism and a rootless aesthetic code of beauty.

If history can temporarily paralyze our understanding of the Good and the True, as it does today, 'the unexpected wonder of the beautiful will suddenly burst forth, clearing secret ways for itself so as to bloom in their place and work for all three' (NPL). Solzhenitsyn's 'meta-literature', writing after the flood, should perhaps be seen as belonging to the pentecostal, 'pneumatological' revival announced by the Russian religious philosophers, a time when, 'Dostoevsky's words: "Beauty will save the world", will come to be seen not as a phrase that is gone with the wind, but as a prophecy' (*ibid.*).

This is not a denial of evangelism; it is rather freeing it from its temptations to moralism and rationalism, from its confines of faith without existential content. The Baptist ferment could mark an overall renewal of Russian Christianity: it challenges Orthodoxy to show its own evangelical and prophetic dimension once again, while Orthodoxy can give the Baptists the *mystery of transfigured earth* — the continuity of tradition, the continuity of the land of Russia too, and the pasch of existence, the pasch of matter. The appearance, in the last few years, of Baptist communities who celebrate the traditional Orthodox feasts of Mary is undoubtedly a step towards the incarnation of the Baptist faith and the 'pneumatization' of Orthodoxy. The Mother of God is also the 'Mother of life' in whom the earth becomes the 'body of God'. Solzhenitsyn's work is in itself another step. Perhaps one day we shall see that Alyosha the Baptist and his brethren were precursors, like the other Baptist long ago. Precursors of a new revelation of the human face of God in icon and eucharist, and thereby in the icon of every face and the eucharist of every meeting.

The mutual integration of evangelism and Orthodoxy could come about in the Spirit as the beauty of Christ. As Dostoevsky also wrote: 'There is nothing more beautiful than Christ'.

12 The letter to the Patriarch

While the letter to the Patriarch Pimen and the fact that Solzhenitsyn had his children baptized are evidence of his will to belong to the Russian Orthodox Church, he nevertheless brings a spirit of mature and passionate criticism to bear on it. He writes as an outsider who has come in, but without sharing the claustrophobic atmosphere of the ghetto; as an 'evangelical' who has turned to Orthodoxy, but who retains a feeling of the need for reform within the Church, if not of the Church.

The Russian Church in 1914

His observations on the Church on the eve of the First World War and the Revolution, in *August 1914*, refer to a time when the whole body of the peasantry — who still made up three-quarters of the population — were still steeped in Orthodoxy. 'The clear light of Christian ethics had for a thousand years formed out customs, the course of our lives, our judgments, our folklore, and had even given our people their name: 'Christians', *Krestiane*, meaning 'peasants', from *'Khristiane'*, meaning 'Christians' (LtP). The country parish formed a solid community in which all were companions in toil and brothers in faith: 'Travelling along country roads in central Russia, you begin to understand why the Russian countryside has such a soothing effect. It is because of its churches. They rise over ridge and hillside, descending towards wide rivers like red and white princesses' ('A journey along the Oka', SPP, p. 203). In another prose poem, 'The ashes of a poet', and through the mouth of Agnia in *The First Circle* (FC, p. 157), Solzhenitsyn stresses the taste for beauty of a Church that always built its churches and monasteries 'in the most superb places', as if to sanctify the beauty of the earth, as in Christ 'heaven' and 'earth' are no longer separated. The Church shone on the natural cycles of life through its liturgical prayer, recalling man to his eternal dimension: 'People have always been selfish and often evil. But the angelus used to toll and its echo would float over village, field and wood. It reminded man that he must abandon his trivial earthly cares and give up one hour of his thoughts to life eternal' (SPP, p. 203). This, claims Solzhenitsyn, was the element in his life that raised man above the level of a beast.

Solzhenitsyn, unlike the Slavophiles of yesterday and the Russophiles of today, does not idealize the peasantry. In *August 1914* he comments on their fickleness, their temper, which was often savage, thir tendency to pillage, their lack of national feeling. Ivan Denisovich, who still has traces of his village upbringing, shows a typical mixture of faith in one God — thundering Jupiter rather than the father of all mercies — 'Hear him thunder and try not to believe in him' (LID, p. 94), and remnants of archaic cosmogonies: each month, 'God crumbles up the old moon into stars' (*ibid*.). But Solzhenitsyn also remarks how Orthodoxy can produce peasant types who are open to the infinite and deeply human. Such a one is Blagodaryov, the soldier whom Vorotyntsev picks out as his orderly, and who becomes his freely faithful companion: independent, wise and cunning, he is a cantor in his village church, and so has a fund of both religious and popular songs at his command. In the midst of disaster, he can organize an admirable and serene funeral service. This is the greatness of the Church: to have taught the people the final prayer that, in Christ, can open the portals of death and send the dead man to the 'eternal memory' of God (A14, p. 510).

But the days of this traditional peasantry were numbered. The general mobilization of 1914 merely accelerated a process of displacement that had already begun with the dawning of the industrial revolution. In the early years of the twentieth century, the drift to the towns was already a major social phenomenon. The urban *intelligentsia*, and then, gradually, the workers, were won over to a rationalism that the lack of a deep-seated humanism, and perhaps Orthodox atavism also, turned into a fiercely anti-theistic secularism. Varsonofiev observes that a priest, even an educated one, could not be considered an intellectual (A14, p. 426). Agnia's mother and grandmother, well before the revolution, had not gone to church, 'they had never observed the fasts, never gone to communion, sneered at priests and never missed a chance to make fun of a religion which had so easily come to terms with serfdom' (FC, p. 157).

So the Church, if it was to pass on the faith in this new context, had to come to terms with personal conscience, and to show that Christianity was able to be the leaven in the dough of urban, industrial civilization. With true prophetic force, the religious philosophers of the day worked out the main lines of a creative spirituality. They showed that the religion of the person and of freedom could exist within Christianity, and that nothing — work, art, politics, *eros* — need be a stranger to the breath of the Spirit. Through 'religious philosophy societies', they drew closer to a Church in which academic theology was also experiencing a renewal. The ordination of Paul Florensky, a great mathematician and religious philosopher, in 1911, became a sign of the times. Responsible laymen co-operated with the hierarchy in preparing for a local Council that would re-establish the Patriarchate and reform the structures and teaching of the Church. The preparatory documents envisaged a renewal, along community lines, of parish structures, which had become an empty formula in urban society, a progressive switch from Slavonic to Russian in the liturgy, and a revision of liturgical rites which, elaborated by monks, were ill-adapted to current conditions.

August 1914 carries traces of all this work. Varsonofiev, who is a religious philosopher, and Andozerskaya, an historian whose very objectivity leads her to recognize the role of the spiritual in social life, are evidence of the existence of a highly cultured movement free from the sectarianism of the traditional intellectuals. The priest giving Extreme Unction to a dying man in the hospital at Neidenburg, feels the meaning of his ministry with his whole being: 'How many, many times in the last few days had he not intoned the familiar words in a low voice, yet each time with sincerity and without sounding bored' (A14, pp. 358-9). Irina Tomchack is an interesting example of the enlightened Christian. Lively, well-educated, humorous, she goes into the meaning of the liturgy, humbly practises repentance, reads and has read to her the life of St Seraphim Sarofsky, witness to the real transfiguration of man in the light of the Holy Spirit (*ibid.*, p. 42). Yet there is a certain precariousness, not to say ambiguity, in her spirituality: she has an excessive taste for portents (*ibid.*, p. 44), a tendency to add half-understood Hindu doctrines to the gospel message, defects typical, in fact, of the spiritual revival of the time, and condemned by religious philosophers such as Berdyaev.[1] Her Christianity has something of the cultural luxury of a superstructure: it is an untested Christianity.

The funeral meal and the Easter procession

The war, followed by the Revolution and its successive upheavals, prevented this renaissance, which was always limited to small sectors of society, from bearing fruit. Uprooted by the war, torn from their traditional structures in the schools of the Revolution, the peasant masses began to turn away from the Church. The elements of the old rural structures that had been reformed were finally carried away by the collectivization of land, which meant the end of the most educated peasants, learned both in faith and in traditional culture. Four million dead, fifteen million deported, most of the village churches closed, the priests classed as *Kulaks* and treated accordingly: this was the toll of the crisis of 1929-32 that Solzhenitsyn evokes in *The Gulag Archipelago*.

The definitive installation of Stalinist totalitarianism, with the great trials of 1937-9, led to practically all churches being closed, not only in the country but also in the towns, where Christian intellectuals were a particular target. Any possibility of witness to the peasant masses then being systematically evicted and forced into the towns was thereby removed. In 1929, the Church had been forbidden any sort of intellectual activity, and this ban was confirmed in the Constitution of 1936. Ideocracy, in effect, cannot afford to be tolerant; from its point of view, Christianity is no more than a hangover from the past whose disappearance should be hastened. Ideocracy itself, while not a religion of salvation, at least sees itself as a liberating gnosis; it establishes an irrational correlation, which it then affirms with correspondingly increased rationalism, between total determination of the person by material factors and exaltation of man as a demiurge with unlimited potential. 'Scientific atheism' was made a compulsory subject in all schools, and higher education could not be completed without successfully undergoing an examination in this 'subject'. Specialized lecturers made regular tours of offices, factories and collectives. The mass media, leaflets printed in millions, and a systematic campaign in all places of collective activity (including amusements) impregnated the entire intellectual atmosphere with the ruling ideology. The aim was to show atheism not as a mere philosophical conviction, but as something 'scientifically' proven. The process of secularization in Russia was not only hastened by the extreme speed of industrialization, after recovery from the 'de-industrialization' brought about by the Revolution and the Civil War, but was also psychologically systematized by the almost obsessive implanation of 'a-theoracy'.

The Second World War produced a huge national and religious upheaval, with many people returning to the faith or daring once more to practice the faith they had silently kept, and even atheists being converted. Striving for national unity in the face of the invaders, the government relaxed its ideological restraints and established a *modus vivendi* with the Church. In 1941, there were only a few hundred churches open; by 1959, this number had increased to 22,000. But just when the relaxation of the status of the new collectives under Khrushchev was leading to a new wave of exodus from the country to the towns (the population of the latter overtook that of the former in 1960), and when the decay of the official ideocracy was leading young intellectuals to turn to the East or to Christianity for inspiration, the renewal of Orthodoxy in the towns was reversed by a new wave of persecution. No blood was shed, but in a process of strangulation, 12,000 churches were closed between 1959 and 1964, and a further 3,000 have been closed since.

All this adds up to the complete disintegration of the old rural Christianity, a process that Solzhenitsyn clearly records. The journey along the Oka, which begins with the evocation of the churches that give the landscape its character, leads to a note of desolation: the churches are dead, empty, their walls and roofs growing weeds, their domes showing their ribs, 'the cemetery is hardly ever cared for, its crosses have been knocked over and its graves ransacked; the ikons behind the altar have faded from a decade of rain and are scrawled with obscene graffiti' (SPP, pp. 203-4). A ritual of life has been lost, and its remnants, as the case of Matryona shows, have not much meaning, being merely symbols and superstitions. Ivan Denisovich is astonished to see a young man cross himself. That must mean he came from one of the new territories annexed after the Second World War: 'A West Ukrainian, that meant, and a new arrival too. As for the Russians, they'd forgotten which hand to cross themselves with' (LID, p. 16). For Ivan, God is no more than the thunderer who crumbles up the old moon to make stars. But the scene where Solzhenitsyn shows the death of a tradition most cruelly is probably the wake that follows Matryona's burial. The rites are dead, incomprehensible, like the honeycomb that has to be eaten with a spoon in memory of the departed, and the *kisel'* before which all stand and sing 'In Eternal Memory': 'They explained to me that traditionally this had to be sung before the *kisel'*. With vodka, and more vodka, the talk becomes more lively, and no longer about Matryona. Finally, 'In Eternal Memory' is sung again, three times, but by now, 'the voices were hoarse and out of tune, the faces were drunken, and no-one any longer put the slightest feeling into their "Eternal Memory" ' (SPP, p. 44). Nor is much to be expected, it seems, from the few remaining country priests. At Matryona's funeral, when the weather is bad, 'The priest and the deacon waited at the church, refusing to come out to meet the procession on the way' (*ibid*.). It has to be said: there is precious little left of the Russia of the shrines and the pilgrims, the peasant Russia beloved of Slavophiles.

But while the brutal building of an industrial society and implacable persecutions have broken the traditional believing society, they have also produced a host of martyrs, and led to a poignant revival of faith, particularly in the towns and the camps. 'Not so long ago', Solzhenitsyn wrote in his Nobel speech, 'hundreds of thousands of Christians gave their lives for their faith in God, in the course of persecutions that yielded nothing to those of ancient Rome'. It was the poor women, above all, who saved the Church then. Matryona's superstitious faith is deepened by suffering into a sort of sanctity. Agnia, a convert, and Stephanie, who keeps her faith, are shining witnesses.

The Easter procession at the patriarchal church of Peredelkino as it has taken place in recent years, shows this purified Church ennobled by suffering. The courtyard of the church is invaded by a noisy throng, forcing the believers to huddle close to the walls. That the writer catches sight, among the believers, of 'one or two Jewish faces', is another sign of the times; many Jews in the Eastern territories were converted to Orthodoxy after the Second World War, bringing the Church the indomitable prophetic energy of their race. There are only a few who dare to take part in the procession in this raucous, cynical atmosphere, and the composition of the group that precedes the clergy is highly significant: two laymen first, 'asking the comrades to leave as much space as possible', then, 'an elderly . . . churchwarden, carrying a heavy cut-glass lantern fixed to a pole'. Following him, 'ten women in pairs' who carry thick lighted candles, 'elderly women with faces set in an unworldly gaze, prepared for death if they are attacked'. Two of the ten, however, are young — 'the same age as those crowding round with the boys', and, Solzhenitsyn comments, 'how pure and bright their faces are' (*ibid*., p. 106).

Those who stand around and make fun of the procession are no longer the militant atheists of the thirties, 'who snatched the consecrated Easter-cakes out of people's hands, dancing and caterwauling and pretending to be devils'. The new generation is 'just idly inquisitive' — yet how barbarous! They buy Easter candles and use them to light their cigarettes, they jig about to their transistors. They are neither violent nor openly blasphemous, yet their whole attitude is a moral outrage: 'Their lips twisted into a gangsterish leer, their brazen talk, their loud laughter, their flirting and snide jokes, their smoking and spitting – it all amounts to an insult to the Passion of Christ' (*ibid*., p. 105).

The writer's conclusion from this scene is sombre in the extreme: industrial civilization and ideocracy, by preventing the transmission of any spiritual values to these young people, or simply by destroying respect for dissident minorities, have simply bred an aggressive barbarism in the younger generation, from which all that can be expected is that one day they will, 'turn and trample on us all. And as for those who urged them on to this, they will trample on them too' (*ibid*., p. 108).

And yet . . . not all are like this. Some are not smoking, which at least shows some elementary respect. Some just have 'simple, credulous faces', and, 'a lot of these must be in the picture' (*ibid*., p. 107).

Questions for the Church

'The Easter Procession', written in 1966, might be seen as the starting-point for Solzhenitsyn's famous open letter, written during the Lent fast of 1972, to the leaders of the Church, in which he asks them this question: What is the Church doing in response to this problem of the young, how is it passing on its faith, when the Baptists, in the teeth of at least as strong a persecution, are evangelizing students, technicians and workers?

He is not addressing the bloodied remnant of a Church that existed between the two World Wars, but thinking of the popular, 'established' Church of the late fifties, with all the strength of its fifty million faithful. He has harsh things to say of it: instead of resisting on the basis of its legal position, as in Poland, this Church has allowed its churches to be closed, given up trying to reach the young, and itself dismantled its parish structures. For every church left open, twenty have been abandoned, and twenty more destroyed. Some villages are left without an open church within a hundred miles or more. The North is left almost without churches, 'this North that, from time immemorial, has harboured the inestimable patrimony of Russian culture, and which undoubtedly constitutes a storehouse of faith for the future' (LtP).

As for the towns: even if some are still open in the provincial capitals, hundreds have been destroyed in a massive process of destruction that was still in full flood in the early sixties. Most large cities in the provinces, with populations of several hundred thousand, have only two or three churches left. The new towns have none.

And most of the bishops, Solzhenitsyn claims, have simply allowed this to happen. Yet the fact that there were some who did not proves that the pressures were not irresistible. Solzhenitsyn quotes the case of Hermogenes of Kaluga, who fought every inch of the way on the basis of Soviet law, and managed to keep all his places of worship open. And what happened to him? 'Shut up in a monastic prison to this day'. There are others, though Solzhenitsyn, in his passionate outcry, does not mention them. There is Paul of Novosibirsk — and he was relieved of all pastoral care in 1972. And a few more — but only a few.

Even when lay people have petitioned the bishops to keep church and prayer centres open, they have been ignored. The twelve inhabitants of Viatka who gave an appalling picture of their plight received no reply, and the reprisals taken against them increased.

The second great criticism is that the Church has abdicated from its responsibility to teach the faith to children and adolescents. Since the early sixties, baptism has been accompanied by a civil registering of the parents, and what possible canonical justification can there be for this, which simply exposes them to extra surveillance and public sarcasm and ridicule? Yet worse than this is that the baptism of the newly-born child is in fact the end, rather than the beginning, of his incorporation into the ecclesial community. Any catechesis is strictly forbidden; he is denied access to liturgical services, to communion, sometimes even to the church precincts. The 'normalization' of 1943 allowed catechesis of children, which had been forbidden altogether by the decree of 1929, inside church during services. During the sixties, the 'Council for the Affairs of the Russian Orthodox Church responsible to the Council of Ministers of the USSR' forbade children to attend services in any form, through verbal instructions which ran counter to the law. And Solzhenitsyn comments: 'And you, princes of the Church, you accept this! Worse still, you collaborate in it, proclaiming it "an authentic sign of freedom of conscience and of religion"! You agree with those who force us to hand our children over, not to neutral hands, but to the blows of basic and mischievous atheist propaganda' (LtP).

The final criticism is that, at the moment when the Baptists' success was seen to stem from their organization in brotherly communities, the Orthodox Church permitted the dismantling of its parishes, which had already become hollow shells for the thousands of faithful who flocked to the too rare churches. In 1961, State pressure forced priests and faithful to hand over the running of their parish, which was entrusted to an executive lay body appointed *de facto* by the civil authorities, and, more often than not, dedicated to the task of destroying the parish from within. Even if this body, in most of the churches that remained open, was neutralized and as it were encysted by the clergy and faithful, it still placed the opposition at the heart of the parish, reducing it to a prayer-gathering and a place where the sacraments were distributed instead of an authentic community. The priests no longer had control over parish funds, with the result, says Solzhenitsyn, 'that the poor are pushed out of the church porches, and there are no funds with which to repair the leaking church roofs'. Priests are allowed — for how much longer? — to celebrate the liturgy, but only on condition that they do not come outside the church. If they want to take communion to a sick person, they have to ask the civil authorities' permission.

The pietist temptation

For Solzhenitsyn, this behaviour of at least part of the hierarchy has its roots in a deep-seated failing of the Russian Church: a pietism of evasion, which disguises its inability as pseudo-Christlike suffering and leads to a total divorce between liturgical and spiritual life on one hand, and ethics on the other.

This criticism is levelled with its full force at those who were responsible for the 'Christian' Empire, the 'Orthodox' monarchy, in 1914. The grotesque General Artamonov, instead of taking the proper defensive measures when the enemy attack is imminent, tells his men to pray to their patron saints, and then is horrified when they know nothing about them: 'Well, then, pray to the Mother of God while there's life in you' (A14, p. 241). Then he hastens to surrender. The Commander-in-Chief of the Russian armies, Grand Duke Nicholas, covers up for him: 'Of course there will be the most rigorous enquiry. But he is . . . a deeply religious man' (*ibid.*, p. 619).

The Grand Duke is also a believer. He is delighted that he can keep his General Headquarters at Baronovichi, which is little more than a railway junction, because of the 'extraordinary, almost impossible, and therefore mystic coincidence' that it turns out to have a church dedicated to St Nicholas, his patron saint, '— not St Nicholas of Myra, whose shrines were to be found all over Holy Russia — that would have been quite unremarkable — but the Blessed Nikolai Kochan, fool-in-

Christ and miracle-worker from Novgorod' (*ibid.*, p. 611). This was a mystic sign, and the Commander-in-Chief felt that he should not spend long away from this favoured spot, so as to have ample time to meditate on the wonder of it. This man of good will, but no will power, is forced to work with a headquarters staff 'who had been wished upon him and who were more of a hindrance than a help' (*ibid.*, p. 610), and with a battle-plan he had no part in devising. He hastens to forget the disaster in East Prussia to celebrate the capture of Lvov, forgetting, there too, that the Austrian army had been allowed to get away: 'Gentlemen, the Mother of God has not abandoned our Russia' (*ibid.*, p. 645).

A still worse example is the telegram — which is authentic — sent by the Tsar to the Grand Duke after the annihilation of the Russian Second Army in East Prussia: '. . . But we must submit to the will of God. He who endures to the end shall be saved' (*ibid.*, p. 621). There is one further message in this time of doom, which the Grand Duke reads out, 'The Tsar informs us that he has ordered the icon "The Blessed Virgin appearing in a Vision to the Holy Father Sergius" to be despatched immediately to General Headquarters . . . What a joy this is!' (*ibid.*, pp. 621-2). St Sergius, of all people, who sent two of his monks to fight for the Grand Prince Dmitri . . . 'It's a *moral* issue', Vorotyntsev comments fiercely, 'To drive one's people unprepared to the slaughter is something far beyond the considerations of mere strategy . . . None of *them* ever go to the front line to see for themselves'. They think they can evade responsibility by glorifying other men's deaths. 'They're quite ready to endure four or five more massive defeats on this scale — but by then only the Lord above will be able to help them!' (*ibid.*, p. 626).

'Praying kneads no dough' (*ibid.*, p. 622). One has to become responsible. Praying may teach one to want to learn, and kneading dough well may be a prayer, but God cannot be expected to take man's place.

The figure of General Samsonov pinpoints this overriding temptation and pathetic temptation of Russian Christianity. When the situation deteriorates, Samsonov turns to prayer, but not only in order to be able to stand back from events and take clearer decisions: he expects precise directions from God about what to do, as though God, in the Monophysite tradition, should replace Samsonov's intelligence, professional competence, and freedom of decision. And when disaster encroaches, when militarily there is nothing for it but to take a group of shock troops and break out of the still tenuous pincer movement, thereby saving thousands of lives and thousands more from being taken prisoner, Samsonov prefers to reel with the blow, and transpose the disaster on to a religious plane in a Christ-like attitude: 'It would have been a relief to him to have fallen on his knees and cried out: "I am the culprit — I sent you to your destruction!" A weight would have fallen from his heart if he could have taken all the guilt on himself . . .' (*ibid*., p. 307). And this is what does in the end, thanking his men, and receiving from them, 'looks of equal goodwill' (*ibid*., p. 448), taking his leave of them with noble humility. He had given up the thought of fighting while it was still possible: 'His was the helplessness of high position' (*ibid*., p. 450), and Vorotyntsev, wondering how he had failed to notice it before, sees, 'the look of pre-ordained doom in Samsonov's face. For all his great bulk, Samsonov was a sacrificial lamb' (*ibid*., p. 448). His bulk should have made him a colossus among warriors, yet here is this colossus abandoning his men, wanting to be no more than a sacrificial lamb. The lamb who bears the sins of the world? Yet the main current of Orthodox spirituality has always stressed Christ's heroic struggle in voluntarily accepting death in order to overcome death, the fact that his suffering is only an expression of victory. Samsonov's very death, at once sacrifice and suicide, confirms this ambiguity: one does not lay down one's life by taking it. The breath of the Spirit is here competing with the icy blast of millions.

It is possible to condemn the general tenor of Russian spirituality by emphasizing its accent on the Cross and forgetting its equal stress on the Resurrection, by concentrating on the almost aggressive thirst for humiliations of some of the 'fools-in-Christ', the mystery of suffering, not to say abjection, in Dostoevsky. It then appears as complaisance in suffering, a dualism in which access to the 'next world' involves the rejection of this, culminating not in the transfiguration of St Seraphim, but in the *accidie* of Stavrogin. Yet a close study of the spiritual history of Russia cannot lend support to this view; what comes across most strongly is rather the sober and virile character of its holiness, the power of transfiguration it has often achieved, its capacity to inspire history. In the early days of Russian monasticism, even if Anthony of Kiev prayed in a grotto, Theodosius made his monks be of service to society and spread learning. The fourteenth century Sergius, whom the Russian Church has taken as its model of holiness, was a striking example of balance between contemplation, active love and effective intervention in history. He and his numerous disciples cleared new lands, copied Greek manuscripts, defended the poor against the powerful, gave heart to a whole people and inspired a movement of national liberation. It was thanks to them that Russian culture rose to the heights of the great works of Theophanos the Greek, Andrey Rublev and Master Denis.

Even though it was prevented from reaching the same sort of synthesis, the philokalic renaissance of the nineteenth century showed the same tendencies: the *starets* Ambrose of Optino helping everyone, peasant, worker, engineer or philosopher, to lead a life of creative service to society; Seraphim Sarofsky refusing to sanction withdrawal from history, but counselling inner peace and witness in the midst of the world. The cultural influence of the 'hermitage' at Optino shines through the work of Dostoevsky, to name but the best-known of those who came under its influence.

The enslavement of the Church by the State, which Solzhenitsyn also attacks, is something alien to the Orthodox tradition, which from St John Chrysostom to St Gregory Palamas and Metropolitan Philip of Moscow, who stood up to John the Terrible, has always not only defended the spiritual independence of the Church, but carried out its duty to speak up for justice and truth in the moral and social spheres. 'A study of Russian history over the last few centuries', Solzhenitsyn concludes, 'leads one ineluctably to the conclusion that it would have followed an incomparably more human and pacific course if the Church had not renounced its independence, and if the people had been able to hear its voice' (LtP).

Its enslavement by Peter the Great was only made possible by the fact that it had been historically isolated for two centuries. It was the first major Church to fall into Orthodoxy's chief historical sin: religious nationalism. In its case, this quickly became hypertrophied in Russian messianism, with the myth of Moscow as the Third Rome and the Third Empire, 'Third' here being used in the sense of definitive. Despite the long resistance of the hermits from beyond the Volga and the fools-in-Christ, witnesses to evangelical freedom, Russia became a sort of Christian Tibet where rites acquired an almost magical value. The seventeenth century schism of the 'old believers' was brought about by the adherents to 'national traditions' reacting against a badly-conceived return to some sort of ecumenism. Their merciless repression by the State, in whose wake came Peter's 'cultural revolution', turned the Empire, in the eyes of a significant portion of the population, into an anti-Christ reigning over a world of perdition in which only suffering, and sometimes even suicide, could be good. The same seesaw, within a half century, from veneration of the 'white

Tsar', the indispensable defender of the faith, to detestation of the Tsar as 'anti-Christ', might well underly the nihilistic 'all or nothing' attitude that recurs, in various forms, among the sectarian *intelligentsia* of modern Russia.

Having despised the Church in the eighteenth century, the Empire sought to use it as a prop in the nineteenth, and in the end used it as its 'dominant ideology'. But it was a dormant Church, and many civil and religious leaders deluded themselves with the idea that it could retain the patriarchal, communitary character of the country parish outside the main current of European history. Far from enlightening faith through an awakening of the individual conscience and an appeal to intelligence and freedom, they sought to preserve the Russian people from such rationalistic emanations from the 'rotten West'. In this context, the *startchestvo* reform could not bear fruit, and the decline at the end of the nineteenth century left the Church in the grip of pietism based on an individualistic and sentimental ascesis incapable of influencing contemporary culture on one hand, and the lullaby of its liturgy, from which the preaching of the Word of God had been banished, on the other.

The lie

The attempts by the Catholic intellectuals of the first decade of the twentieth century to give the Word of God back something of its ethical relevance were swept away, with them, by the Revolution. The reforms sketched out by the over-hasty Council of 1917-18 — elections of bishops, full lay responsibility at parish and diocesan level — were weakened by a schism of left-wing groups compromised with the regime and finally nullified by the virtual disappearance of the Church between the wars. The Church that rose again thanks to the Second World War did so in all its old structures, even more conservative than before. It thought only of clinging to its traditions and rites, produced no innovatory thinking, and managed to be at once a paradoxically established Church in an 'a-theoracy' and an archaic cultural backwater carefully marginalized by the State.

This return to tradition was a return to the ways of Russia under Peter the Great, at a time when the myth of the Russian Empire was in some sense being reborn under Stalin. In *The First Circle*, Solzhenitsyn notes how the 'Father of Peoples', 'had been very gratified at being mentioned in the Church's prayers as the "Leader Elect of God" '

(FC, p. 144). He remarks too on how the bishops had joined in the general chorus of praise on the sixty-ninth birthday of the man who held fifteen million people in prison camps in the Soviet Union alone (*ibid.*, p. 111). But why wonder, when the Church had long remained silent in the face of the serfdom that was the shame of Russia in the eighteenth and nineteenth centuries?

Between 1953 and 1959, the Church once more enjoyed a certain degree of internal autonomy. But in the Sixties, the 'Council for the Affairs of the Orthodox Church', created principally to supervise the material upkeep of places of worship in a State-run economy, became, despite its constitutional separation, a sort of atheist ministry of worship whose main objective seemed to be to isolate and asphyxiate the Church while outwardly using it to further 'peaceful co-existence'. 'The administration of the Church, even the nomination of priests and bishops, with a marked preference for the least worthy, in order to further the self-destruction of the Church . . . all this is decided in secret at the Office of worship' (LtP).

The fact that part of the hierarchy belong to such a system leads to the situation where the Church is living a basic lie. These men allow churches to be closed, children and adolescents to be excluded from catechesis and worship, the canonical parish statutes to be dismantled. They ignore petitions from the laity. Bishops and priests who denounce or prevent violations of the law by the Council for the Affairs of the Church have their right to exercise their ministry taken from them. We have already mentioned the cases of Hermogenes of Kaluga and Paul of Novosibirsk. Solzhenitsyn mentions that of two priests, Nicholas Echlimann and Gleb Yakunin, who, in two letters, one addressed to the Patriarch Alexis and the other to the Soviet authorities, have simply and gently, *told the truth*: 'These two priests asked for anything in their letters that was not in accordance with the truth to be corrected . . . What reply did they receive? One of unheard-of brutality. (The representatives of the hierarchy) punished these priests for having told the truth. They relieved them of their right to carry out their priestly ministry' (*ibid.*).

At the same time as this was going on, the representatives of the Moscow patriarchate, in Rome, Geneva, in front of western journalists, told everyone that the situation of believers in Russia was excellent. They stifled protestations from groups of lay people to the Churches of the West and the UN, whilst vigorously denouncing injustices elsewhere, in full accord with Soviet policy. 'The Russian Orthodox Church indignantly rebukes the injustices perpetrated in distant countries of

Africa and Asia, but when it comes to those that corrode our own country, not a word!' (*ibid*.).

One can debate the diplomatic opportunism of such an attitude. Solzhenitsyn's attack goes deeper: he is denouncing *the death of a language* and *the destruction of an ethic*. We are back, it would seem, with the pietistic degeneracy described in *August 1914*. What is the Patriarch Pimen, a man of sincerity in prayer and extreme weakness in carrying out his responsibilities, but another 'sacrificial lamb' suffering from 'the helplessness of high position'?

The leaders of the Russian Church defend their approach by saying that it ensures a certain 'survival' of the Church. This is admitting that they give the liturgy and the sacraments an importance in themselves, divorced from any ethical considerations, just as they give their own ministry an importance in itself, divorced from any collaboration with priests and people. In Russia today, the Orthodox Church, against the whole of its tradition, is clericalized to the extreme and reduced to sacramental automatism. Its inability, or refusal, to speak a word of truth in history leads to the liturgical embalming of the Word of Truth. Hence the challenge from a vigorous Russian Protestantism. Hence, too, the terrible question, which only God can answer, but no man can avoid: 'How can the hands of those who tell lies celebrate the Holy Eucharist?' (*ibid*.).

Solzhenitsyn replied to those who called his challenge rash and premature much as he replied to the Secretariat of the Union of Soviet Writers, who had just expelled him, in November 1969: 'Wipe the faces of your watches! They're slow on our time. Draw back your heavy, costly curtains! You don't know that dawn has already broken'. 'The sinister period, without hope or way out' of mass terror has been rolled back. Men of courage can do much to humanize Soviet society by ensuring application or revision of the law: 'In the final analysis, the true destiny, the definitive fate of our country depends on the answer to this dilemma: will the right of the strongest carry public opinion with it, or the strength of right?' (*ibid*.). The time of bloody persecutions is over; all that is at risk today is loss of material goods, and 'The Gospel shows us the way we should follow: that of sacrifice' (*ibid*.).

What of the present? Solzhenitsyn's letter is no less prophetic now than when it was written. Nevertheless, it is only fair to say that the 'sacrifice' Solzhenitsyn wrote of is being lived by hundreds of thousands of lay people for whom the apostolate of the laity is a daily reality, and by thousands of admirably dedicated priests who take it upon themselves to visit the sick and perform other good works. And by some of the bishops, even.

Yet the lesson is still to be learned. A spirituality without ethics, a liturgy without proclamation of the Word of God, and a Word of God without word of man may make up a moving Eastern 'tradition', appealing to Westerners avid for the 'sacred', but they are still a betrayal of the Gospel. There are two opposing temptations here: the Western one to downgrade religion to morality, and the Eastern 'orthodox' one to shut it up in a mysticism of evasion. It is time for a mutual exorcism, for a fusion of contemplation and active love, not in order to escape from history, but to set out its limits and its future.

NOTES

1. *The New Religious Consciousness and Social Reality* (St Petersburg, 1907) — in Russian; and, *The Spiritual Crisis of the Intelligentsia* (St Petersburg, 1910) — in Russian.

PART FOUR

History

13 The structures and limits of history

History: elusive or too soon found

On its own level, or on its own surface, perhaps, history seems impossible. Most of us live in the present. We are spectators at the scene of a discontinuous present, put on by the mass media and advertising, and then put back on the shelf, since change is the rule of the game. Even if one can close one's ears and eyes to this fleeting spectacle, how does one transmit, bring back, bring to mind those moments of the past in all their existential substance, with their anguish and hope, the now withered possibilities of their 'here and now', and 'highest points' of consciousness and decision, as Solzhenitsyn calls them? Péguy once observed that a few years after the event he could not make a young man understand what the Dreyfus affair had meant to those who saw it as a question of conscience. This continuity is the theme of Solzhenitsyn's story 'The Right Hand'. Seriously ill, a veteran of the Civil War, who has lost his right hand, drags himself as far as a hospital; a young secretary, with the indifference born of knowing the rules, refuses to admit him: it's not the right time, and it can't be an emergency since he has walked there himself. She is reading a comic, and the old certificate with which the veteran tries to attract her attention means nothing to her. Yet this unappetizing piece of paper is redolent of all the epic struggle and all the tragedy of the Revolution. It tells that this man was part of a 'Special Detachment' of implacable warriors who rode down their enemies without mercy (SPP, p. 133). The same gulf exists between the old soldiers and those who stayed behind, between the victims of mass terror and the younger generation, 'because of the things I could never tell them and which they would never find out' (*ibid*., p. 126).

For some, history is but a prolongation of natural history, an *inevit able* sequence of events. But even though some structures are susceptible to some form of scientific analysis, history itself is still contingent. It springs from the interaction of human freedoms and of circumstances that can either be left to sink of their own weight or else be overcome and transformed by the power of the Spirit. This is what Solzhenitsyn sets out to show in *August 1914*: the 'knot' of fate and freedom that makes up contingent history gives the lie to the universally accepted myth of the inevitability of the October Revolution.

This myth has plunged Soviet society into a state of historical amnesia. The past has been anathematized. The works of the first two decades of this century, which contained a spiritual vision of the contemporary world, have been banned, destroyed, lost. And if the best-known churches have been kept as museums — and thereby removed from actuality — how many more have been destroyed!

But it is not just a question of churches and the new barbarians who buy Easter candles to light their cigarettes. The monument commemorating the battle of Kulikovo is likewise abandoned ('Zakhar-the-Pouch', in SPP, pp. 109-22). Yet Kulikovo was where Russia, in 1380, checked the Mongols for the first time in history, thereby assuring the future safety of Europe from the nomad hordes of Asia.

There is now a renewed quest for memory in Russia, and in order to help this on its way, deepen it and free it from the temptations of nationalism, Solzhenitsyn set out to destroy the principle of the inevitable nature of the Russian Revolution, or at least of the course it took in October 1917.

The contingency of the October Revolution

Needless to say, there was no lack of explosive elements in Russian society in 1914. The peasants, who accounted for three-quarters of the population, had hardly begun to play any part in the life of the nation. As General Nechvolodov, who has tried to awaken a sense of national consciousness in the Russian people, remarks in *August 1914*, 'The fact is that most of the people don't understand what Russia means. Nineteen out of twenty of the people have no conception of the idea of the fatherland' (A14, p. 213). What Dostoevsky called the 'strength of the earth', a strength that Western Europe had once felt, but re-absorbed, whether through a population shift into towns and industry, as in England, or by making land and education available to the peasants, as in France.

In the Russia of 1914, this explosive force went hand-in-hand with one from the present: the new urban proletariat experiencing the first upheaval of industrialization, made up of former peasants lately snatched from the impersonal protection of archaic communities and so particularly vulnerable to any -isms to replace it, particularly secular messianisms. It was as though Russia faced the joint possibility of peasant revolt and industrial unrest at the same moment, social dramas that Western Europe separated by at least two centuries. The third explosive force of the time, which plays a considerable part in Solzhenitsyn's historical novel, was that of the sectarian *intelligentsia*. This narrow group, devoid of feeling for history or for the State, preached an absolutism that led to total rejection of the society of their day in favour of a vision of an ideal society, always in the future, where all oppression would vanish, and all evil with it. Solzhenitsyn stresses their virtues, their disinterested quest for the good, but also shows that their systematic opposition to any form of power only held the germs of a new, and far worse, form of tyranny.

Worst of all were those who actually held power. Throughout the book, the Tsar, his family and the leaders of the State and the army, are shown as cut off from reality, isolated, enmeshed in petty intrigues. They also unwittingly secularized Christianity into a 'dominant ideology' and tried to sublimate their own helplessness in sentimental piety . . .

And yet, Solzhenitsyn insists, there were many positive factors in the Russian scene in 1914. Since the beginning of the century, the ecnomy had experienced an uninterrupted period of expansion that led Alexander Blok to write that 'the star of a new America' was rising over Russia. Solzhenitsyn describes this 'take-off' in regions he knew (he was born there): those that run from the lower Don to the Caucasus, through the steppes of the Kuban. He creates true self-mde men, like Zachary Tomchak, who started as a shepherd in the Caucasus and built his fortune — 'though this had been achieved purely by his own sweat and muscle' — starting with the dozen sheep given him by the farmer he worked for (*ibid*., p. 48). Now he has 'disc seed-drills from Siemens, cultivators for digging potato trenches, and those new ploughs which were pulled on long cables between traction engines' (*ibid*., p. 45) . . . not to mention a car. The secret of his success was to have divided up the steppe into rectangles protected with windbreaks formed by rows of acacias — a dent, this, in Stalinist mythology, since this 'invention' was attributed to the 'Father of Peoples'. In fact, many regions were in the grip of an agricultural awakening. The reform of 1906, which allowed peasants to leave the communities and develop their own lands, a reform balanced by the growth of credit, marketing and production co-operatives, together with a massive emigration to Siberia where a whole class of innovatory pioneers emerged, and the mechanization of agriculture in the 'Black Lands' of the Ukraine and Kuban, led by peaceful German colonists, produced the record agricultural production of 1913, which was not to be equalled for many decades.

This awakening of agriculture was paralleled by the explosive growth taking place in the towns. Solzhenitsyn quotes the southern, exuberant Rostov, with its trolley buses, up-to-the-minute shops, and modern buildings, 'of a kind that was rare enough even in Moscow, the walls of its upper floors almost entirely of glass' (*ibid*., p. 574). In passing (*ibid*., p. 592), we learn that Moscow is growing too while respecting the character of its past, and only the war has halted progress on the new underground – another sideswipe at Stalinist mythology, which clamed all the credit for this enterprise too.

Towards the end of *August 1914*, Solzhenitsyn evokes the world of the engineers, who are shown as builders of a better world, free from the trammels of ideology. Arkhangorodsky, a leading member of the Jewish community in Rostov, an engineer who builds mills and silos, discusses progress with Obodovsky, founder of the engineers' Union and a theoretician of development. A just distribution of goods, he maintains, only makes sense in the context of continuing economic growth. Obodovsky, a former anarchist now turned economist fiercely devoted to the common good, tells the engineers: 'In general, we have two main tasks of equal importance . . . the development of productive forces and the development of voluntary social institutions' (*ibid*., p. 594). And he concludes: 'Give us ten years of peaceful development and you won't recognize Russian industry – or Russian agriculture for that matter' (*ibid*.). These two men, one the practical builder, the other the investigator and co-ordinator, 'shared a common engineer's spirit which like some powerful, invisible wing, lifted them, bore them onwards and made them kin' (*ibid*., p. 592), in a common quest for justice as well as construction. For them, private initiative must be combined with 'rational political measures' capable of channelling profits to where they are most needed (*ibid*., p. 602), all within the framework of the underlying history of the country, its national and spiritual continuity: Obodovsky quotes Dostoevsky and his intuition of the importance of Siberia for the future of the country (*ibid*., p. 596).

Economic development was closely linked to a population explosion: the population of the empire has almost quadrupled in a century, passing the hundred million mark towards 1900, and reaching 160 million in 1914. 'Do you know what Mendeleyev calculated', asks Obodovsky, 'He worked out that by the middle of the twentieth century the population of Russia would be well over three hundred million, and a Frenchman predicted that by 1950 we should have three hundred and fifty million!' (*ibid*., p. 597). Reasonable predictions at the time, brought to nought by two World Wars, the Civil War, frightful famines, millions dead as a result of collectivization and the concentration camps, so that in fact the population had only reached one hundred and eighty million by 1950, only increasing again at the end of the period of mass terror.

The 'Russian renaissance'

Obodovsky's evolution typifies a growing divergence of views among the *intelligentsia* with the expansion of the middle classes. Since the beginning of the century, the sectarian intellectials, who had gained stength from the spread of a technical education heavily biased in favour of science, were being replaced in the centres of intellectual influence by a new generation deeply imbued with European culture. This led to the growth of an open atnosphere in which, to reverse a well-known tag, hypostasis was replaced by hypothesis and ex-communication by dialogue. This was the beginning of the 'Russian renaissance' in which Russia became fully herself through integration into European culture, while striking a balance between her new creativity and the spirit of the highest achievements of her tradition, which the thrust of technological civilization had threatened to engulf. Never had so much interest in the researches and achievements of Europe been shown. Strindberg, Matisse and Picasso were appreciated and noticed in Russia at a time when they were scarcely known in their own countries. At St Petersburg university, students studied Latin, Germanic and Celtic languages and literature. The magazines that Innokenty Volodin discovers in his mother's library — *Apollo, The Golden Fleece, The Scales, The World of Art, The Sun of Russia, The Awakening* — are full of translations (FC, p. 419). Study of Europe helps study of Russia: the discovery of a school of French painting free

163

of naturalism encourages interest in Icons; interest in the Middle Ages in the West is reflected in the increase in Byzantine studies, with a growing appreciation of the influence of Byzantium on early Russian culture. New schools of art, new discoveries in science, new schools of thought . . . Poetry, barely tolerated under the domination of the sectarian *intelligentsia*, now lends its colour to drama, the novel and philosophy, in a triumph of the sense of aesthetic and spiritual gratuitousness, a feeling of the irreducible nature of the personal experience of beauty, love and death. Symbolist poetry, celebrating the mystery of beings and things, and 'acmeist' poetry, sparser, more ironic, finding the 'acme' of meaning in the unexpected happenings of daily life, both flourish. Soloviev and Nietzsche are studied alongside Marx, whom many people are now learning to read in a critical, properly scientific way.

All this was not without its dangers, and there was a tendency to escape into the realms of the marvellous and the occult. Interest in the mystical Russian sects increased, and the confusion that made Rasputin's fortune was only an extreme, or demonaical, expression of this tendency. The 'new religious consciousness', fruitful and ambiguous at the same time, sought to unite Christ with Dionysus, taking a religious approach to Nietzsche. Yet, despite the confusion, there was a real spiritual renewal in progress, brought about mainly by lay people, those 'religious philosophers', who, having explored atheism to the full, turned to Christ, to the Spirit, not from pious conformism, but as a result of their very experience of freedom of thought, seeing the light of divine energy in the 'communing' freedom and man, the 'holy flesh of the earth' and 'the transfiguration of *eros*'.

In *August 1914*, Solzhenitsyn sketches the growth of this 'renaissance' in a series of historically significant touches. Veronika and Yolya read *Apollo*, and, to the scandal of their elders, go anywhere for their own enjoyment and pleasure: 'To an art exhibition, or a lecture on the values of life . . . or a discussion on "The Problems of Sex" ' (A14, p. 562). If Yolya has a tendency to quote modish poets and be influenced by 'Symbolist rubbish', Veronika shows a compassion going beyond political affiliation to take in all who suffer, whether in a 'good' cause or not. Irene Tomchak, as we have seen, searches for a conscious faith, rooted, despite its flirtations with Hinduism, in the highest expression of Orthodox spirituality, that of St Seraphim Sarofsky. In Moscow, the neat, pretty Olda Andozerskaya has just been made Professor of Western Medieval History, a sign both of the new position of women, and an approach to history that gave a place to spiritual values because of its respect for sources. Varsonofiev, the 'astrologer', is in fact a religious philosopher in the true sense of the term, and the best illustration of Solzhenitsyn's own philosophy of history.

The thinkers of the 'renaissance', after the Revolution of 1905, began to replace a spirituality of evasion with one of incarnation, and to take the measure of their own historical responsibility. In 1909, in the collection of *Landmarks*, Berdyaev, Bulgakov, Struve, Frank and others called the intellectuals to an examination of conscience, to a truly historical discernment of spirits: if we are to avoid disaster, they claimed, the time has come to stop trying to assuage man's thirst for the absolute with secular messianisms, to give the absolute its due by recognizing man's spiritual dimension. Berdyaev diagnosed a sort of feminine passivity in Russian sensibility at the time, and asked what virile force would come to espouse it − or rape it: either the violence of the most hardened revolutionaries, fanatics inspired by the ideals of the 'Grand Inquisitor' and secularizing the eschatological atavism of the people; or a virile, creative spirituality, mobilizing this fertilization for the historic tasks ahead − just as Gandhi was beginning to place the spiritial energies of India on the historical scene.

So nothing was fixed in 1914: history was still open, and this is why Solzhenitsyn attaches so much importance to the responsibility of those in positions of responsibility − the men who plunged Russia into an absurd war just as 'the lush and prosperous years had started to come' (*ibid*., p. 72), and who, unable to look after the peace, were to prove equally incompetent at waging war.

Only war, in fact, and a war marked by reverses from the first major battle − that described in the book − allowed the explosive forces of the past and the present to join together, obliterating ten years charged with quite different promises, but needing, as Obodovsky said, another ten years to bear full fruit.

The irrationality of history

For true understanding of history, man must be more than an historical being, and be aware of this fact. He must reach the 'ark' of spiritual understanding, symbolized by the silent, withdrawn, almost monastic 'monkey house' on a Sunday evening: 'From this ark . . . it was easy for them to survey, as from a great height, the whole tortuous, errant flow of history; yet at the same time, like people completely immersed in it, they could see every pebble in its depths' (FC, p. 358).

What emerges from this vantage point is the irrational nature of history: 'History is *irrational*, young man. It has its own, and to us perhaps incomprehensible, organic structure' (A14, p. 429), says Varsonofiev, the mouthpiece of the 'renaissance', and, perhaps, of Solzhenitsyn himself, who used almost the same words in his 'Letter to Three Students': 'Our reason is not great enough to explain, understand and foresee the march of history — and as for trying to plan it . . . that has been shown to be absurd'. Faced with ideologies that claim to explain everything, the liberating way is that of scepticism: 'It's a way of ridding the mind of dogma — that's its value' (FC, p. 51), 'a way of getting at people with one-track minds' (*ibid*., p. 89). The risk, in a rather obvious paradox, is that scepticism itself will become systematized. Allied to an Asiatic type of detachment, it can produce a cyclic conception in which history, somewhat as in Marxism, but on different lines, becomes naturalized — not by insertion in a supposedly dialectical process of evolution, but through identification with the inevitable cycles of the cosmos, in such a way that 'revolution' no longer means a novelty, but simply a turn of the wheel: the timeless turning of the stars. In *The First Circle*, Ruska Doronin propounds a cyclic theory of history reminiscent of the disillusioned wisdom of Ecclesiastes: 'An age comes, an age passes . . . The sun rises, the sun sets . . . what has been will be again, what has been done will be done again' (Eccles. 1.4-9). 'History is so monotonous it makes you sick to read it', he says, having read his Mommsen, and ready with examples from antiquity to prove his point. Everything has already happened: 'They put Gnaius Nevius in fetters to stop him writing plays in which he said what he thought. And the Aetolians proclaimed an amnesty to lure emigres back and then put them to death' (FC, p. 88).

The advantage of his analysis is that it takes up the classical analysis of power, both in itself and its effects: the hypnosis it spreads and its corrupting effect on those who exercise it. Liberty without law leads to anarchy, and anarchy to dictatorship; an analysis that, in the pessimistic Calvinism of Protestant democracies (often monarchies), made a useful contribution to the system of 'weights and counter-weights' devised to limit the exercise of a power both necessary and corrupting. Ideologies, on the other hand, forgetting this reality inseparable from power, see it only as an effect and an instrument, which can be used in an unlimited way if the aim is to bring about unlimited freedom. But, as Nerzhin remarks, scepticism 'can never give a man the feeling that he's got firm ground under his feet' (*ibid.*, p. 89). This firm ground is the spiritual consciousness of man in communion with man, and it shows the structures and limits of history, and first, its basic rhythm.

Slow history

For Solzhenitsyn, this rhythm is that of *slow history*, with its own 'organic structure' gradually worked out by 'the bonds between generations, bonds of institution, tradition, custom' (A14, p. 430). In this passage, Varsonofiev uses two images: the tree with its imperceptible growth and the river flowing steadily on. Solzhenitsyn's work is full of examples of this organic history. A well-built, matured city, with trees and running water: the central Asian city (Tashkent, no doubt) where the 'old doctor' of *Cancer Ward* lives, in which great trees form tunnels over the pavements beside which fresh water runs in paved streams, and the low, wide houses sit in their own spacious gardens (CW, p. 443). The park 'obeyed its own laws' (A14, p. 33); the Orthodox Church slowly implanted beauty in the lives of the peasants, giving a liturgical gravity to the steps in life leading to a dignified death (*ibid.*, p. 510).

There is also the slow history of the aristocratic virtues of the old Europe, a Christian humanization of warrior rites, enabling them to stylize and thereby limit violence: think of the conduct of war in the eighteenth century, a parenthesis of high civilization between religious and ideological conflicts. *August 1914* shows affectionate glimpses of this international aristocracy at the moment when total war was about to put paid to its existence for ever. There is the meeting of 'two far-flung descendants of the French aristocracy, from two different phases of their unhappy history of political emigration – Bourbon and Huguenot' (*ibid.*, p. 389). More important, there is the unexpected meeting between the Russian colonel Vorotyntsev and the German general von François. The former is probably of aristocratic lineage; if he clings to this it is from nostalgia for the age of chivalry rather than from personal pride – a code of chivalry was beginning to hold sway in the Russia of Kiev, then was crushed by the Mongol invasions and vanished from Russian society, till the despised officer class re-introduced it in the nineteenth century. Von François, descended from noble Protestants exiled from France, is inspecting forward positions, in a car, with a few officers and a machine gunner. Vorotyntsev, who has rallied a handful of Cossacks, is trying to gauge the extent of a 'gap' opened up in the badly shaken Russian line. The two groups appear over the brow of a hill together, just avoid opening fire on each other, and instead engage each other in a conversation not devoid of humour and full of politeness: once they have been introduced, they cannot shoot each other; when the Russians are riding away, the German machine gunners could have mown them down, but von François considers this 'unthinkable after their civilized encounter, and utterly unseemly for a great commander who was about to take his place in history (*ibid*., p. 383).

Slow history, too, is what has formed the culture and wisdom of the old doctor in *Cancer Ward*. In his case, of course, the tragic destiny of Russia since 1914 has played its part, but one can still feel the continuity of high European culture in both his learning and the family atmosphere that surrounds him — 'bourgeois' culture in the patrician sense the word took on in the free towns of the Low Countries and the Rhineland. The description is reminiscent of a Vermeer interior, despite the twentieth-century objects: the painted parquet floor, the large light drawing room with the open grand piano, the dining room with fronds of vine clinging round the windows and an expensive radio, the book-lined consulting room . . .

It would seem that the highest values worked out by a few in the course of this slow history gradually work through to the good of many, in a complex rhythm of withdrawal and communication far removed from the demands for immediate equality of the ideologues who try to rationalize history. Reason, says Varsonofiev, is an axe to the living tree of history (A14, p. 429); it can be used to prune the tree, but cannot make it grow better: it cannot seize what the roots take from the soil and the leaves from the air — life itself. Turning to the river image, he says that a brutal interruption can only break the flow: 'Then along come some clever people who say it's a stagnant pond and must be diverted to another and better channel: all that's needed is to choose a better place and dig a new river bed. But the course of a river can't be interrupted — block it at all and it can't flow any longer' (*ibid*., p. 429). So a revolution that is not content with pruning the tree, or straightening the course of the river, but has to mutilate the one and block the other in its quest for totality, breaks the creative continuity of history and brings the mud from the bottom to the surface.

This is what the Russian Revolution did, through its excesses, killing or exiling the men of the 'renaissance', then devouring all its own initiators except one. Even faces have changed, Solzhenitsyn notes in an admirable observation of 'slow history': 'and no camera lens can ever again find those trusting, bearded men, those friendly eyes, those placid, selfless faces' (*ibid*., p. 405). Berdyaev made the same observation in his *Spiritual Autobiography*: 'A new anthropological type appeared, lacking the goodness, gentleness and vagueness, too, of Russian features before: clean-shaven, hard, aggressive and energetic faces'. One can understand why, today, Russian intellectuals struggling to safeguard memory and freedom are growing their beards — Solzhenitsyn among the first. They are trying to recapture the spiritual continuity of Russian history, a virility devoid of cruelty, inseparable from respect and kindness: the virility of the husband, not the rapist.

Universal order and the spiritual vocation of man

The currents 'are not to be found on the surface, where every busy little half-wit casts around for them', Varsonofiev adds (*ibid*.). Human history, like man himself and the symbolic tree, draws life from the 'earth' below and the 'heaven' above, beyond the relatively clear zone reason hacks out for itself and tries to dominate. The laws of the perfect human society are only to be found in 'the total order of things. In the purpose of the universe' (*ibid*., p. 430). In, that is, the biological, animal, truly *natural* reality that contemporary ethnologists are rediscovering in the footsteps of certain traditionalist thinkers of the last century. Today we know that codified, even ritual language, hierarchic structures and group territorial foundations exist among the animals; furthermore, that the laws that regulate these societies are found at all levels of creation, in ecological systems or living organisms, with two tendencies confronting each other in permanent tension like the *yin* and *yang* of ancient Chinese cosmology: the tendency to inertia and decay — enthropy, and that to unification in complexity — negenthropy. Human society is rooted in animal society, and life in physico-chemical matter, but there is nothing 'reductionist' in this, since biology, in order to understand living organisms, has to use 'informational' and cybernetic notions found in ecology and ethnology, which evidence the omnipresence of a Wisdom and a Word reflected also in human understanding, so that our most complex sciences — informational and cybernetic — are in a way merely an attempt to understand these. Solzhenitsyn, among the science fiction elements in *Candle in the Wind*, posits a 'social cybernetics' which, taking the structures of life and society — the 'total order of things' — into account, would facilitate positive action in history, while respecting both history and the freedom of the human spirit.

In fact, 'he who would play the angel plays the beast'. Ideologies that disregard this 'plan of creation' in fact succeed only in implanting its worst features run riot — no society could be more rigidly codified and stratified than that of Stalin's Russia; it is only if we accept the order of things, even without commanding a 'social cybernetics', that we can re-create the necessary tensions, grope towards equilibrium and sometimes, for a time, towards transformations.

Man, and therefore his history, is rooted not only in the earth but also in heaven. The laws of the perfect human society are to be found in the total order of things, in the purpose of the universe *and in the destiny of man*, Varsonofiev adds. Because man's inner heaven is not empty, because spiritual experience is real, because his understanding is the image of God, he can make the creative strength of the Spirit burst through the mechanics and deadweight of the earth — not in any 'idealist' sense, but in the biblical sense of the 'Spirit who gives life'. Personal existence, the historian Andozerskaya reminds her listeners, is not determined entirely by environment: 'There is, too, the spiritual life of the *individual*, and therefore each individual has, perhaps in spite of his environment, a *personal* responsibility — for what he does and for what other people around him do' (A14, p. 568). Individual existence is not an isolated existence, immured in one's own ego-centricity. Solzhenitsyn's thought, in the mainstream of Russian spirituality, is as averse to individualism as to collectivism. If the *individual* is a fragment of humanity hardened on the outside and rotten within, the *person* is to be found — not without looking — in communion. This coincidence of essential unity and diversity in the person is designated by the Russian religious and philosophical concept of *sobornost*, springing from the divine source of the Trinity, three persons in one, the foundation and orientation of all negenthropy. In the Trinity, says St John Damascene, 'the persons are one, not to merge into one another, but to contain one the other', each containing the unity not only through his relationship with himself but equally through his relationship with the others. This trinitarian vision, becoming human and divine in Christ and the Spirit, rather than an institutional concept, gave Russian religious philosophers their framework for celebrating the mystery of the Church. So the deeper a man looks into himself, the further beyond history and into God he goes, the more, too, he enlarges the whole of humanity, of which he is a unique mode of existence, giving the totality of history a unique face.

This dialectic of unity in diversity is reflected in the construction of *August 1914*. The first half of the book gives an intimation of a totality: we are drawn into a field of centrifugal forces, the rapid succession of scenes with men and regiments caught up in the immense course of flux and reflux enlarges out understanding and sensibility to the dimensions of a huge army. In the second half, on the other hand, the lines are drawn in and the action centres on a few characters who interiorize the multiplicity of the first part. And the depth that allows this communing interiorization is symbolized by the forest of Grunfleiss which belongs to God alone, is 'simply God's forest' (*ibid*., p. 487).

Cuts and knots

The lasting creations of history always stem from a few people inspired by divine energies. One thinks of the great monks of the West who guarded and nourished the creations of Byzantium and of Western Christendom; of the open, creative holiness of a St Francis of Assisi, the spirit that made possible the first stirrings of the Italian Renaissance and the great cultural achievements of Greece, Serbia, Bulgaria, Russia and Romania from the thirteenth to the fifteenth centuries. The liberation of Russia itself from the Tartar yoke and the expansion of culture that followed were made possible by St Sergius and his numerous disciples, who plunged into God's forest and from there educated a whole people. Olda Andozerskaya gives a more cosmopolitan example of this basic law of history: the development of European civilization from the root of the Middle Ages, which her progressive students refuse to study, claiming that politically, Western history and any example they can draw from it begin with the French Revolution. One would go back to the Age of Enlightenment, but 'what on earth have pilgrimages to Jerusalem got to do with it? What use is paleography?' Andozerskaya's reply returns to the image of the tree: the philosophy of enlightenment, she says, 'is only one branch of Western culture . . . it grows out of the trunk, not from the root'. The root is 'the spiritual life of the Middle Ages . . . Mankind has never known a time, before or since, when there was such an intense spiritual life predominating over material existence' (A14, p. 567). History takes its creative dynamism from spiritual experience; it is a dialectic of the human and the divine, a continually renewed tension between man's spiritual destiny and the total order of things. Her vision is close to that developed a few years later by Nicholas Berdyaev in *A New Middle Ages*: modern humanism, he says, is only the working out of the spiritual energies accumulated by the Middle Ages; once he has exhausted this capital and proclaimed the 'death of God' — with its ineluctable concomitant of the 'death of man' — man is left with a choice between a take-over by anti-Christ or a replenishment of his spiritual sources which would permit the resurgence of 'a new Middle Ages'. This would not be a sort of 'eternal return' of the earlier one, but a transfiguration of the discoveries of Marx, Nietzsche, Freud, in the spirit — the Holy Spirit — of the earlier Middle Ages, so that, freed from their 'reducing' limits, they could take their place in a new 'divine-humanism'.

So the 'organic' continuity of history is nourished by spiritual, 'upward' cuts, brought about by the exercise of personal freedoms that allow good to act. It is hindered, on the other hand, by 'downward' cuts, in which other freedoms give themselves over to idols and release the forces of separation and chaos. The spiritual cuts make history a process of continual creation; the idolatrous cuts hand it over to chaos and death.

Solzhenitsyn, inspired by Pushkin, completes his images of the tree and the river with that of the *knot*, which is more directly concerned with personal freedoms. The 'knot' ties circumstances in which ancient choices are objectified to new forces with their destructive force. So *August 1914* describes the 'knot' in which the old Russia, whose best and worst aspects are typified in Samsonov, struggles — 'a sacrificial lamb' — in the grip of outside forces. Samsonov is 'Holy Russia', Russia 'before Peter the Great', and he is conquered not so much by his own failings — except that he loses heart too soon — as by the incompetence of those around him, incapable of fusing the spirit of tradition with the disciplines required by modern times. So he humbly says farewell to his men, as if asking their pardon, and wanders into 'God's forest', stripped of his epaulettes and decorations, a 'sacrificial victim' and no more. However ambiguous this sacrifice, it is by no means without grandeur. Across his path come Lenartovich, believer in a mythical revolution, for whom the old man and the old Russia he stands for are no more than an object of hate, their humility no more than a weakness that must be rooted out, and Vorotyntsev, also a man of the times, but a man of faithful memory and creative fidelity too. There is nothing absurd for him in Samsonov's death; he knows how to embrace the spirituality of his people, how to entrust a dead hero to the 'eternal memory' of God; he escapes from the pincer movement into the future, the future that Solzhenitsyn and so many others are trying to bring about today.

History is marked out by a line of great 'knots', great crosses like those ancient Russia set up along her borders. In them, the organic continuity is tied to the cuts that either renew or destroy it. Once the tangle becomes inextricable, there is a cut to a different level and a new age begins. It is one of Solzhenitsyn's great intuitions to have seen that since the beginning of this century, and particularly since 1914, the world has moved, 'into a new era: that the entire atmosphere of the planet − its oxygen content, its rate of combustion, the mainspring pressure in all its clocks − have somehow changed' (A14, p. 122). Now 'the stars themselves have moved into new conjunctions' (*ibid.*) and history has moved into the era when the techniques, ideologies and nihilism of the West have encircled the globe and mankind faces a new set of final questions.

History as a 'metanoia' and a communion of saints

The nihilistic experience of the twentieth century became flesh − cancerous flesh − in the concentration camps. Societies who lived through this terrible experience did so, as Solzhenitsyn notes in the first chapter of *The Gulag Archipelago*, in silence. All were 'struck dumb' − those who were arrested and those who turned aside. In antiquity, a slave was defined as *aprosopos*, 'faceless', literally, one who cannot be seen. Whole sectors of humanity were thereby plunged into nothingness, Communists and Jews in Nazi Germany, *Kulaks*, 'saboteurs' and 'traitors' in Soviet Russia. The silence of those days, whether of fear or ill-will, today seeks to become the silence of oblivion: executioners, informers and inquisitors, 'insist on burying their bloody past in a sack and dragging it behind them into the future, without a word, without a verdict, without a moral judgment from anyone . . .' (Declaration of 18.1.1974). The function of history here is one of *metanoia* − change of direction, redirection of heart and will − on both the personal and collective levels. *The Gulag Archipelago*, a symphonic history in which Solzhenitsyn orchestrates the recollections of two hundred and twenty-seven ex-prisoners with his own, has this liberating *metanoia* as its sole aim. It is in the first place his own confession, as an active participant in a certain conception of the world and social organization. He confesses that he was an officer, with the extreme privileges of rank, and added harshness, almost to the point of implacability, towards the men under his command. He confesses that after the capture of Bobruisk, when he passed a prisoner, a soldier from Vlassov, stripped to the waist and bleeding, whom a member of the Special Detachment was whipping forward from horseback, he just averted his eyes when the man was crying out for help.

This is why, now that eight years of prison and forced labour have opened his eyes to the truth about man, Solzhenitsyn feels compelled to call his people to an implacable examination of conscience. The abortive process of de-Stalinization showed up the abscess in society, but failed to drain it. What is needed is the courage to seek the origins of totalitarianism in Lenin and even Marx — and in oneself, so as to root them out of one's own thought and language.

Consigning the horror to oblivion threatens in effect to poison the Russian people and the Socialist movement. A friend of Solzhenitsyn's, writing in the *samizdat* under the pseudonym D. Blagov, called his efforts a real psychoanalysis of history, in which he likens the Soviet concentration camp system to, 'a terrible event in man's past, repressed into his subconscious and lodging in his psyche as a dark secret . . . "forgotten", but still capable of causing neurosis. When he is enabled to remember, when the secret psychic illness is laid bare and brought to the conscious level, his cure will be possible'. But just 'taking stock' of the situation is not enough; what is needed is a genuine conversion, from ideology to a system that recognizes the whole man, including his spiritual dimension.

The Gulag Archipelago seeks to cut through this rejection of history in which both those responsible and those who suffered to become the silent generations take refuge. The terrible experience that millions experienced, and that caused the death of millions, an experience still undergone today by at least thousands of political prisoners, has to be restored, communicated, *told* in all its *truth*. An undertaking surely unique in world literature? Solzhenitsyn's powerful, spare art here bears less relation to the novel or to tragedy than to the *liturgical mystery* in which the past is made present in its permanent meaning: a vast liturgy of the Good Friday of history, of the crucifixion and descent into hell of so many innocents. The history that leads through *metanoia* to the communion of saints is first and foremost the history of the humbled. No man, no nation, no community can today ignore this process of purification that requires us to seek the intercession of the excluded, the accursed, the crucified. To refuse the truth is to give death the victory, to abdicate to the nothingness we feel complicity in bringing about. Only history restored as in a liturgy can open up the communion of the living to us.

14 History versus ideologies

A smuggled philosophy

Solzhenitsyn's thought, and more so his whole sensibility, are far removed from those of Marxism. Not from the properly scientific 'Marxist' contribution, which can take its place in an 'open' dialectic, nor from the demands for justice and community often associated with some form of Marxism, in Russia at the time of the Revolution and today in various parts of the Third World, but from the philosophy, not to say mythology, that Marxism seems to harbour.

The 'truth' of Marxism lies in its revelation of certain economic factors underlying the collective life of humanity, but, having discovered the role of these factors, it then systematized this role into a 'total' conception of history. Before the Russian Revolution, Russian religious philosophers had already pointed to two logical fallacies in this construction. The first consists in blurring and limiting the dialectic by declaring it materialist; this is basing the whole on the part: one component part of complex reality is *a priori* made the mainspring of everything − history is finally irreducible to the struggle between matter become conscious (we do not quite know why) in man, and unconscious matter − nature. The second error is then to give an established fact a causative value. That the economic element forms the infrastructure of our existence is an established fact, like the fact that the foundations of a house hold it up. But to give this infrastructure a causal value in relation to all the other structures of history, thereby depriving them of any roots of their own in reality,

The spirit of Solzhenitsyn

is to move from a judgment of fact to a value judgment and to fall into a pre-critical mode of understanding. Novgorodtsev, whose major work, *On the Social Ideal*, appeared in the year of the revolution, was the chief critic of these logical errors.

Before him, Bulgakov[1] and Berdyaev[2], who knew Marxism from the inside, condemned its philosophical and mythological content smuggled in under a pretendedly scientific umbrella. This package involves blocking all spiritual ways open to man, denying transcendence, identifying reality with matter, which is given all the qualities of spirit, the whole wrapped in the secularized dyanmism of Judaeo-Christian messianism.

Solzhenitsyn's thought belongs in this spiritual line, with its understanding of Marxism, combined with some knowledge of the views of Albert Camus. His main theme is the emergence of a spiritual consciousness in an environment dominated by ideology, an environment described in *The First Circle* from top to bottom, from the omniscient Stalin to Spiridon, the near-blind orderly at the special prison; from the fear-ridden 'Father of Peoples', all-powerful but looking into the abyss, to this peasant who has been through the mill of history but who knows that there are limits beyond which one cannot go without becoming a beast.

Stressing the irreducible nature of consciousness and conscience, Solzhenitsyn sketches an open dialectic, unresolved since at this point there can be no 'synthesis' but only the 'bottomless pit' of the person from whence stem the multiple relationships that are objectivized in history. Hence all aspects of history, all its components, far from being explicable on the basis of one of them, are held in a constant balance and continual tension around this inaccessible centre. Freedom of the spirit and the 'power of law' (LtP) are therefore of equal importance with economic and social changes in the positive woking-out of history.

The new commonplaces of ideology were already appearing in 1914. 'The environment is always at fault, so all you have to do is change it' (A14, p. 568); 'We are molecules of the environment' (*ibid*.). Varsonofiev observes that the revolutionaries regard those who look for the meaning of life, concern themselves with religion and inner development as 'scoundrels': 'These *narodniks*, in trying to save nothing less than all the people, refuse to save themselves until that goal is reached' (*ibid*., p. 425). This is echoes by the cry of a revolutionary in *The First Circle*: 'What we must do is free mankind from all this sophistication!' The final stage is reached with the apogee of Stalinism: ideology is no longer bold speculation or persecuted opposition but the total State, the pedagogy of the implacable, the implacable primacy of the greatest number. How many generations had to learn, like Ruska Dorodin, that ' "pity" and "kindness" were concepts to be despised or derided and that the word "conscience" was only part of the cant used by priests?' (FC, p. 315). What we have to face is 'the fact that there is a law of big numbers' (*ibid*., p. 298). Lansky, a successful literary critic of the last years of Stalinism, has to face questioning by the prosecutor's daughter Clara, who, though part of the Soviet 'establishment' herself, is, with the disconcerting directness of youth, making a number of disturbing discoveries. She is a 'free worker' at the special prison, and finds the prisoners bear no resemblance to the monsters the police authorities had made them out to be. So she suspects they may be victims of injustice, and tells Lansky so. His reply is to deny the importance of the individual in history, which reigns as a terrible yet benevolent deity, whose laws are revealed only to party members — the gnostics of history. They efface their egos before it, and so must those who suffer — this in 1950, when there were more than fifteen million people in concentration camps in the USSR. 'Nobody can do just what they want', he says, 'only history does what it wants' (*ibid*., p. 298). We are capable of grasping the general process, and of following the general trend of events, but 'the vital thing' is to see — the final *gnosis* — 'that it's both inevitable and necessary'. So if some people suffer, 'often through no fault of their own', we have to accept this as a 'fact of life', an illustration of the law of big numbers; and: 'the bigger the scope of some historical development, the greater the possibility of particular errors'. These are of no more significance than traffic accidents or the damage caused by an earthquake.

One is reminded of the theodicy — the 'justification of God' — worked out by the scholastics with arguments borrowed in part from classical philosophy: one must consider 'the whole', and the cries of the damned make an interesting counterpoint in the harmonies of paradise. Reminded, too, of the revolt of Ivan Karamazov, or of Albert Camus, faced with the suffering of innocent children; of the revolt of Soren Kierkegaard, in the name of individual existence, against the majestic Hegelian system that only recognized 'moments' of the historical manifestation of reason.

The living God is neither hypostasized history nor the Almighty of the theodicies. On the Cross, God took man's part against idols. This is the God Solzhenitsyn recognizes.

With Clara, he has only one comment to make to these gnostics of history: 'The law of big numbers might be tried out on you!' (*ibid*., p. 299).

Flight into the past and the future

The mythic quality of classical Marxism, which is the secret of its appeal, offers a 'utopia' (the fact that it states the contrary only reinforces the clandestine nature of the utopia). Through a universal cataclysm, a sort of immanent death-resurrection, the proletariat, the collective Messiah and only true 'Christ of history', will ensure the transition from the reign of need to that of freedom, till a state of perfect understanding between man and man, and man and nature is reached.

The Russian religious philosophers contested the very idea of a final outcome in history. For them, the roots of evil go deeper, and the necessary struggle against evil will never end. They saw that in the rest of Europe, despite their absolute proclamations, the Marxists were in fact engaged in patient labour to improve the lot of the working classes: the Erfurt programme replaced the Communist Manifesto, Bebel was accepted rather than Bakunin, Jaurès rather than Guesde, not to mention the Labour movement in Britain . . . In Russia itself, the First World War intervened before socialist thought had had time to mature; laicized and utilitarian, Marxist utopianism joined forces with a messianism of Christian origin (but corrupted by the heretical identification of the 'people of God' with the Russian people) in a mood of collective atavism. Once the Revolution had taken place, Marxist thought, enmeshed in its own logomachy, was incapable of understanding, let alone controlling, the way the new society evolved. It celebrated heavenly achievements and condemned infernal betrayals, but neither this super-history nor this infra-history was capable of embracing the all-too-real hell of the camps.

Solzhenitsyn clearly recognizes this incapacity. Clara declares outright to Lansky that she is sick of seeing plays about the evils of the bourgeois world, about lecherous, rich old men buying young working-class girls: 'It's just fighting with shadows − all this was fifty or a hundred years ago, but we're still supposed to get worked up about it. You never see plays about what's happening now' (*ibid*., p. 298). Solzhenitsyn's novels and short stories, on the other hand, show us some of the realities of Soviet society in the fifties and sixties, a society suffering from deep-seated evils, while full of youth, promise and dedication. The bureaucratic Party oligarchy lives in luxury, sometimes at the expense of the State. The condition of the workers and the peasants, on the other hand, while improving, is still precarious, which seems to lead to a prevalence of theft, and — thanks to a major break in the transmission of values with the installation of industrial society — a certain moral decadence seen in 'drunkenness, bad treatment of children, domestic quarrels, refusal to work, delinquence and occasional senseless crimes' (*The Testament of Varga*).

The growing numbers of the middle classes withdraw into the little world of private or family interests, seeking a *'petit-bourgeois'* way of life. They show virtually no sign of any taste for freedom or civic responsibility. Yet Solzhenitsyn shows us admirable, though desperately overworked doctors, teachers inspired by the meaning of goodness and beauty, political officials who try to operate 'in council', intellectuals, particularly scientists, passionately looking for the meaning of life; there is a patriotism still tinged with nationalism but concerned with wider values, a sorrowing, deepened Christianity, increasing the number of the 'just' in secret, and that amazing reserve of true humanity formed by all those who have been through hell and not become wolf-hounds . . . Even if barbarism is on the increase among the young, there are those like Clara who are not blinded by their privileged position and who ask valid questions. And barbarism need not be a destructive force; it can be an openness to the Spirit, if true witnesses to the Spirit can be found.

Marxist ideology, however, is not only orientated to the past in its efforts to ignore the present; it also seeks to divert attention from it by exalting the future in the shape of the 'communism' in which future generations will finally find happiness. This notion of a history orientated towards a happiness always set in the future was criticized by the nineteenth-century scientist and visionary Fedorov, for whom the notion of progress that immediately disqualifies its antecedents is a 'parricidal' concept, and a perfect society based on it could flourish only 'in the cemeteries'. For several of Solzhenitsyn's characters, too, happiness is 'after all . . . a relative term' (FC, p. 46), 'a mirage' (CW, p. 476), and we can have no idea of how future generations will see it. Shulubin tells us how he paid for his family happiness, when his children 'spat on [his] soul' (*ibid.*), how he 'took books which were full of truth and burnt them in the stove' in order to preserve his happiness. And his tortured conscience has struck him back with cancer of the rectum, as though to punish him and his family for wanting 'enough loaves of white bread to crush them under our

179

heels', for their obstinate will to survive. And 'as for the so-called "happiness of future generations", it's even more of a mirage . . . Who has spoken with these future generations? Who knows what idols they will worship?' (*ibid*.). Sufficiency does not bring happiness; neither does caring about it for ourselves and for our children: 'If we care only about "happiness" and about reproducing our species, we shall merely crowd the earth senselessly and create a terrifying society' (*ibid*.). The only way is through a personal ascesis, through sharing out now what we have not enough of. In that way we can talk of 'happiness', the sort of happiness that spreads 'light': 'So may you continue to flourish, my friends, and may your light shine!', Kostoglotov writes to the Kadmins (*ibid*., p. 322).

The link between violence and the sacred

Except for Easter, the 'Feast of all feasts' central to Russian Orthodox liturgy, the sacrality of myth is inseparable from violence in its exaltations of collective existence: the death of a scapegoat, the totalitarian intoxications of our century culminating in the concentration camps and total war — or the excesses of a faceless sexuality that jeers at the image of the person . . . In Marxist ideology, this secret link between violence and the sacred is expressed in a real litany of hate: 'What would you do without "enemies"? You would no longer be able to live, without your "enemies"; hate, hatred that leaves racial hatred nothing to envy, that's the sterile air you breathe' (Letter to the secretariat of the Writers' Union, 12.11.1969). The class struggle, which exists but is not the whole story, can become a sort of racial curse used to explain all the evil in human society, and Solzhenitsyn attacks this distortion of an idea. The inmates of the cancer ward discuss someone who has profiteered from the war, and Rusanov comments sententiously: 'if you dig deep into such cases you'll always find a bourgeois social origin' (CW, p. 435). This incenses Kostoglotov: 'That's not Marxism. It's racism', he retorts. And comparing his calloused hands with the 'white and puffy' ones of the 'proletarian' Rusanov, he goes on: 'Did my father give me a different sort of red or white corpuscle in my blood? That's why I tell you yours isn't a class attitude but a racial attitude. You're a racist!' (*ibid*., p. 436).

The link between violence and the sacred pushes back the limits to the death-wish set by great civilizations. In *August 1914* it is nationalist passion that mocks the 'rules of war' inherited from liberal, aristocratic Europe. The humanitarianism shown by the Russian commander when his troops occupy Allenstein — 'War was something that was waged by two different sets of uniforms — total war would have exceeded the bounds of humanity' (A14, p. 284) — contrasts with the hatred and contempt shown when the Germans retake the town: the inhabitants, carefully left alone when the Russians moved in, shoot at them from all the windows when they are forced to retreat, 'and a machine gun opened up from the lunatic asylum, still hung with a notice in Russian requesting that the inmates should not be disturbed' (*ibid.*, p. 402). When the fate of the Russian army is sealed by the German pincer movement closing in, the Germans shoot the seriously wounded, tie prisoners to cannon, and organize a sort of concentration camp:

> = The novel solution — a *concentration* camp!
> = The fate of men for decades to come.
> = The herald of the twentieth century. (*ibid.*, p. 556.)

Here is the intuition that the First World War meant the dawn, no longer in a few prophetic writings, but in the very stuff of history, of the *era of nihilism*: 'Dostoevsky's devils . . . roam the world', corrupting men's minds 'by denying the existence of universal, fixed norms of good and evil, of justice and injustice, on the pretext that "everything is relative", everything changes, and the only rule of conduct to follow is to do what benefits the "party" ' (NPL). Only this era of nihilism allowed the spread of totalitarian regimes and transformed Marxism itself into totalitarianism: when it was just one element in the rich complexity of European civilization it had been capable of other interpretations and other applications.

Two Communists in the time of Stalin

Solzhenitsyn offers two examples of militant Communists motivated by longing for justice and community, and suddenly enslaved, degraded by the idolatrous nature of ideology: Zotov in *An Accident at Krechetovka Station* and Rubin in *The First Circle*.

Vasya Zotov, since the outbreak of war and the invasion of Russia — we are in Autumn 1941 — has no aim other than to serve: 'His insignificant life only meant something if he could help the Revolution' (SPP, p. 139). Transport Officer at an out-of-the-way station, ashamed of not being at the front at his age, he has kept himself above all the spivvery, intrigue and transient love affairs of the support zone. He has left his wife pregnant in occupied Byelorussia, and has no hesitation in declaring, despite taunts, that he trusts her and will remain faithful to her. At the post office, where he goes to read the papers, he meets a young woman, Paulina, whose husband is away fighting at the front. They follow the news together with passionate interest, and he excitedly reads articles by Ehrenburg (that Barres of the Russian front) aloud to her. A very pure friendship springs up between them: 'He had become attached to Paulina, her child and her mother in a way that in normal times would be impossible' (SPP, p. 153). He would not dare 'even to touch her white hand', 'Not because of her husband or his wife, but because of the sacred bond of grief that united them' (*ibid.*, p. 154). In this way, Paulina becomes 'his conscience'. He devotes all his time to his duties: the whole life of the country, the whole revictualling of the front depend on good co-ordination of rail traffic; in his free time he is working on a report for the Defence Commissariat on how to make Rail Transport Officers more effective.

In the special prison of *The First Circle*, Lev Rubin, a party member up to the time of his arrest, remains a convinced Communist. He is a young academic, a philologist who specializes in Germanic languages; also a warm character who makes friends easily. He speaks *Hochdeutsch* impeccably, and when the occasion demands can manage Middle German dialects as well (FC, p. 21). He feels German writers to be relations, and, though he has never been there, seems to know the little towns along the Rhine as though he had long been affectionately walking their streets. The first time he appears in the novel, he is 'carrying a Mongolian dictionary and a volume of Hemingway in English under his arm' (*ibid.*, p. 25). He feels the need to share everything, and without friends, 'suffocates'. In prison, it is true, 'it seemed to be his fate that his friends did not share his outlook, while those who did were not his friends' (*ibid.*, p. 226), but he accepts this state of affairs, managing to remain true both to his friends and his ideas: 'When the light of battle was not in them, his eyes were almost feminine in their softness' (*ibid.*, p. 53). In the war, his knowledge of German earned him a place in the 'Section for the disintegration of enemy armed forces', but in order to convince the Germans of the wrongness of their ways, he had to get to know them, and his gift for friendship meant that he ended up by loving them. After their surrender, he tried to defend them, just as he now intervenes with the prison authorities on behalf of the small group of German prisoners. This sympathy and moderation, at a time when the law of 'an eye for an eye, and a tooth for a tooth' reigned supreme, earned his arrest, trial and imprisonment.

So Zotov and Rubin are both sincere, unselfish, deeply human Communists, not in spite of their Communism, but because of it. Both, moreover, rise above the political sphere: Zotov through his experience of a love that is non-erotic in inspiration, a personal encounter of two people sharing in a universal grief; Rubin through his friendships and his vast learning. Yet both make Communism an absolute, a powerful secular religion that claims to slake their thirst for a total experience. Zotov venerates Stalin, 'the omniscient, omni-potent Father and Teacher who was always there, who foresaw everything, who would do all that had to be done, and would never let it happen' (SPP, p. 138). And when 'it' — the German advance — does happen, a fact he cannot fail to know about, anguish grips his heart, then he is ashamed of his anguish, seeing it as a lack of faith. Besides his armed prophet, he has his Holy Writ, which he carries everywhere with him in his soldier's kitbag, like pilgrims did with the Bible in the previous century. But it is not the Bible, it is the first volume of *Capital*. At Krechetkova, he is at last able to find time for this 'cherished book': 'once he had mastered even this first volume and committed it in its noble entirety to his memory, he would become invincible, invulnerable, irrefutable in any ideological combat' (*ibid*., p. 155).

Rubin, who has passed thirty, has a far more complex past, in which he has already been forced to sacrifice his intellect on the altar of the party. When he was sixteen, a cousin whom he admired persuaded him to hide some printing type. The type was found and he was arrested; he covered up for his cousin and pretended he had stolen it. For this he was given fifteen days in prison. Fifteen tragic days which marked his record. In prison, he heard the convicts curse the 'Stalinist butchers'. But the weight of the secret is too much for him in the end. Both his cousin and the prison inmates, have been Marxists in opposition groups, and how can one be a Marxist on one's own, or in small groups? So, having come to understand that 'in this complex age socialist truth sometimes progresses in a devious, roundabout way' (FC, p. 24), he is persuaded to confess and denounce his cousin. He is then enlisted to play his part in the great ritual of hate — the process of collectivization, in which four million peasants died. He transferred the messianic feelings of his ancestors to Communism; in the special prison he composed a poem on the long march of the Hebrews guided by Moses. Moses was the only one to see clearly: 'Moses, who knew that in the end they would come to the promised land, was right' (*ibid.*, p. 209). Moses today is Stalin, and Rubin, a willing convict, concludes that the State cannot exist without a well-ordered system of punishment, for as long as its wandering in the desert lasts. He is working on a grand secret project, the establishment of a series of 'civic temples' which would not only lend dignity to the feasts of the New Jerusalem, but would be used for weddings, name-giving to the newly-born, entry into adulthood, true Communist 'initiation sacraments', which have in fact been developed in Russia, and more so in East Germany. These civic temples would dominate towns and villages, the ritual would be looked after by specially chosen 'ministrants' of irreproachable life and thought, and all the senses would be brought to bear on enhancing the occasion: 'by impregnating the air with a special aroma, by choral and other musical performances, by the skilful use of coloured glass, spotlights, and tasteful murals . . .' (*ibid.*, p. 506). This Russian Jew shows himself more Russian than Jewish and unconsciously transposes the whole liturgical gamut of the Orthodox Church to the benefit of the new ideology.

The mystery of idolatry has no place in the lives of the Soviet 'establishment' — the Rusanovs, Makarygins and Kabalygins: their sole concern is power. Idolatry is the concern only of the pure in heart, the noble minds who absolutize the relative.

The chance of the trains brings Zotov to a meeting with a soldier who has escaped one of the pincer movements that characterized the German advance, Tveritinov. He is getting on in years, well-educated, an actor, and Zotov feels a certain pride in talking to someone of this eminence. But he mentions Stalingrad, and Tveritinov has the natural reaction of someone approaching fifty, and asks vaguely: 'Sorry . . . Stalingrad? What was it called before?' (SPP, p. 183). That does it: 'Something in Zotov snapped and he suddenly froze': only a traitor could ask such a question, insinuate such sacrilege. He has Tveritinov arrested. He, having destroyed his papers during the retreat, knows what is in store for him. And Zotov, turning round for a last look at the man he has handed over to the sacrifice, sees 'the despairing face of King Lear betrayed . . . "You're making a mistake that can never be put right" ' (*ibid.*, pp. 188-9).

Rubin's destiny is to perform a similar act. He is researching into a means of identifying human voices on the telephone, and is made to listen to the recorded voice of Innokenty Volodin warning the old professor on the 'phone. The authorities do not know who made the call, and hope Rubin can identify the caller from among several suspects. At first, 'Rubin couldn't help liking this man who had been brave enough to telephone a flat under surveillance' (FC, p. 236); but then the idolatry mechanisms come into play: '– perhaps "drug" was a code-word for something else' (*ibid.*, p. 237). And above all: 'But objectively, although this man had imagined he was doing good, he was in fact working against the forces of progress' (*ibid.*, p. 236). Therefore, he, Rubin, 'must rise above his personal feelings . . . He must rise above his personal misfortune' (*ibid.*, p. 237): the moment of ascesis, man rising above his nature. The ascesis is misdirected and the rising above not into communion, but the impersonal history whose priests are the security police officers, the thugs who keep Rubin in prison, makes him see the thugs as 'objectively the embodiment of progress' (*ibid.*). And in the end, Rubin identifies the voice as belonging to Innokenty, the innocent.

The myth of the superman and the myth of the people

When one rejects the 'clandestine philosophy' of Marxism, there is a growing temptation to oppose the individual of genius to the masses, to emphasize the will-to-power by ennobling it with creativity. This almost Nietzschean temptation is embodied in Sologdin in *The First Circle*. Almost unnaturally good-looking and intelligent, he believes that, 'a great idea can only be generated by a single, enlightened mind' (*ibid.*, p. 208). For him, the people are 'dull, drab', less than full men, 'totally absorbed in their joyless daily round' (*ibid.*, p. 467). 'The great temple of the human spirit' has nothing to do with the masses: 'Only outstanding individuals, shining forth like lonely stars in the dark firmament of our existence, could embody the higher meaning of life' (*ibid.*). Particularly demanding of himself, Sologdin imposes the law of the 'last inch' on himself: once the essential point of a creative endeavour has been reached, that is the moment to redouble one's efforts. His calm and solitary researches lead to a decisive breakthrough just when the authorities of Mavrino are hoist with the petard of rashly-given deadlines. He is then in a position to manipulate these puppets at will and decide his own future, and this he does with clear-sighted and detached cynicism.

Halfway between Rubin and Sologdin, Nerzhin represents Solzhenitsyn's own quest for truth between Marx and Nietzsche, between collective forces and the genius of the individual. As a young man, he had been fascinated by the refinement of the intellectual

The spirit of Solzhenitsyn

elite: 'nobody mattered unless he was highly educated and had an all-round knowledge of history, science and art' (*ibid.*). But the camps showed that these highly educated individuals did not thereby naturally form a moral elite: 'these delicate, sensitive, highly-educated persons, with their love of the beautiful, often proved to be craven cowards, very good at finding excuses for their own despicable behaviour and turning into wheedling, two-faced traitors' (*ibid.*, p. 468).

So Nerzhin henceforth reserves his admiration for the people, in an amlagam of the populism of the old *intelligentsia* and the Marxism of Soviet Russia: the two myths of the peasant and the proletariat. Now the only people who matter for him are, 'those who ploughed the land and forged the steel, or worked wood or metal with their own hands' (*ibid.*). He looks to them for true wisdom, 'and so he came back full circle to the fashionable idea of the previous century about "going to the people" ' (*ibid.*, p. 469). But in the camps, he has personal experience of 'the people', and comes to see that populist or Marxist lyricism about them is misplaced: there is no immaculate conception of the proletariat. These peasants and workers have lost the continuity of the old wisdoms in the course of collectivization, which killed off a whole culture, and the precipitate rush to the towns, but have not acquired a new set of personal values to put in its place: 'Few of them had the sort of beliefs for which they would willingly have sacrificed their lives' (*ibid.*). They are more likely than he to be taken in by informers, and naively credulous toward the authorities – starting with Stalin, from whom they constantly hope for an amnesty. They are also 'much more eager for small, material things: for instance the sour millet cake, occasionally given as an "extra", or a pair of unsightly prison trousers if they looked a little newer or brighter' (*ibid.*). So, 'the only solution left, Nerzhin now felt, was simply to be oneself'. 'It was only character that mattered, and this was something that everybody had to forge for himself . . . only thus could one make oneself a human being' (*ibid.*, p. 470).

This is the course Varsonofiev advises for the two young volunteers on the brink of a tragic history – perhaps in order to exorcise it, perhaps in order that it might bear its true fruits. The personal order, he tells them, is more important than the social: 'The word "develop" has a better and more important application – we should develop our soul' (A14, p. 428). Man's duty is first and foremost to perfect the development of his own soul, 'for who knows when one of you may not be fated to catch an echo of the true, the secret order of the world'.

This development is not solitary complacency or the aesthetism of an élite. It allows one to 'catch' and therefore to 'perform' true justice. Nerzhin, once he has lost the populist 'illusion' and realized that, on the level of history alone, 'beyond this there was nothing, nobody' (FC, p. 496), strengthens his own inner resources, his soul, an thereby becomes a part of the people. He approaches Spiridon, the orderly of the special prison, neither as an inferior, nor as a superior, but simply as an equal: 'He could not look down on, nor look up to this peasant . . . indeed he now literally sat by his side, shoulder to shoulder' (*ibid.*, p. 483). Consequently, he finds in this man from whom history has stripped all the layers of dead skin, an example of the 'perfect development of one's own soul'. On one side, he has a passionate attachment to the land and to his family; on the other, a tranquilly coherent possession of the 'virtues': 'He never slandered anyone, never bore false witness . . . He only killed in war. He could never have brought himself to steal the smallest thing from anyone' (*ibid.*, p. 479). He has a simple, direct phrase to describe his method of distinguishing between good and evil: 'the wolf-hounds are right and the cannibals wrong' (*ibid.*, p. 486), a direct limitation on human action unknown to the ideologues, but one that one cannot ignore without becoming a cannibal, as Solzhenitsyn wrote in his 'Open Letter' of 14.6.1970.

The apprenticeship of Sasha Lenartovich

If the apprenticeship of history — history *versus* ideologies — is shown in condensed form in the case of Gleb Nerzhin, *August 1914* gives another example of apprenticeship, this time spread over the events of the book, and without a definite outcome, in the case of Alexander (Sasha) Lenartovich.

Born into a family of revolutionary intellectuals, and having lost his father at an early age, Sasha is brought up by his maternal uncle (whose Christian name he bears), who is later executed as a terrorist. Towards the end of his boyhood, he was overcome by the excitements of the events of 1905: 'the new dawn seemed to be breaking, the longed-for moment to have come — but then the light was extinguished and stamped out' (A14, p. 347). From then on, his thirst for the absolute is both awakened and usurped by revolutionary messianism:

187

'his heart beat faster at the thought that soon that vital *something* would happen: that it would burst forth, illumine and transform life in the whole of Russia and throughout the world' (*ibid*., p. 346). He studies law, a militant in a revolutionary circle, and has nothing but contempt for Russian history. Called up with the rank of ensign, 'his uniform hung around him like a sack' — an expression of his disgust with the army — and his expression as he looks at his troops is 'one of boredom' (*ibid*., p. 148). In Neidenburg, when the Russians have captured it, the soldiers hasten to put the fires out, but Sasha, 'an ensign wearing the badge of a university graduate, with a slightly supercilious but keen expression which belied his rather languid way of moving' (*ibid*., p. 147), stands apart and takes no interest in the proceedings. Talking to a doctor who has exhausted himself treating the ever-increasing numbers of wounded, he develops the principle of 'the worse, the better', explaining that, 'you have to stand back and take the long-term view if you don't want to be fooled by appearances' (*ibid*., p. 149). The doctor is a man of history, that is a realist, prepared to compromise when service to people is at stake: 'Russia needs workers, practical men'. Lenartovich is a man of ideology, ruled by his secret passion for all or nothing; like Lenin, whose concept of war was similar to his, he ignores the nation and those around him for the sake of the 'general' advantage of humanity. 'What — and shore up the whole revolting system?', he exclaims, 'It should be smashed to fragments without mercy! We should be knocking it down to let in the light!' (*ibid*., p. 149).

Yet when the first serious battle comes and the Russians try desperately to escape from the German advance and threatened pincer movement, he feels involved. He tries to rationalize this feeling — on aesthetic grounds first: 'there was undoubtedly a kind of horrible beauty in the thunder of gunfire' (*ibid*., p. 350), but this is the gunfire 'from one's own side', and it appears to be winning the day. When the attack comes, and the men move forward in the early morning mist, 'every man threw himself into the spirit of the attack, and Sasha with them'. He feels the common bond of suffering and pride, and, to his surprise, takes a prisoner.

It is his first victory as a man, not a victory of words and wit in an argument, but 'won with his body, his own arms and legs' (*ibid*., p. 352). 'He now felt buoyed up by a surge of confidence'; he feels the dawn of a new sort of truth in him that has nothing to do with ideology: 'on a morning like this it was joy enough simply to sit and look'. He remembers past moments when he has had glimpses of a similar feeling: opening his eyes to the freshness of morning light, the southern colour of apricots, a bicycle ride with the fresh wind on his face, books that are companions in humanity, not works of ideology, women — that woman, girl, Yolya, who does not believe in the Revolution but whose whole demeanour has the beauty of a dance . . . 'And now — he had to carry on and defend Russia, that damned country of his' (*ibid*., p. 354).

But the feeling does not last. The little local victory is but a minor detail in the general Russian rout. Lenartovich rejects his new feeling of 'brute joy' and returns to his old hatred of the only true enemies, class enemies. He decides to desert. But soon he is literally knocked off this new position, as an enemy barrage hurls him face down in the mud. When he raises his head, he finds Vorotyntsev, who is to be his new master, who sums him up: 'This young student who despised military service might make a good officer yet. He was tall and good-looking and held himself well' (*ibid*., p. 476). He does not question what Sasha is doing there, or give him orders, but simply puts a proposition to him: 'Do you want to stay here? Or will you come with us? We are going to break through the lines . . .' Sasha, whose mouth is still full of earth, feels acceptance overcoming his resentment: 'With your permission'. And Vorotyntsev 'harshly' then sets out the rules: 'I warn you, we share all our duties without regard to rank. There ar the fit and the wounded, that's the only different among us'. Like a good teacher, he has won Sasha's allegiance by appealing to his main interest — equality. He agrees to the conditions, but his acceptance is soon put to the test.

The men Vorotyntsev has met and taken command of are carrying the body of their colonel on a stretcher. They loved him, and — with peasant ignorance of distances — want to bury him on Russian soil. Vorotyntsev takes up one of the front poles of the stretcher and asks Sasha to take the other. He wants the officers to take their part in this procession which celebrates the very order of life: the father fighting at the head of his troops and 'laying down his life for his friends', and the mother, the earth waiting to receive him. For Sasha, this is a double challenge. First he has to overcome the sheer physical stain: 'All his life, Sasha had cultivated his brain as being of prime importance; he had never had time to exercise his body' (*ibid*., p. 507). 'Gritting his teeth as he carried the stretcher, he picked out a tree ahead of them which he could reach before asking to be relieved. Then he would carry on for another stretch'. Then it is a challenge to his rationalism: 'why was he giving in to the ridiculous obscurantist notions of these peasant reservists from the darkest corners of Russia?' (*ibid.*, p. 506). These are the people, but in their historical, not mythical, embodiment. In the end, the grave sanctity of the scene chokes Sasha, and he bursts out: 'Colonel, why must we carry this dead man? It's sheer superstition!'. For him, the colonel is just a 'dead man'; his old aggression comes back: if the wounded lieutenant dies, he says sarcastically, they'll have to carry him too, 'and I can tell from his face that he's a Black Hundreder'. He tries to involve Vorotyntsev in his rage, but he remains calm and detached and tells him two things: that in a country whose very existence is threatened political disagreements are 'just so many ripples on the water', and that for an officer the choice is simple: 'the difference between decency and swinishness, Ensign'. What Lenartovich makes of this maxim we are not told.

NOTES

1. *From Marxism to Idealism* (St Petersburg, 1903); *The Two Cities* (Moscow, 1911); *A Philosophy of the Economy* (Moscow, 1912).
2. *Problems of Idealism* (St Petersburg, 1903); *Sub Specie Aeternitatis* (St Petersburg, 1907); *op. cit.*; *op. cit.*

PART FIVE

Struggle

15 Justice and truth

The just

An authentic involvement in history can remain 'invisible forever' (A14, p. 431). Anyone in the humblest, most peripheral positions — prisoners, the sick, abandoned old women — who can penetrate to its deepest layers becomes a spring of living water in the desert of human suffering or flat contentment. It is they who, unseen, patiently restore the tissues of being in the face of the forces of incoherence and death.

'It is without doubt because of the intercession of the Christians that the world still survives', wrote a second-century apologist. The hidden influence of the saints saved the order of things and human society from disintegration. The prayers and love of the poor, the innocent, the 'fools-in-Christ', reveal the eucharistic centre of being, the icon of the face hidden under the mask, and allow the divine energies to act in the world. God, the hidden God, sacrificial Love, who suffered death in public in the flesh, raises all flesh to life in secret: he too, and first and foremost, can only operate in history in a way that remains 'invisible forever', through these unknowns who open themselves to the Unknown, becoming sharers in his open crucifixion and hidden resurrection.

From the time of Constantine onwards, this ministry of suffering intercession and disinterested love has largely been concentrated, particularly in the East, in the monastic vocation. In Russia, the figure of the *starets* was familiar throughout the nineteenth century. These 'grand old men', all welcome and love, were discerners of spirits, and, like Jesus in the gospels, liberators from sin, telling people that they were more than their sin, they were persons: 'go and sin no more'. The last recognized *starets* in Russian history was Father Alexis Metchev, who died in 1923, not a monk, but a married priest. Today, organized monasticism has been reduced to a shadow of its former self by the joint attack of State atheism and the brutal transition to an industrial society. But there are still the anonymous just outside the monasteries who continue this 'invisble' commitment. Humble people, but the righteous, 'without whom, as the saying goes, no city can stand. Nor the world' (SPP, p. 47).

Matryona, as we have seen, typifies the difficult transition-period rural Christianity is going through in Russia today: few churches left, fewer priests, no effort at evangelization and renewal. In this climate, where superstitions naturally proliferate, it is all the more moving to see the occasional emergence of a conscious faith, a brotherhood that knows no bounds. This applies to Matryona. Her life has been one long process of being torn between two rival brothers. The one she loved disappeared during the First World War. Believing him dead, she married the other. But the first comes back and appears at her door with an axe in his hand. In the end he is pacified; fratricide is avoided, and his anger turns to malicious resentment.

When her husband is killed in the Second World War, he exploits her. Defenceless, all her children dead at an early age, she is eventually forced to concede the outhouse (timber-built and therefore capable of being dismantled and transported) which adjoins her cottage and which was one day to have been their bridal chamber. Not only does Matryona give in to this request, despite the avarice and vengeance lying behind it; she even helps with the clandestine transportation. In the dark, in deep snow, she is killed by a train while trying to get the sledge over an unguarded crossing, and dies as mangled as she would have been by the axe.

Old and ill, unable to cope with the bureaucratic officialdom that is gradually wearing her down, Matryona has kept a deep faith, though mixed with peasant superstitions. She always asks God's help as she starts work, and blesses her lodger, the narrator, with a 'God go with you' as he sets out for the school where he teaches. She prays in secret, showing nothing, in obedience to the gospel precept. But above all, she is willing to help. Everyone knows this, and everyone takes advantage of her, but she does not mind. She helps 'without a trace of envy', and 'won't take any money' (*ibid*., p. 21). When the collective is short of labour and the peasant wives refuse to work overtime, the chairman's wife comes to look for Matryona. She goes to help, and stays. Any distant relative or neighbour can enlist her help at any time: 'She would abandon her private affairs, go and help her neighbour'. The women form teams to plough up kitchen gardens in turn, and Matryona is again always called in to help — 'equally indispensable'.

Alyosha the Baptist, in Ivan Denisovich's camp, is another of the righteous. Like the apostle Paul, whom he quotes, he is ready 'not merely to be bound but even to die for the name of the Lord Jesus' (LID, p. 140). Having reached a state of inner freedom, he can give thanks for being imprisoned. He is also always ready to help. 'You could count on Alyosha. Did whatever was asked of him' (*ibid.*, p. 88). And while in *August 1914* a pseudo-Christian piety was invoked to cover up all failings, and the Empire at its last gasp used Christianity as its 'dominant ideology', Alyosha is an authentic witness to the Lamb sacrificed since the beginning of time, the Lamb who takes away the sin of the world, whereas Samsonov is only the 'sacrificial lamb' to the extent of his dreadful ineptitude. The Russian feeling for 'kenosis' is here restored in its evangelical authenticity.

Ingmar Bergman, writing about his film *Cries and Whispers*, which is itself a long meditation on death, says that in our civilization, dedicated to metaphysical 'silence' (*Silence* being the theme and title of an earlier film of his), in which the person is reduced to a cry without an echo, only the humble righteous, such as those Solzhenitsyn evokes, can keep the ways of hope open and give a man a little strength to live and die. In the film, which is otherwise proudly and totally atheistic, the servant-girl Anna. perhaps because she has lost her own daughter, establishes a bond of pity and love with her dying mistress that transforms the latter's death into a sort of mystic birth. Writing about the little Baltic island on which the film is set, Bergman recalls an old woman of eighty who is a sort of Anna — and a sort of Matryona: 'Her fate has been a terrible one, but she has remained full of warmth and life. She is a human being in the fullest sense of the word'. And, he adds, 'as long as people like her exist, we can hold back from despair'. If 'the heavens are absolutely empty', if, that is, the old images of God are dead, 'every human being, or nearly every one, carries a sort of sanctity within himself' — 'the light that is within us', as Solzhenitsyn calls it in the gospel phrase; and the 'marvellous', the mystery, is revealed anew 'within us and in our relationship with other people'.

In the olden days, says Solzhenitsyn, it was the sound of church bells tolling for the Angelus that 'raised man above the level of a beast' (SPP, p. 204). Nowadays, when so many of the bell-towers have crumbled and the bells are silent, it is the presence of men like Alyosha who, even in camp conditions, can remind Ivan Denisovich that man has a spritual dimension: 'If everybody in the world was like that,

Shukov (Ivan Denisovich) would have done likewise. If a man asks for help why not help him? Those Baptists had got something there' (LID, p. 88). With instinctive symbolism, Solzhenitsyn places Ivan next to Alyosha in the sleeping hut and above Tzesar Markovich. Alyosha is the innocent: 'Unpractical, that's his trouble. Makes himself nice to everyone but doesn't know how to earn anything' (*ibid*., p. 142). Tzesar, an influential person in the film world before his arrest, keeps useful contacts, receives parcel after parcel, has got himself a 'cushy' job and lives in the warm in an office where he can have pleasant conversations on matters of aesthetics. Ivan knows how to make himself useful to him, to hold his place in the parcel queue, to hide his bag during searches, so that he is given worthwhile crumbs from this rich man's table: dry cakes, a lump of sugar, a slice of sausage. Is it too fanciful to see him between 'the kingdom of God' and the 'kingdom of Caesar'? He can be quiet and listen when Alyosha talks of God, of Christ and of prayer, though he is not convinced. He is 'not against God', but cannot accept the idea of heaven and hell, perhaps because the traditional symbolism loses its meaning when history takes on a metaphysical dimension and hell is let loose on earth . . . Above all, he dislikes the evasion of history that characterizes Baptist spirituality. The inner freedom that makes the convict camp a positive reality for Alyosha is not enough for him: there is also history with its responsibilities, and the overwhelming taste sensation to be derived, after the long fast of the camp, from a single slice of sausage.

But despite his verbal sparring, Ivan loves Alyosha, and 'he who receives you, receives me', Jesus said. In Alyosha, in his life rather than in his words, Christ is not the imperious judge who creates a paradise to reward and a heaven to punish (leading Voltaire ironically to praise the inquisitors for lightening God's work by taking it upon themselves to torture men on this earth), but Christ in the hell of men, he who 'never says "No" '. There is only 'Yes' in God, as St Paul wrote. The necessary compromises of history do not degrade man so long as there is this tension between the kingdom of God and the kingdom of Caesar, which preserves men's spiritual stature, their double rooting in earth and heaven.

'Pravda'

Some have a spiritual vocation to play a part in politics: this is where Solzhenitsyn's spiritual vision shows itself to be so much broader than the narrowly 'vertical' one of the Baptists. If any one lesson emerges from *August 1914*, it is that those in positions of responsibility are actually responsible, and can be held accountable for their responsibilities, as Vorotyntsev does with Samsonov, and later with the General Headquarters Staff. Seeing the incomepetence of the generals from the first battle — and the higher their rank, the worse they become — the author observes in a sad parenthesis that, '(In which case there might appear to be some consolation in Tolstoy's conviction that it is not generals who lead armies, nor captains who command ships or companies of infantry, not Presidents or leaders who run States or political parties, were it not that all too often the twentieth century has proved to us that it *is* such men who do these things)' (A14, p. 400). So throughout the book the condemnation of the Imperial regime stems from its incapacity to master what history has entrusted to it, through its failure to come to terms with the creative elements in society.

If one is to play a responsible part in politics, the first requirement is to adapt oneself 'to the slow process of history, by work, by persuasion, by gradual change . . .' (*ibid*., p. 606). With this criterion in mind, it is easy to see which characters in the book set themselves in real history, and which, by denying or failing to recognize this history, risk its disintegration. Those who deny it are the ideologues. Those who fail to recognize it are the Commander-in-Chief, Grand Duke Nicholas, and his Staff, and also the Tsar, who shrugs off with a pious phrase the thousands whose death he has been incapable of preventing.

One has to commit oneself to history as a realist artisan, capable of submitting to its matter in order to transform it, but in a light that comes from beyond, the light of the virtue of *'pravda'*, 'justice-truth'. Solzhenitsyn re-activates this admirable word, usurped by the regime, and previously mortgaged by the populists and the socialist revolutionaries. He re-activates it by rooting it in spiritual consciousness and stripping it of all populist illusion. The short story *For the Good of the Cause* has as its protagonists communists in various positions of responsibility in a provincial town. Some of them have taken upon themselves to encourage the students of a technical college to build themselves the new buildings they desperately need. Others, the town delegation, pompous careerists, offer the buildings, without telling the college, to a research institute which is looking for a regional headquarters. When the chief inspiration of the college, the teacher Lydia Georgievna, learns of this incredible piece of double-dealing, the quality she constantly invokes in her protestations is that of *pravda*, in which justice and truth are united against injustice and lies. It is

195

iniquitous, she says, to deceive the students in this way: 'The kids will think, and think rightly, that we're afraid of the truth' (SPP, p. 91). She goes back beyond the current ideology to the original ethic of socialism, and quotes Lenin — the Lenin of the original outbreak of the Revolution: 'Lenin taught us not to be afraid of speaking freely: "Free speech is a healing sword"!' (*ibid*.).

For Solzhenitsyn, this ethical requirement has to be stripped of ideology and rooted in transcendence. If politics is 'relative', the justice that must inspire it is not in the least relative (*Letter to Three Students*). Acting with justice is 'living the truth'. There is no point in inventing a justice 'for the convenience of the earthly paradise' we imagine. True justice, which is inseparable from truth, is more than this: 'There is a justice which existed before us, without us and for its own sake. And our task is to divine what it is!' (A14, p. 431). We 'divine' it through awakening our conscience, which, enlightening people in communion, becomes 'that of humanity as a whole' (LTS). *Pravda* is then no longer an ideological concept, but respect for and service of the truth of beings and things. It indicates a political morality based on the affirmation of God and the individual conscience, which cannot be reduced to historical conditioning, but can rather condition history because it is based on God.

The truth Solzhenitsyn talks of is not the truth of the ideologues, but that of persons in all their dignity and royal freedom. If we are to 'divine' this truth, we must become capable of rendering selfless service. We must overcome that desire for possession which makes the other an object, and that fear — quickly turned to hate, which makes him a scapegoat. The other can be an individual or a collectivity; it makes no difference: if God exists, and if beliefs are worth more than life — which they are if we are prepared to die for them — then the individual cannot be seen just as part of a whole; rather, society and history are dimensions of the individual. So the first requirement in the service of *pravda* is a personal ascesis as a way to 'spiritual harmony' through mastery and metamorphosis of our passions. This is why Varsonofiev considers the 'development of our soul' more important than development of the social order, since it alone can open the way to man's truth, to his spiritual calling.

One cannot over-emphasize the point: Solzhenitsyn's whole attitude is radically *anti-ideological*; he seeks not reductive knowledge, but the inspiration of spiritual knowledge which, as all the mystics say, is an 'Unknowing'. Ideology is violence: first intellectual, then historical. *Pravda* is active love, inventive and creative, never discouraged because its source is always near. Violence goes with lies, with the totalitarian desire to explain away and distort the whole of man. 'Once the lie is unmasked, violence appears in all its repulsive nudity, and its evil spell is broken' (NPL).

Solzhenitsyn's basic message is the importance of the spiritual dimension: not in the sense of an evasive pietism, but of a creative spirituality that alone can change the course of life because it alone can change the meaning of death. This means replacing the myth of the Revolution − considered as an abstract ideal − by the patient, multi-sided reality of a creativity that alone can question and renew the bases of our civilization.

In *Candle in the Wind*, when the African Kabimba gives vent to his hate, the hatred of the Third World for the rich who 'will never understand how the rest of humanity lives', Alex, who has spent ten years in prison through a judicial error, explains gently that neither resentment nor expectation of a liberating cataclysm can be creative: 'We have lost a hundred years or ten, never mind how long; we have been offended, humiliated, but it is not our business to seek revenge. And why should we? We are richer than they'. Richer, 'through having suffered. Suffering is the rootstock of the soul. Those who have everything always suffer from poverty of spirit. So we are now going to build, without haste'.

Violence and its limits: Solzhenitsyn and Camus

The need to 'build without haste' in no way excludes that for indignation and revolt when the situation demands it. Kondrashov-Ivanov, the visionary painter of the castle of the soul, also praises the great rebels of Russian history: Peter the Great, the Decembrists, the revolutionaries of the 'Will of the People'. And Nerzhin adds the name of Jeliabov, the Christian revolutionary, and that of Lenin.

Solzhenitsyn's work is full of these rebels who, regardless of risk, shout the truth out to the powerful of the world, wrenching 'the burning arrow' of indignation from their breast (A14, p. 645), as Vorotyntsev does in front of the *Stavka*, the General Staff bogged down in jealousies and impotence: 'knowing that all was lost, having nothing more to fear, free of all inhibitions . . .' (*ibid*., p. 644), feeling at one with the dead and the wounded, trying to speak for them, he calls those in the highest positions of responsibility to account for their responsibilities: 'all we Russian officers bear a responsibility for the history of Russia' (*ibid*., p. 645). As Nerzhin does in his struggle to force the authorities of the special prison to give the prisoners the rations due to them under the regulations, or to force them to give those about to be transferred to a worse prison the last meal that they were trying to deprive them of: 'it was a symbol of their human dignity' (FC, p. 693). As Grachikov does when the party delegation tries to take away the building the students have built for themselves, facing up to a Stalinist bully, threatening to resign to go and do 'any kind of unskilled work' (SPP. p. 98), and finally wringing a compromise out of him. As, finally and above all, Solzhenitsyn has done by the challenge thrown out by his books and other writings.

Creation can, under certain circumstances, provoke a revolution, but this is never more than one result, one aspect — and perhaps not a successful one — of a deeper evolution. (England, after all, evolved in the course of the eighteenth and nineteenth centuries, without major upheavals, into a country with better democratic institutions than those achieved in France at the cost of three revolutions . . .) The more a revolution sees itself as the mythical Revolution, the more liable it is to bring the 'long and insane process of destruction' (A14, p. 605), and the greater the process of disillusionment as the original impulses give way to a form of slavery as bad as the one it replaced: 'In no more than ten years a whole people loses its social drive and courageous impulse, or rather the impulse changes the sign from plus to minus, from bravery to cowardice' (CW, p. 471). We must wait for the publication of the forthcoming 'knots' for a better knowledge of Solzhenitsyn's thoughts on the Russian revolution. He will certainly try to 'discern the spirit' in its history, to distinguish the part played by truth-justice from that played by violence and lies. Between now and the end of the century, we are all, but particularly the Russians, called to this decisive winnowing on the threshing-floor of the Spirit, of the history that, as Pasternak said, 'was born of the motherhood called Russia'.

For the present, it would seem that Solzhenitsyn's attitude to revolutionary violence is akin to that of Camus. In his speech for the Nobel prize, he acknowledged the influence of his thought on the relationship between culture and politics.

Like Camus in his 'southern thought' (*pensée du midi*), Solzhenitsyn affirms at once the irreducible nature of evil and the need to struggle against its successive manifestations. 'Iniquity did not begin with us. Nor will it end with us', but also: 'You shouldn't have searched in the village, but in yourself' (A14, p. 569). Camus writes: 'Man must mend

. . . all that cán be mended. After which, children will still die without good cause' (*The Rebel*). The best politics will never quell the indignation of Ivan Karamazov. To believe that evil can be abolished is to fall victim to the illusory dream of an absolute good that then has to be imposed by totalitarian means. But to abandon the struggle is to acquiesce in injustice.

The man who wishes to retain his humanity — and preserve that of his adversary — in political struggle, must, says Camus, be 'conscious of the limits', those limits that Solzhenitsyn says we cannot transgress without becoming cannibals. If necessary, he will fight to preserve the independence of his country or for a non-mythic revolution, but 'under certain conditions': violence 'must keep . . . its provisional, burglarious character, be always tied, if it cannot be avoided, to personal responsibility, to immediate risk' (*The Rebel*). Camus introduces the same ethical criterion as Solzhenitsyn in *August 1914*: 'the difference between decency and swinishness'. In his *Letters to a German Friend*, written during the occupation, when he was taking an active role in the Resistance, he accepts that he uses violence against violence; but there is a difference between the violence of freedom fighters and that of the society that produced the concentration camps and the gas chambers: the difference between decency and swinishness, between the honourable course and the dishonourable.

So both Camus and Solzhenitsyn refuse to accept that the voice of conscience can be silenced, even for a moment, in the name of efficacity. 'It is a short-sighted view to think that one can live on the basis of force alone, constantly overruling the objections of conscience', wrote Solzhenitsyn of the treatment imposed on non-conformists in certain psychiatric hospitals (*Open letter*, 15.6.1970). And he could have signed this decisive formula of Camus': 'There are two sorts of effectiveness: that of the typhoon and that of sap' (*The Rebel*).

Unlike Camus, however, and because the ultimate for him is not absurdity but Love, Solzhenitsyn sees the royal way as one of personal sacrifice, ultimately of martyrdom if needs be. He thereby aligns himself with the Tolstoyan Gandhi, but without adopting his systematic recipes, knowing only that the alchemy of the void in which history metamorphoses itself in vain can become a eucharistic 'trans-signification' every time a man, or men, interiorize and crucify violence in the crucible of their 'heart' and transmute it into love, into a creative force. Gandhi held that spiritual energy alone, released through silence and fasting, had the re-integrative power to equilibrate and overcome atomic disintegration. In his speech for the Nobel prize, the Christian Solzhenitsyn accorded the same 'negenthropic' power to the 'word of truth', quoting the Russian proverb, 'A single word of truth weighs more than the universe'. But the word can become *pravda* only through the silence of a dedicated life and a death freely accepted: 'It is only through personal sacrifice that we will come to reform the wold about us' (Letter to Fr Serge Jeludkov). The death of a witness, when all seems lost, is itself the sign of a secret resurrection: the shaft of transcendence striking through to prevent history closing in on itself or humanity idolizing itself, letting light in on the unsayable and so on to a future. The last word on the service of truth-justice is the acceptance of martyrdom: 'no-one can bar the road to truth, and I am ready to face death to help it forward on its way' (*Letter to the Writer's Congress*, May 1967).

16 Beyond myths: socialism, nationhood, universality

A moral socialism?

If Socialism means not the inevitable result of supposedly rational laws controlling history, as classical Marxism would have it, but a refusal to abandon man to economic determinism and production for its own sake, in the name of man's spiritual calling, then Solzhenitsyn would seem to be making the great vision of a 'moral socialism', as described by Shulubin in *Cancer Ward*, his own. Shulubin is someone who has fallen from high position, but he is also, even in his flesh, a martyr to his senses, and this gives him the right to be heard. He looks like an owl, a night bird who cannot face the light of the sun — or at any rate could not in the dark night of Stalinism — and also a symbol of wisdom. This 'old Bolshevik of 1917' considers the error of the Marxists of his generation to be that: 'We thought it was enough to change the mode of production and people would immediately change with it' (CW, p. 473), and has now come to see that: 'You can't build socialism on an abundance of material goods, because people sometimes behave like buffaloes' (*ibid*.).

So he has come to rehabilitate pre-Marxist revolutionary thinkers in his own mind — anarchists like Kropotkin and populists like Mikhailovski. Their inspiration is overtly ethical and they stress the unique character of the individual. They would have society organized on socialist lines to ensure maximum development of each individual in a context of community. Mikhailovski tried to develop a 'subjective sociology' capable of discerning the morality, or immorality, of social phenomena. He called for 'struggle for individuality' and saw the struggle between the individual and society as one of the motors of history. Kropotkin, a constructive anarchist, dreamt of the elimination of all forms of power that constrained the individual, and saw the basis of a free society in the sort of 'mutual aid' that existed in pre-capitalist times and still survived in the rural communes of Russia.

Elsewhere, Shulubin points to the fact that Lenin felt the same ethical urge when, between April and October 1917, he escaped from the impotence of exile and saw history opening up before him, before he was dragged into the bitter fatality of power which led him to become the pioneer of the concentration camp system. His *April Theses*, like *The State and the Revolution*, written in August and September 1917, condemn Marxist determinism *de facto* and extol the value of freedom, making a man capable of judging economic facts according to moral criteria and then bending them to his needs. The best commentators were not wrong: Antonio Gramsci, for example, who was to become the great theoretician of Italian Communism, wrote that Lenin was not 'Marxist' in the sense of historical materialism, but that he had spontaneously rediscovered the idealist roots of Marxism, 'which, in Marx, had been contaminated by positivist and naturalist elements' (*Avanti!*, Milan, 24.11. 1917).

In fact, when Lenin wanted a model for the new society, he looked to the Paris Commune, which was inspired by 'non-authoritarian' French socialist principles and in no way by Marxism. The suppression of the army and the police, the election and dismissal of officials by all the citizens, would allow the establishment of institutions 'in which freedom of opinion and discussion would not degenerate into trickery'. Representative institutions would stay: 'We cannot conceive a democracy without representative institutions', but widened in their scope. The 'second infallible means' to be borrowed from the Paris Commune in order to transform the State from a master into a servant was the equalization of administrative salaries (including those of 'people's commissars', i.e. ministers) and working men's wages. This is the point Shulubin recalls in a discussion in which Kostoglotov has brought up the essentially 'non-egalitarian' nature of Soviet society. A professor of philosophy has come to join the little discussion group, but his thought seems to be very conformist, and it is him whom Shulubin wants to shake. ' "There's one point I remember . . . No official should receive a salary higher than the average pay of a good worker. That's what they began the revolution with". "Is that so?" ', asks the professor in surprise, ' "I'd forgotten that" ' (CW, p. 439).

Significantly, Solzhenitsyn hardly ever quotes Marx, but often quotes Lenin, whom we know he read assiduously in his camp, from an eye-witness who was a fellow prisoner of his. And the Lenin he quotes is always that of the initial revolutionary fervour, before the objectivization of dictatorship, the Lenin who was not to come back to this mood till the last months of his life when, faced with the brutality of Stalin and so many others, he asked himself sorrowfully where men's moral qualities came from, since they did not seem to stem from their political and social conditions.

So Shulubin concludes that we need a consciously moral socialism in which, 'ethical demands must determine all considerations: how to bring up children, what to train them for, to what end the work of grown-ups should be directed, and how their leisure should be occupied. As for scientific research, it should only be directed where it doesn't damage morality . . .' (*ibid*., p. 474). Grachikov, facing the local Stalinist delegate in *For the Good of the Cause*, echoes this requirement: ' "Communism will not be built with stones but with people . . ." he shouted' (SPP, p. 97). This is the only passage in Solzhenitsyn's work in which an echo of Maoism can perhaps be found: with this difference — that Maoism is a concept that denies the freedom of the individual and his transcendent dimension, whereas Solzhenitsyn's ethic is one of liberty, and spiritual liberty at that.

This, in fact, is the nub of the matter. The weakness of Shulubin's case, as of that of Kropotkin, Mikhaylovski or the Lenin of 1917, is that they could not clearly recognize the spiritual nature of the individual, that man is rooted not only in society and nature, but in the depth of the Spirit. The failure of the Revolution, which Shulubin can diagnose clearly enough, does not send him back to this depth; with his still purely immanentist outlook, his only escape from despair is to point to the length of time any natural evolution takes: 'Man is a biological type. It takes thousands of years to change him' (CW, p. 473). He cannot see the call, the leaven, in Christianity; only the debatably 'Christian' parties of the West or the illusory recipies of Tolstoy. In the same way, Kropotkin and Mikhaylovski remained positivists, and never consciously rejected the materialist postulates of Marxism. All were incapable of spiritually operating the transformation, with its recognition of the transcendent dimension in man, that their aspirations sought. The individual, for them, remained the product of social and natural evolution.

Without a spiritual dimension, in fact, *where* was he to find the strength to rise above economic facts so as to control them? Shulubin, instead of establishing, or recognizing, a tension between man's spiritual and his social dimension, builds a *utopia*: that of general 'goodwill' in a ghostly society that obeys only the dictates of the highest values. Kostoglotov, the basic Marxist, objects: 'Where is the material basis for your scheme?' But it is not only economics that is missing here; it is the whole of man's animal nature, his will-to-power and even his death wish. If they are forgotten, they will take over, however far away the utopia remains. In 1917 Lenin dreamed of a society without police and almost without a State, organized in a federation of 'soviets', developing and broadening the representative institutions of 'bourgeois' democracy, in which anyone with a minimum level of education could take his turn in administration and industrial management. In 1918, the Constituent Assembly and all parties were dissolved, beginning with the most revolutionary ones except for the Bolsheviks; the worker's movement was halted and a State capitalism took over, with the beginnings of dictatorship, State security police and the first concentration camps. Then came, *with no real break*, the Stalinist terror.

Spiritualizing the earth

Between the moral utopia of Shulubin and the comment, so typical of both East and West today, that: 'There has to be an economy, after all, doesn't there? That comes before everything else' (*ibid.*, p. 475) lies the position adopted by Vladimir Soloviev, whom Solzhenitsyn quotes several times — as does Shulubin, without seeing how far he is from the philosophy inherent in populism or anarchism. 'Vladimir Soloviev argues rather convincingly that an economy could and should be built on an ethical basis' (*ibid.*), he claims. This point merits closer examination. The economic views of the great religious philosopher of the end of the last century are to be found particularly in the seventh chapter of his treatise, *The Justification for Good*, originally published in Moscow in 1898. The economy, he holds, has its own inner logic, but its objectives should be set, in a continual endeavour, by man's spiritual calling, since it is man's mission, as created *Logos*, to organize and spiritualize the earth: 'In a living society, and one with a future, economic elements are bound together and determined by moral ends'. The great achievement of socialism is to have rehabilitated matter, but historical materialism limits the scope of this rehabilitation by its insistence that man is no more than matter. The affirmation of man's spiritual dimension is alone capable of giving the insights of socialism their true significance, since, 'matter has the right to be spiritualized by man'. 'The real solution to the economic question has to be found in a moral relationship between man and material nature, conditioned by a moral attitude towards both man and God'. Material riches, therefore, 'cannot be regarded as the sole aim of man's economic activity'. Production should be subordinated to the human dignity of the producers on one hand, to their possibility of developing meaningful human relationships within the production process — what Ivan Illich calls 'conviviality' — and, on the other, to a mastery over material nature that is also respect for it and communion with it: man must refrain from, 'taking advantage of it, exhausting it, laying it waste', must learn to improve it and give it 'greater fulness of being'. Soloviev's remarkable insight, which makes him so relevant today, was that the crisis brought about by changing technology is not so much one of the means of production but of its very nature. This is why he defines production formally as: a reciprocal action of men in the physical sphere, which should, in conformity with the moral law, ensure that each and every one can live a dignified life, develop himself in all spheres, and which is in the end destined to transfom and spiritualize material nature'.

That, if one wants a definition, could also be Solzhenitsyn's socialism.

The working out of the scheme, however, is by no means simple. Kostoglotov confides to Shulubin that, 'out there, in the camps, we used to argue that there was a lot of good in private enterprise' (*ibid.*, p. 472). When the latter objects that it 'gives birth to people who are no better than beasts, those stock-exchange people with greedy appetites completely beyond restraint', he replies: 'Well, to be quite honest . . . I've found people with greedy appetites beyond restraint in our society as well' (*ibid*., p. 473). In the latter part of *August 1914*, Obodovsky says that while he had earlier been preoccupied by the qustion of distribution, he now sees the main problem as being one of creation (A14, p. 602). He stresses the power of private initiative, quoting the example of the new agricultural industries springing up round Rostov, and the 'intelligence, education, foresight, experience and organization' of a few businessmen and engineers. What is needed is, in most cases, not the replacement of private enterprise by cumbersome State bureaucracy, but 'rational political measures' to ensure that if anyone makes unearned profits, 'that money is channelled elsewhere'. Even Shulubin admits that private enterprise can be 'very flexible', and can, within strict limits, be useful, provided its dynamism is channelled into an ordered economy.

Solzhenitsyn is by no means given to unqualified acceptance of a set of formulae claiming to establish who is right and who wrong. The bases of industrial civilization − over-emphasis on production, exploitation of nature − its temptation − growth for growth's sake − and its inhuman results − gigantic techno-structures that deprive man of his humanity and despoil the environment − scarcely seem to differ in East and West, and both bear an equal share of responsibility for the tragic lot of the Third World. In both societies, the organic structure of the people is vanishing, with a mounting tide of barbarism among the young, who live by dreams of power and pleasure, ignorant of the contribution that can be made by a real culture, a real popular culture devoid of vulgarity because nourished by spirituality.

This is the situation evoked in the play *Candle in the Wind*, set outside the East-West conflict the better to describe the moral bankruptcy of the 'developed' societies. The real problem is not the choice between socialism or capitalism − though Solzhenitsyn's deep instincts incline him more to the original inspiration of the former. It is how to base a civilization on communion, how to form a society in which the individual can rediscover his creative power, his ability to set his own objectives and so control the whole of the economic sphere.

Working 'in council'

There is therefore a need for constant endeavour to introduce meaningful communication and co-responsibility into human relationships.

Solzhenitsyn points in this way to the original spirit of the Russian Revolution which produced the 'soviets', the councils in which no one voice was dominant. A nostalgic harking-back, *au fond*, to the *sobornost* beloved of Slavophiles and the people's commune. But for Solzhenitsyn there has to be a vertical dimension as well as a horizontal one; in the examples he gives, co-responsibility is always organized round a 'vertical' presence – not 'paternalistic', but 'fatherly': fatherly in the sense – originally revealed by Christ – of one who inspires, fructifies, sets an example and then retires to allow others to fulfil themselves. Such a presence is Colonel Pervushin, who has transformed his regiment into a loving community and who in the end lays down his life for his flock: 'He is like a father to his men: they will follow him' (A14, p. 516). Another such is Fyodor Mikheyich, the Principal of the college in *For the Good of the Cause*, a man proven in the war, in which he was twice wounded, who sees the role of a leader as being not to impose his own ideas arbitrarily, but to act as: 'the essential focal point for a group of people who trusted each other and worked for a common aim' (SPP, p. 67). Grachikov, the secretary of the town Committee, loves the college: he would like to have a chance of studying there himself, to learn something among young people and from them, too, something useful that he could do outside his bureaucratic working-hours. But he is a special sort of bureaucrat, since he likes to 'listen to other people's opinions. It was against his nature to end conversations and meetings by giving orders; he tried to convince his opponents to the bitter end, so they would admit, "Yes, you're right", or else prove to him that he was wrong' (*ibid.*, p. 81). And when his superior, the secretary of the regional party committee, notices this 'weakness' and reproaches him: 'You're too soft. You don't act the Soviet way', Grachikov stands his ground: 'Quite the contrary. I work in the Soviet way – I consult the people'.

In *August 1914*, the example of working in council is given by Vorotyntsev when disaster has destroyed the traditional discipline of the army, and the only way an officer can command allegiance is to earn it. He tries to persuade a strong detachment, which has lost all its officers, to hold a position from which they can cover the retreat of a large part of the army. How is he to talk to them? And what can he say? What sort of appeal will they respond to? Decency – the criterion he is later to throw at Lenartovich – they would not understand. The Tsar, they might understand, but as a myth, and he, who in any case despises the present Tsar, is not going to mystify them. God? That would be blasphemous: God is not the God of the Russians alone, and these men would realize that. The fatherland? For most of them, 'their "fatherland" scarcely extended beyond their local district'. So he tries to put himself in the place of these grim, sullen men, 'in their sweaty greatcoat-rolls', and decides simply to tell them the truth, man to man, and ask their advice. He decides to 'give them a straight-forward, truthful account of the position, to describe the whole situation and explain the military objective; regulations forbade an officer to talk to rank and file like that, but in reality it was the only proper way to do it' (A14, p. 376). So he tells them: 'For just as long as it takes the waggons to get the wounded out of the town we must plug that gap. We must hold out until evening. There's no-one else to do it except you'. So his appeal is to self-denial, to service, the evangelical counsel to 'lay down one's life for one's friends'. And suddenly, the closed, exhausted, hostile faces light up with under-standing and sympathy: '— the spontaneous smile of pity for a wounded bird'. And when he asks for volunteers, everyone volunteers.

Later, when Vorotyntsev meets the ten men from the Dorogobuzh Regiment carrying (because 'they had decided') two stretchers, one with the dead body of their colonel, and one with a wounded lieutenant, another 'council' is held. The ten men, against all the rules, gather round the two officers and do not hesitate to take part in the discussion on what to do. 'This is good'; the lieutenant thinks to himself, 'this is the right way to treat soldiers. If they have to share the risk of getting killed, they should be granted equality in every-thing else' (*ibid.*, p. 499).

Again, a leader emerges spontaneously in the chaos. It is a mere battery sergeant-major, Terenty Chernega, who ranges the guns in batteries and organizes the defence of a dyke along which several regiments have to escape: 'Chernega galloped up and with a wave of his arm, as though casting a thousand roubles to the wind . . .' And the gunners obey him, give up their ideas of fleeing, accept the risk of their own lives that others may live, because, 'Chernega's generous spirit of self-sacrifice spread like a violent contagion' (*ibid.*, p. 438).

The true team leader is the one who sets the rhythm of the work, gets his men into their stride, so that 'after working like that' each one 'felt an equal to the team leader' (LID, p. 91). True teachers, like Lydia Georgievna in *For the Good of the Cause* get their authority from a sort of inner light: her pupils 'loved everything which was sincere. Anyone could see from her face that she was saying exactly what she was thinking' (SPP, p. 56). They work by example: 'she would never tell anyone to do something she was not ready to do herself', and her pupils 'had come to know her and love her especially as a result of the months spent on the building-site'. They refer to her by her diminutive, Lidochka, but she can maintain the sort of distance that allows her to give them 'a gentle tap on the shoulder' as a mark of her trust (*ibid*., p. 57).

But perhaps the most detailed and illuminating examples of co-responsibility are found in the doctor-patient relationships described in *Cancer Ward*. The 'old doctor', still a model and counsellor to many of his ex-pupils now in charge of departments in the hospital, thinks a doctor should be, 'the kind of person to whom (people) can pour out the fears they have deeply concealed or even found shameful' (CW, p. 455), in a relationship that shows both reciprocity and, on the part of the doctor, a loving, soothing, fatherhood. He has a long interview with each new patient, gets to know him, so that 'then he could treat each patient as a subject on his own' (*ibid*., p. 457), because, 'you see, the organism isn't divided'. This means that, 'the doctor should be a single subject as well!', unified in openness and knowledge: a single conjointure of intelligence and heart. He even thinks that it is not a bad thing if the specialist contracts the disease he usually treats, so that, once he is cured, he can feel from the inside of his patients, as it were.

Kostoglotov, taciturn, observant and circumspect from his years in the camps, rejects the − reassuring but infantilizing − myth of the infallible doctor. In hospital with cancer, he complains: 'they just give me the treatment as if I were a monkey' (*ibid*., p. 44). So he studies medical books on the subject in order to understand the jargon of the doctors consulting at the foot of his bed, shaking them out of their lordly goodwill, asking for reasons, trying to become their 'reasonable ally' (p. 318). He wants the doctor to tell him his tentative diagnoses and doubts, so that the two, doctor and patient, can work together 'in council', and the patient can try to make an intelligent contribution to his own cure, since, as the 'old doctor' said, 'the organism isn't divided', and the cure of the body cannot really be accomplished without the co-operation of the soul: 'Don't be afraid, just explain. I'm like an intelligent soldier who has to understand his mission before he'll fight' (*ibid*., p. 78). Only Vera finally gives in to this demand for reciprocity; to make Oleg accept a course of treatment that is necessary but might leave him permanently impotent, she talks to him from the depths of her own mind, tells him her secrets, what makes life meaningful for her, and wins his free consent to the treatment.

The multiplication of possible occasions for the exercise of co-responsibility, of human-scale social developments in which this living communication can take place, would be a worthy platform on which to base a political struggle. But these possibilities and developments cannot be envisaged without a change in man, or without a Church acting as a workshop of love in which hearts of stone are gradually changed into living hearts.

Towards human unity in diversity

It is not impossible today to contemplate a 'radio-active earth' on which 'the last bipeds stagger about, dying one by one'. The very risk of bringing this situation about makes us realize that 'we belong to the human race before all else', gives a feeling for a 'one and indivisible humanity'. But if it takes the fear of general annihilation to bring us to this realization, this is because humanity is becoming materially united, but not spiritually. Solzhenitsyn's appeal, expressed most strongly in his speech for the Nobel prize, is that from now on we should 'acquire a universal outlook', a universal consciousness 'to express the irreversible march of the nations of the whole world towards unity', a march that must be given a spiritual character. Without this, we shall not have unity in diversity, but in incoherence and chaos: 'entropy, the point of departure for universal extermination'. Today, there are too many opposing scales of value in the world. We are quartered by 'this disparity in the rhythm of life, this divergence in vibration'. A humanity with two hearts cannot survive any more than a man with two. Faced with the impotence of international institutions, the caution — even cowardice — of experts, the impossibility — at least in the short term — of finding a properly religious witness to the Good and the Beautiful that the world will listen to, Solzhenitsyn addresses his appeal to artists, and in the first place to writers. Only beauty can today strike an immediate echo in all men's hearts; only the work of art, which represents victory over the forces of death — above all when it describes them — a deepening of the experience of being and a participation in a general rebirth, can give men back the taste for life and compassion for their fellow men. The one heart of humanity already exists: it is just a question of making its beat heard; it exists in 'universal literature, an immense heart beating to the rhythm of the suffering of the world and its tragic destiny' (NPL).

This process of unification, if it is not to be the 'levelling' of 'entropy', needs meetings, exchanges, diversity, the whole living variety of languages, cultures and countries. The concept of 'world-wide' becomes a faceless abstraction unless it expresses a *universal specificity* in which each individual is supported by 'the whole weight of the experience of others', in which each community on the march can transmit its 'vital experience' to others. Humanity would be as impoverished by a levelling-out of its historical particularities as by a series production of human beings without individual faces: 'Nations constitute the riches of humanity in its collective personifications. The least of them glows with a unique colouring and incarnates a particular reflection of the creative intentions of God' (*ibid.*).

So Solzhenitsyn rises above the traditional Russian opposition between the partisans of universality (which often looks like the West from there) and those of nationalism: the opposition which produced th struggles between 'slavophiles' and 'westernizers' in the last century, and still produces conflict between 'universalists' and 'Russian-ists' among the Soviet *intelligentsia* today. Significantly, both groups reacted strongly against the publication of *August 1914*; the first accused Solzhenitsyn of 'Russophilia', of 'excessive attachment to the soil of Russia', while the second, particularly the underground but tolerated review *Vietche* (1972, Nos. 4-5), denounced him as a Germanophile slandering the people and the army of his own country.

He is in fact simply one more in the line of those great Russian writers who have never been more universal than when they are being most Russian. (The same can be said of most creative artists, whatever their country of origin.) In the trinitarian movement of 'negenthropy', the national and universal scales are mutually interdependent. The universal gives national feeling an opening in friendship to other nations, makes it feel the need of other cultures and other races; it purges it of temptations to nationalist idolatry, collective narcissism, murderous biologism and the igominy of racism. National feeling can cure universalism of ideological abstractions, and universalism can cure nationalism of idolatrous passions; the one becomes real and the other open. Each nation can then set about its own task modestly, in a spirit of openness to and respect for others, at the opposite extreme from the sorts of messianism that seek to expand national pride to universal levels.

Solzhenitsyn is also a Christian writer, and so for him the only created being that reflects the absolute is man: the individual. Only the individual person is the image of God. From this point of view, the nation is but a dimension of the person, and can only be one 'image of the image' among others, to use a Patristic phrase describing the earth. So Sanya, a young pacifist at the beginning of *August 1914*, enlists and goes to war because he feels 'sorry for Russia' (A14, p. 16).

In the human unity reconstituted in Christ, the Gospel commands us to love our neighbour. The nation is the stage at which a country and the people who live in it are made our neighbours, not to mention those who have lived in it and now rest in its soil. Today above all, when technology and ideology present us with grey caricatures of universality, we need these simple roots: in a people, a country, a language. This is Solzhenitsyn's cry: 'All my life, I have had nothing other than the soil of my country under my feet, I have felt nothing but its sorrow and have written about nothing else'. This is why he belongs to all of us, too. This fidelity to his own country enriches all meetings, all exchanges, all the fates of those who so often today are left homeless or exiled. It conjoins cultures, makes nations more open and universality richer and more thinking.

Motherland-fatherland

The fatherland is first the territory man needs, like an animal. In one of his prose poems, Solzhenitsyn describes an ants' nest made in a rotten log, which he threw on to a bonfire without noticing that it was alive with ants. Then, seeing the ants 'tumbling out and scurrying around in desperation', he rolled the log to one side, so that many of the ants managed to escape. But, 'strangely enough they did not run away from the fire. They had no sooner overcome their terror than they turned and circled and some kind of force drew them back to their forsaken homeland'. Many of them climbed back on to the still-burning log, 'ran about on it and perished there' (SPP, p. 202).

The fatherland is then the place where man feels the maternal bounty of the soil – motherland, rather than fatherland. Solzhenitsyn comes from the South, from the steppes bordering the Caucasus mountains. He celebrates the beauty of the mountains and the sun 'flooding every inch to the very horizon' (A14, p. 19). But for him the 'true heartland' of Russia is 'the forest country . . . which starts north of Voronezh' (*ibid.*, p. 18). He describes it in simple, almost humble words, far removed from the lyrical praise of wide-open spaces which so many Western writers see fit to lavish on Russia. For him it is not a Eurasian expanse but a European nation, an old Christian land in which man's work and prayers have united earth and heaven 'without confusion or separation'. Broader than most, of course, and particularly richer in forests, so more secret and more open to unconscious impulses; but the beauty he sees in it is that of the parts that are 'gentler, smaller in scale and given variety by woods and hills' (*ibid.*, p. 19); 'unassuming, temperate, unscorched by the sun, seen through a haze of thin sunlit rain, or in the spring floods with the muddy field and forest roads, a quiet land where the simple forest tree is so useful and necessary to man' (CW, p. 160). In *Matryona's House*, the narrator is returning from the 'hot, dusty wastelands' of central Asia. He is looking for the 'very heartland' of Russia, 'where it was not too hot and where leaves rustled in the forest' (SPP, p. 9). In a village market, early in the morning, he comes across a woman selling milk; he buys a bottle and drinks it on the spot. He is surprised by the way the woman speaks: 'She did not so much talk as sing in an oddly touching way and her words made me feel nostalgic for Asia. "Drink, drink, your heart's athirst" ' (*ibid.*, p. 11).

A primeval scene: solitude, the woman, the mother tongue, mother's milk, the *motherland*: 'I just wanted to creep away and vanish in the very heartland of Russia – if there were such a place' (*ibid.*, p. 9). But the motherland does not swallow him up: it is a Christian land, a land for people, it leads him to Matryona, a mother as her name suggests, but a spiritual, humble mother, a 'mystagogic' mother who gives him the evangelical witness of service and faith.

So the fatherland is also a meeting-place for people, a sketch of communion among people – not the mythical 'people' of the populists, but all the several individuals stretching back over the centuries, woven together by the thread of memory, hope and sacrifice.

At the now abandoned memorial to the battle of Kulikovo, when Russia acted as Europe's shield against the Mongol hordes (*Zakhar-the-Pouch*), a group of workers and intellectuals meet and come together in their fidelity to the past. The first admires the workmanship of the nineteenth-century memorial, the second explains to them what the battle was about.

The fatherland is in fact a memory that forms the beginning or 'trial-run', to use an expression of Péguy's, of the communion of saints. This memory is enshrined in a language, which fashions and enriches the soul. So the great literature of a country is 'the living memory of a nation. It maintains and reactivates its forgotten history . . . preserves the language and soul of a nation' (NPL). The Russian tragedy is that its literature of the twentieth century has been 'broken in its continuity by the intervention of power' (*ibid.*), thereby depriving a nation of its memory and producing generations who 'are born, live and die dumb'. Solzhenitsyn has set out to restore this broken continuity; this is the aim he set himself in *The Gulag Archipelago* and the group of historical novels of which *August 1914* is the first to appear. But his endeavour goes deeper than this: he has set out to restore areas lost to the language itself. The language of *August 1914* is difficult and not always appropriate. But in its epic moments, it rings out loud and clear: it might be called 'Church Russian'.[1] It digs back into the linguistic strata of the Slavonic of the liturgy, 'the language of prayer and benediction'. A constructional language, rooted in the earth, in the *arkhe* of history — not in the sense that it is archaic, but basic — while at the same time intimately linked to spiritual life in its liturgical, communicant expression. This is the language of Blagodaryov, peasant and Church cantor, the language of the legend of the Holy Face, the icon 'not made by the hand of man', which Solzhenitsyn places in the heart of the forest where Samsonov is going to kill himself and so many men die. Through the mediation of a people that was, and in parts still is, steeped in Orthodoxy, Solzhenitsyn rediscovers a liturgical existentiality, a liturgical language, a biblical language, a language that allows him to show the eucharistic meaning of men's actions, as the Apostle enjoins. A *language of roots*, too, in the strict sense, which forces the reader to look carefully for the original meaning of the words used, through an approach to language not unlike that of Heidegger, that other witness to the seriousness of existence.

The Church-forest

The Church is the infinitely discreet presence that maintains the tension, asssures the circulation of life, between the spiritual and economic realms on one hand, between the national and the universal on the other. It keeps society open to the dimension of the infinite, unites men in the gratuity of adoration, fills their hearts with joy and compassion. When society seeks to take refuge in its demiurgic pretension, the blood of the martyrs prevents the exclusion of God and blesses the earth nonetheless. The Church, while it sanctifies each national culture — and in Russia has even fashioned the language — and while it suffers with each of the peoples confided to its care, reminds them that none of them can identify itself with the people of God, none can collectively call itself the messiah — a permanent Russian temptation that led Berdyaev to remark that having failed to produce the Third Rome, Russia gave rise to the Third International.

Solzhenitsyn expects much of the Church, and calls it brutally to account when it fails to live up to its responsibilities. Here our concern is not with what he expects of it, but with what he has known how to express of its mystery. We have already referred several times to the 'host of witnesses' who throng his novels. Perhaps the place to end is in the forest. This, in Solzhenitsyn's work, is surely the most striking symbol of the presence, silence and blessing of the Church. For the forest itself is silence and blessing. Without it, nothing would grow. It is the primordial sanctuary, in which hangs the icon of the Holy Face, the face of God made man, given up for us, but never to be captured by us. The forest of Grunfleiss, in which twelve warriors, given 'a sense of freedom and security' by the forest (A14, p. 509), bury a dead hero, committing him to the 'eternal memory' of God, and thereby themselves find the strength to escape from the German 'pincer movement'. In which Samsonov, in his agony of soul, is kept company by the 'one small star' (*ibid.*, p. 488) that could be seen through the clouds. The forest in which Agnia deciphers mysteries. The forest in which Matryona waits for the returning exile to show him that the world and history have no meaning except in holiness.

NOTES

1.   V. M. Zaloyets, 'Les frontières du roman', *Août quatorze jugé par les lecteurs russes* (Paris, 1973), pp. 43-4.

PART SIX

The quest continues

17 The Gulag Archipelago, Lenin in Zürich, the political writings

I would need a whole book to do justice to the works of Solzhenitsyn published in the West since his exile, particularly *The Gulag Archipelago* and *Lenin in Zürich*. It sould be a different book; for they serve to root his work still more strongly in the Russian and Soviet reality of this century. It would have to concentrate as much on his reflections on the birth and growth of a totalitarian system as on his universal spiritual message. Here, I can only suggest ways in which the spiritual study I have made of his writings is extended by these two works.

The composition of *The Gulag Archipelago* is contemporary with that of the novels, short stories and plays I have examined in the body of the book. Written between 1958 and 1968, it represents the tragically fertile soil in which the writer's creation was rooted at this time, when he often violently refused to have a biography of him written, when he wanted to be just one *zek* among many, a 'son of Gulag', and the liturgical and prophetic voice speaking for so many silenced voices.

The Gulag Archipelago was a striking confirmation of the conclusions I had reached. There is the *leitmotiv* of the wheel, which I had seen as symbolizing history unleashed and all-destroying in *August 1914*. This *leitmotiv* runs through the whole of the Second Part of *The Gulag Archipelago*, 'Perpetual Motion', which is prefaced with these verses by Wilhelm Müller: '. . . the wheels/which never like to rest,/the wheels! . . ./They dance in merry ranks . . ./the millstones!'. And the same symbol, one could say, runs through *Lenin in Zürich*, from the powerful wheels of the locomotive pulling out of a Galician station at the beginning to the wheels of the train in which the Bolshevik leaders cross wartime Germany with impunity on their way back to Russia.

Another detail: I have quoted extensively from Soloviev who is only referred to by a secondary character in *Cancer Ward*. But *Gulag* tells us how Solzhenitsyn came to know the great philosopher: through one of the two 'Russian boys', so impressively cultured, but already close to death, whom he met in his first camp, just outside Moscow, in the old monastery of The New Jerusalem (what irony, and what prophecy!). One of them quoted from Pasternak, but mostly from Soloviev's *Meaning of Love* and *Justificiation of Good*.

Gulag confirms my theory that Nerhzin of *The First Circle* is the writer himself. One of the most inexplicable passages in the novel — Nerzhin's voluntary departure from the relative comfort of the *sharashka* (special prison) towards the lower circles of the concentration camp hell, is illuminated by an extraordinary scene recounted in *Gulag*, Part III, ch. 5: it is night, and Solzhenitsyn, alone — this is the most privileged period of the *sharashka*'s régime — lights a great bonfire in the grounds; he feels the original, paradisiacal splendour of fire, symbol of *Sophia*, wisdom, and the deep incandescence of things, as I tried to show in my examination of the chapter in *The First Circle* where Agnia takes her fiancé one evening at sunset to a little church on a hill overlooking Moscow and is suddenly in ecstasy, on fire. Next to the *sharashka* there is an ordinary camp, and a girl had escaped that day, to the fury of the guard and the women, who will suffer for it. But one girl had sighed: 'At least she can have a good time out in freedom for all of us!'. The jailer had overheard her, and she was being punished, kept standing at attention for hours in the freezing cold. Now she is groaning and weeping to be forgiven. But, 'even in the camp no one was about to say to her, "All right, idiot, come on in" '.

For Solzhenitsyn, as for Nerzhin, this humble martyr was a messenger from the lower circles. One had to descend to these circles in order to witness and to understand: 'To that flame and to you, girl, I promise: the whole wide world will read about you'.

The meaning of Solzhenitsyn's destiny is to be found in this interiorization of the energy of fire; its metamorphosis into prophetic energy through a voluntary descent into hell. *Gulag* not only restores the truth of history, but inaugurates a prophetic history: Solzhenitsyn speaks here like an Old Testament prophet, with the same harsh and burning verve, the same flashes of tenderness and harshness. He calls *The Gulag Archipelago* 'An Experiment in Literary Investigation', but literature here is not an end in itself; its criterion is ethical and spiritual, the irreducible transcendence of God and man. The theme of the rebel who speaks out from the indignation of his heart, from his thirst for 'truth-justice', is particularly strong in Part V, a fresco of the *zeks'* resistance, their revolts often echoing that of the real Russian revolution, that of the spring and summer of 1917, before the Bolshevik distortion set in. Irony, so strong in the great novels, becomes a prophetic weapon in *The Gulag Archipelago*; the ironic reversal overthrows the totalitarian idols and lets good shine through.

As a prophet, Solzhenitsyn calls for collective repentance. This has to begin with oneself; not in the self-indulgent individualism of a Tolstoy, but in organic, and tragic, communion with one's whole generation. (In the Orthodox tradition, remember, the communion of saints is firstly that of 'conscious sinners'.) 'And just so we don't go around flaunting too proudly the white mantle of the just, let everyone ask himself: "If my life had turned out differently, might I myself not have become just such an executioner?" ' (GA I, p. 160). 'Confronted by the pit into which we are about to toss those who have done us harm, we halt, stricken dumb: it is only after all because of the way things worked out that they were the executioners and we weren't' (GA I, p. 168). In the autumn of 1938, in his third year at Rostov University, Solzhenitsyn was summoned by the District Komsomol Committee, with some other Komsomol members, and offered the chance of a brilliant future in the NKVD. He was twenty and a fervent upholder of the régime, and had no obvious objection. But he refused, through a sort of instinct inherited from times 'when morality was not considered relative and when the distinction between good and evil was very simply perceived by the heart' (GA I, p. 161). But as a young officer, after being 'trained like a young beast' at officer cadet school, Solzhenitsyn gave way to the trappings of power, taking pleasure in rank and extra rations. Only later, in camp, does he remember with shame how he threw out orders and punishments, how he failed to heed the cries of a prisoner being dragged along and whipped by a bully on horseback, how, even after his arrest, he refused to carry his own case, since that was something an officer just did not do. In his second camp, Kaluga Gates, just outside Moscow, considering himself still a loyal Soviet citizen, he denounced some fellow inmates planning an escape. The escape may have been unlikely, but it was still a pact with the devil. It was at this point that fate saved him, in the form of his transfer to the *sharashka*.

Prison strips life and man to the bare bones. The 'trusties' quickly acquire a 'sensor relay' that tells them what sort of person they are dealing with from a look, from the first sound of a voice, and so enables them to open themselves completely to those who are open and remain hermetically sealed to those whose minds are closed. Solzhenitsyn became, in prison, a *visionary of the human face*, capable of identifying the righteous instantly from their faces, and of suggesting them to his readers by a truly iconographic literary technique. *The Gulag Archipelago* adds a whole host of the just to stand beside Matryona and Alyosha the Baptist.

If individuals are not recognized as such, if men are categorized by a schematic history, then society disintegrates and the very notions of good and evil, of innocent and just, disappear. Without ideology, evil remains circumscribed: 'The imagination and spiritual strength of Shakespeare's evildoers stopped short at a dozen corpses. Because they had no *ideology*' (GA I, p. 174). Ideology provides evil with the justification it has long sought, gives evildoers a good conscience and transforms fanatics into criminals whose evildoing need in future know no bounds. Ideology is the social theory that makes their actions seem good to them and to others: 'That was how the agents of the Inquisition fortified their wills: by invoking Christianity . . .', and the same can be said of Moslems, colonizers, Nazis, Jacobins. Now the scale is greater: 'Thanks to *ideology*, the twentieth century was fated to experience evildoing on a scale calculated in the millions' (GA I, p. 174).

The lie of ideologies, and of the revolutions they give rise to, or take over, consists in their attempt to suppress the 'carriers of evil' and to establish the reign of purity through violent purging. The introduction of absolute theories into the immanence of history effectively establishes the right to massacre. Then not only are the 'carriers of good' indiscriminately slaughtered as well, since violence is blind, but revolutions, 'then take to themselves as their heritage the evil itself, magnified still more' (GA 2, p. 598). To this, Solzhenitsyn opposes what he has come to see as the central truth of all the great religions of the world: 'They struggle with the *evil inside a human being* (inside every human being). It is impossible to expel evil from the world in its entirety, but it is possible to constrict it within each person' (GA 2, p. 597).

For Solzhenitsyn, a denunciation of ideology means a radical critique of Lenin.

We are all familiar with the Khrushchev thesis, taken up in part by

Roy Medvedev in his study of Stalinism: the tragedy and indeed the catastrophe of Soviet history arose from the character of Stalin. The massacres and deportations, and the concentration-camp system, did not, so it is claimed, originate in Marxism-Leninism itself. The course of the revolution was corrupted by the megalomania, self-deification and pathological suspicion of a tyrant. *The Gulag Archipelago* refutes that reassuring version of history. In fact, it says, everything began with Lenin. It was Lenin who, towards the end of 1917 and at the beginning of 1918, gave the order for 'anti-social elements', 'dangerous vermin', to be wiped out. It was Lenin who set up not only the one-party system but an ideocracy, an a-theocracy, and rigged trials directed at the leaders of other revolutionary parties and at church officials. Lenin was the founder of totalitarianism.

For that reason the representation of Lenin's character in the chapters taken from the 'knots' (*August 1914* and the volumes in progress, *October 1916* and *March 1917*) and brought together in *Lenin in Zürich*, is especially important. Solzhenitsyn portrays Lenin first and foremost as a force, 'a bowstring', an 'arrow from the bow', a 'whirlwind' (*Lenin in Zürich*, p. 90). An hour lost makes him ill. Any meeting or business which suddenly comes up irritates him. Every muscle but even more his mind is 'always tensed ready for action'. So much power is stored up in him that he can 'move mountains and continents'. The tension is primarily intellectual; it cancels hunger and need: 'He could make do with very little food; he generated energy almost without eating' (LZ, p. 87).

But that energy is not infused with peace or illuminated by transcendence, or transmuted into spiritual power. It is directly and fanatically employed in the service of the 'Cause', the only ethical criterion; in the service of ideology, the *gnosis* of human development, the true science of sciences. Then man is conceived appropriately only in the immanence of a supposedly rational history which becomes conscious of itself only in Lenin's fevered brain, the mind of 'the only infallible interpreter, who always knew precisely what was right' (LZ, p. 20). Every day has its truth because there is no transcendence. Nothing surpasses the movement of the masses, the history of generic man.

The certainty of access to absolute knowledge, which alone can act as the foundation of absolute power, always leads Lenin to foster disagreement. He can bear near him only those who share his views without reservation as scientifically demonstrable truth. 'Those left . . . may be the most mediocre, the most insignificant people, but if they are united in single obedience you can achieve anything' (LZ, pp. 50-1). Anything and everything. 'Everything is allowed if there is no God', said Dostoevsky. Everything is allowed for the one who becomes (as Lenin thinks *he* has become) the absolute consciousness and conscience of a mankind called to self-deification. To know the laws of development (and nothing else exists) and to master them sooner or later means obtaining the power to shape that development.

After two thousand years of Christianity in which the perpetual tension between the Kingdom of God and the kingdom of Caesar has gradually given rise to freedom of thought and spirit, man is making a giddy though fascinating regression to armed messianism (abolishing evil by means of evil, ending war by promoting war). In front of the Zwingli statue, erected in memory of another armed prophet in an age of Reformation, Lenin ruminates: 'An excellent combination, the book and the sword. The book, with the sword as its extension' (LZ, p. 64). Zwingli, to be sure, is holding a Bible, but he closed churches, which are now libraries, temples of triumphant rationalism. Lenin replaced the Bible by *Capital*, so the identification of knowledge and power is henceforth wholly justified, and the sword which sometimes usurped the place of the cross can now replace it altogether.
    Western Europe and the United States would seem to have adopted a culture of relativity, dialogue and mutual respect, as is shown by their attachment to 'formal freedoms' and the gradual integration of the working-class into the national community. Lenin's anxiety to start the worldwide revolution in Switzerland or Sweden seems ludicrous. Russia, on the other hand, is vulnerable to a secularized eschatology, to a sectarian anti-culture, for these, the partial and the partisan, have been absolutized. In that alone (for there are other dimensions to the Russian genius) Lenin is deeply Russian, as the Satanic genius Parvus remarks. As early as 1915 Parvus wanted to tear the Zürich exile from his abstract meditations and direct him to his true destiny – a Russian destiny: 'All that Lenin lacked' (thus Parvus) 'was breadth. The savage, intolerant narrowness of the born schismatic harnessed his tremendous energy to futilities . . . wasting his strength in meaningless struggles, with nothing to show except mounds of scribbled paper. This schismatic narrowness doomed him to sterility in Europe, left him no future except in Russia – but also made him indispensable for any activity there. Indispensable now!' (LZ, p. 122). Lenin himself will sense that after the February revolution: 'In Petersburg and in the Soviet there was a vacuum, and he felt its

suctional pull demanding that he fill it with his own power' (LZ, p. 191).

The supposedly absolute knowledge of the relative, before its devastation, puts Lenin into a quasi-pathological state of avidity. Solzhenitsyn's description of Lenin's ever-ranging mind is Kafkaesque. He devours pamphlets and newspapers, indulges in incessant ideological discourse, his mind rushing forward without ever pausing for contemplation. The ducks play on the water and Lenin thinks of Clausewitz — of the laws of armed conflict. Oblivious to the peaceful conviviality of a homely Swiss interior (which Solzhenitsyn describes in a page which recalls the Swiss writer Ramuz), Lenin in the smoke-filled inn tries to show that Switzerland is the most revolutionary country in the world. You can't penetrate Lenin's gaze; and Lenin never manages to enter, with disinterested sympathy, the mystery of another individual's existence. All that now exists for him is the Cause, whose brains, mouth and limbs he is. He knows only those who are for and those who are against the Cause: '. . . there can be no such relationship between human beings as simple friendship transcending political, class and material ties' (LZ, p. 21). 'Only those who saw the Party's needs in correct perspective could hold their places and march at his side' (ibid.).

Lenin gives everyone the sense of a mission, of a struggle which will be right for them. He makes them feel understood, appreciated, but 'then, an hour later, they were already receding, and he would soon have clean forgotten who they were . . .' (ibid.). In the gnosis of becoming, it is the masses which count and not the individual, whereas in the gospel parable nothing is more important than the lost sheep, the individual.

Yet two limit-situations do enter into Lenin's inner world: love and death. Through them transcendence taps at the door.

Love is Inessa Armand, whose presence, or rather Lenin's powerful nostalgia for it, enters into the long soliloquy of exile. Lenin met Inessa in the service of the Cause, but her beauty and vital intensity have made her more fascinating. She will not do what she is told, yet he does not reject her. Lenin who is wholly tension and anxious speculation, who judges everyone and everything according to the one criterion of the Cause, finds in his meetings with Inessa a certain gratuitousness, a truth which is physical, demands attention to the present, and shows the glory and misery of being a man and not the infallible voice of the dialectic. With Inessa, he is no longer the brain and sword of human collective history, but simply himself. Only

Inessa seems unique — for him alone. She gives him a foretaste of a different and unsuspected reality. In him she awakens a physical, intense, and jealous tenderness: a gratitude which is not unpossessive. Even the companionship of struggle becomes amorous complicity. When, for a carefully prepared mission, Lenin has to choose a pseudonym for Inessa, he decides: 'We'll call you . . . let's see . . . Petrova . . . (I'm "Petrov" too — you should remember, if nobody else does. So, through our pseudonyms, we shall face the public united in one person — openly yet secretly. You will actually be me.)' (LZ, p. 26). That is not so much communion as possession — an all-absorbing passion. But sickness and death intervene like a wall of nothingness. Two or three times a year Lenin is struck down and despairs. Much more often he notices insidious signs of anxiety and longing in his head where universal evolution is concentrated as a brilliant light. In front of the grave of the poet Büchner, who lived in the same street in Zürich, he senses the relation between his sickness and death: 'The inscription did not say what he had died of. Perhaps his head had ached like this, ached and ached . . .' (LZ, p. 179). Ultimately, however, for Lenin death is something apart from thought. His ideology ignores it completely. Death — the death of others — is simply one element of the dialectic, whose necessary and happy negativity it amplifies. Death is not *someone*'s death. But when multiplied, when it becomes mass death, it is the negative aspect of the dialectic. Hence Lenin studies the enormous Russian war losses so assiduously. His joy increases with the mass mortality rate. Death on a mass scale was wiping out the hated empire and making ready the way of revolution. The problem in fact was not one of stopping the war, as so many pacifistic socialists wanted, but of fanning the flames and then transferring it where it belonged — to his own country.

As for Inessa, in spite of the suffering which Lenin feels because of the distance between them, and because of her silence, he never thinks for a moment of compromising his own arrangements for her sake. They are too convenient for him and the Cause. He has never thought of going to her, in the self-oblivion of true love, to share her life and to give *himself* as he wishes her to give herself. In Solzhenitsyn's view, Lenin is a petit bourgeois revolutionary. That essentially is why Inessa frightens him. She gives him a bad conscience: 'She was too mercurial, too much a person in her own right, too distracting' (LZ, p. 73). She is too beautiful. And she has children, she wants to live with them, and for Lenin children mean a different way of life: 'He could not, he had no right to let himself be slowed down and taken out of his way by those children' (LZ, p. 73).

Lenin is a fanatical servant of the Cause. He is a divine intellect to whom 'everything is permitted'. He has surrendered to another law. He undertakes the complete enslavement of his wife Nadya. He forces her to undergo long periods of *ménage à trois*, making her a purely functional individual. She becomes an unperson with a face (as the slave was called in ancient Greece – *aprosopos*, without a countenance). She is the serf of a man who talks only of liberation. Transcendence knocks as it does at every man's door, but Lenin never opens up.

The passionate rationalism of Leninist ideology, which closes its bearer to power from above, opens him clandestinely to the powers of darkness, to which he wants to surrender Russia. Solzhenitsyn occasionally evokes in *Lenin in Zürich* the black sea monsters, the behemoths and hippopotami who lurk in the depths of history. It is their imperceptible surface movements and not the supposed mastery of the laws of development which decide Lenin's fate in the end. The man who avoids the protection of banality, of everyday deadness, without surrendering to the power of the Spirit, necessarily succumbs to dark forces: to Behemoth, the beast of the abyss. Lenin in Solzhenitsyn's novel has a double: Parvus, a fantastic character and a true gnostic. He sees the future with a Satanic lucidity which is far-reaching and penetrating in a way that Lenin's vision is not: '. . . there was his grotesque fantasy about the possibility of a socialist party winning power and then turning it against the majority of the people, suppressing the trade unions' (LZ, p. 103).

The manipulator of the 1905 revolution, Parvus invented the theme of the weakest link in the chain which allows the explanation that the Revolution, despite all Marx's forecasts, could break out in a country as under-industrialized as Russia. Parvus has grown immensely rich as the result of financial deals controlled from the Balkans. He is cynical and ostentatious, a sensualist, uninvolved. He has entered the service of the Germans whom be believes he can use to manipulate the new Russian revolution. He predicts the decline of Europe, a confrontation between the United States and Russia, and the rise of the totalitarian systems. Satanic, a human Behemoth, but too intelligent and refined himself to rush into action, he knows that Lenin will be his secular arm in Russia.

The central chapters of *Lenin in Zürich* are devoted to their meeting and to a long discussion between Lenin and Parvus that is very reminiscent of the conversation between Ivan and the devil in *The*

Brothers Karamazov. The very name, or rather pseudonym, of Parvus is characteristic. The Latin word means 'little', whereas Israel Lazarevich Gelfand is gross and heavy, opaque and delicate at one and the same time. Solzhenitsyn does not hide his belief that the man who sees below the surface and discerns the movement of the black monsters in the depths is not Lenin, but Parvus. Parvus initiates Lenin. The 'hippopotamus blood' of Parvus is transfused into Lenin's veins. And Parvus catches 'a gleam in Lenin's eyes which meant that he could see it too' (LZ, p. 136).

Under the ideological justification, the experience of the camps, too, reveals an obsession with power locked in its own immanence. Power, for the mediocre, is often the only passion they know. Deprived of any contact with the 'higher spheres of human life', those in charge of the camps live 'the more fully and avidly in the lower spheres' (GA 2, ch. 4). More than the basic drives of hunger and sex, more even than greed for wealth, what drives them is a thirst for power, for an absolute power (a power, that is, which mimics the Absolute), that reduces them to the level of the beasts, since 'power is a poison' (*ibid*.). The man who is open to transcendence , on the other hand, who listens to the irreducible sign of transcendence in the voice of his conscience, sets limits to power; for him its exercise, though it may be a dangerous trial, is not necessarily fatal. But for those who know no limits because ideology keeps them locked in immanence, power is a fatal poison, from which nothing can save them. So the ideologues and the executioners they justify made the camps a huge machine devoted to the destruction of human beings, body and soul.

But at this point the system is stood on its head. For Solzhenitsyn, just as the camps prove that without God, everything goes, so too they strip man to his irreducible core, the centre of his being and yet something greater than him. They confirm, with an intensity he could not have dreamed of, Berdyaev's great intuition that the reductions of Western culture of the last two centuries have left man with a stark choice between divine-humanity and bestial-humanity; either the death of man must follow the death of God, or God must come back to life in what remains of man. The experience of the camps, where one hands over one's second skin too, reveals (or can reveal) 'the little inner kernel of the soul', the divine spark, 'the weak little spark of God (once) breathed into them too' (GA 2, p. 579).

Solzhenitsyn here challenges other witnesses from the camps, those who, like Shalamov, bring back no message other than of despair.

Shalamov's *Tales from Kolyma* (still unpublished in the West) show the experience of the camps as 'entirely negative', in the sense that 'man only changes in one way: for the worse'. He may have the essence of life shown to him, but this is a vision of such horror that he cannot contemplate it without his heart turning to stone.

Chapter 2 of Part IV of *The Gulag Archipelago* takes the form of a tragic dialogue between Solzhenitsyn and Shalamov, with the first invoking the 'communion of saints', those 'deeply religious spirits' who held firm in the camps. There were also those who were sustained by civil pride, but, he notes sadly, the civic spirit was not very deeply rooted in Russia; those who not only resisted but who stripped themselves down to the 'one thing necessary' were the religious spirits, because they either already possessed, or came to find, a relationship with transcendence, and instead of stiffening with pride or dissolving into despair, came to take themselves back from Another, in whose Cross and Resurrection they shared, coming back to life in the vast crucible of suffering. 'How can one explain that certain unstable people found faith right there in camp, that they were strengthened by it, and that they survived uncorrupted?' (GA 2, p. 606). Solzhenitsyn evokes these 'confessors' in truly liturgical, or more accurately iconographical, terms that remind one of the mosaics and frescoes in which the Christian East used to depict long lines of martyrs carrying candles or palms: '. . . their self-confident religious procession through the Archipelago — a sort of silent religious procession with invisible candles. How some among them were mowed down by machine guns and those next in line continued their march. A steadfastness unheard of in the twentieth century! And it was not in the least for show, and there weren't any declamations.' (GA 2, pp. 605-6.)

Those who were corrupted in the camps, he states, were those who lacked the humble courage of recourse to transcendence, those who 'had already been corrupted in freedom or who were ready for it' (GA 2, p. 608). The camp only uncovers basic tendencies already there, but not needed outside. Stripped to the 'human essence' revealed by the camps, man sees either death or the incarnate, crucified God overcoming death. If corruption was a massive phenomenon in the camps, that was not just because the camps were awful, but because the Soviet people 'stepped upon the soil of the Archipelago spiritually disarmed', knowing neither how to live nor how to die. But this preparation, or lack of it, is not the final determining factor: there is a mysterious choice, which I have tried to analyze in the first two Parts of this book, and which *The Gulag Archipelago* illustrates with examples.

This choice, made all at once or gradually, is between survival and conscience, between the maintenance of biological life 'at any price', meaning 'at the price of someone else' (GA 2, p. 585), and that gesture of love and respect which leads, if necessary, to the laying down of one's own life. Those who chose the way of conscience, Solzhenitsyn admits, were not the majority, 'but fortunately neither was it just a few' (*ibid*.). And these could be recognized only if one looked closely at them; they did not shout it out: 'Dozens of times this same choice had arisen before them too, but they always knew, and knew their own stand' (*ibid*.). 'And do not *all* those who survived remember one or another person who reached out a hand to him in camp and saved him at a difficult moment?' (GA 2, p. 609). Suffering, at least in some cases, did not corrupt, but ennobled, and one could meet men whose clear conscience shone in their eyes, 'like a clear mountain lake' (GA 2, p. 580).

Solzhenitsyn sums up his own experience of conversion in a short poem, written in rhymed verse to make it more easily memorable, in the camp hospital, which he prints in Part IV, chapter 1. Suffering brings back the memories of the church chants of his childhood, the 'good seeds' scattered by the pride of adolescence, with its pretensions to explain everything by a rationalism that was in fact no more than an ideological system borne along by the beating of his heart and the coursing of his blood:

> Blood seethed — and every swirl
> Gleamed iridescently before me,
> Without a rumble the building of my faith
> Quietly crumbled within my heart.

Then came the experience of the camps, and of illness, the edge of death and of nothingness, and a return to an open heart, capable of perceiving 'the even glow of the Higher Meaning': 'Though I renounced You, You were with me!' (GA 2, pp. 596-7). The *metanoia* is not only individual but linked to the destiny of a whole generation, a whole society, a whole people: 'In my most evil moments I was convinced that I was doing good . . . It was only when I lay there on rotting prison straw that I sensed within myself the first stirrings of good' (GA 2, p. 597). Not good in the moral sense, but in the sense of the Being who is love.

The simple, non-intellectual use that Solzhenitsyn makes of the terms good and evil should not lead the hasty reader to assume that he is being moralistic, or even pharisaical. These words have personal and ontological connotations: evil means separation and good means communion, with God and with one's fellows. This is why 'the line dividing good and evil cuts through the heart of every human being' (GA 1, p. 168). Solzhenitsyn makes the meaningful comment, apparently ignored by both his admirers and his detractors alike: 'Let the reader who expects this book to be a political exposé slam its covers shut right now' (*ibid*.). It is not a matter of putting the just and innocent in one camp and 'those with black souls' in another. A 'bastion of good' remains in the blackest of hearts, and 'a corner from which evil has not been entirely rooted out' remains in the best of us. So one cannot extirpate evil by massacring the evildoers, for 'who is willing to destroy a piece of his own heart?' (*ibid*.), but by working for a change in them, through a shining and forceful concept of the Good, of Being. The dividing line between good and evil in all of us is a shifting one: 'One and the same human being is, at various ages, under various circumstances, a totally different human being. At times he is close to being a devil, at times to sainthood. But his name doesn't change, and to that name we ascribe the whole lot, good and evil' (*ibid*.). So instead of judging others, we should try to know ourselves in the light of transcendence. 'From good to evil is one quaver, says the proverb. And correspondingly, from evil to good' (*ibid*.). In one's dealing with others, and one's appreciation of oneself, the last word belongs to the parable of the wheat and the tares.

As for the evil we suffer, it touches a common chord with our deepest destiny, however little we may have lived. In the camp hospital in which he lay after his operation for cancer, Solzhenitsyn met Doctor Boris Kornfeld, who told him the story of his conversion from Judaism to Christianity. He feels that there is no such thing as a completely just man, that the saint is above all a sinner conscious of his failings. He is convinced that, 'there is no punishment that comes to us in this life on earth which is undeserved' (GA 2, p. 594). Not that there can be any correlation between the fantastic extremes of punishment in the camps and what we deserve, but if you 'go over your life with a fine-tooth comb and ponder it deeply, you will always be able to hunt down that transgression of yours for which you have now received this blow'. This proved to be the last speech of the mysterious Dr Kornfeld. In the morning he was found with his head battered in by a mallet. He died without regaining consciousness. He had not been out for two months, 'for fear of having his throat cut'. Who did it and why,

Solzhenitsyn never discovered. This was the time when 'it had recently become fashionable − to cut the throats of stool pigeons'. Something in Kornfeld's last words 'touched a sensitive chord' in Solzhenitsyn, and he asks whether the Doctor might not have expressed a law of spiritual life: 'that the meaning of earthly existence lies not, as we have grown used to thinking, in prospering, but . . . in the development of the soul' (p. 595). If that is so, then those who are being punished most terribly are not the prisoners, but the torturers, for 'they are turning into swine, they are departing downward from humanity' (*ibid*.).

One cannot state that anyone is fixed forever at the level of a beast. Or can one? Solzhenitsyn appears sometimes to doubt. Could evil possess 'thresholds' beyond which there can be no turning back?: 'When . . . he suddenly crosses that threshold, he has left humanity behind, and without, perhaps, the possibility of return' (GA 1, p. 175). Sometimes the face has become a mask. We do not know the extent of damnation. Neither, perhaps, does God himself − only the damned can, closed in on their own nothingness.

Chapter 1 of Part IV of *Gulag*, entitled 'The Ascent', ends with the repeated doxology, *'Bless you, prison!'*. 'All the writers who wrote about prison but did not themselves serve time there considered it their duty to express sympathy to prisoners and to curse prison. I . . . have served enough time there. I nourished my soul there and I say without hesitation: *Bless you, prison*, for having been in my life!' (GA 2, p. 599). But he adds the tragic parenthesis: '(And from beyond the grave come replies: It is very well for you to say that − when you came out of it alive!)', to prevent any non-spiritual interpretation of his thanksgiving.

This Fourt Part, 'The Soul and Barbed Wire', is undoubtedly the finest and most intense of the meditations that punctuate the whole narrative sweep of *The Gulag Archipelago*. Its title page bears this quote from St Paul: 'Behold I show you a mystery; we shall not all sleep, but we shall all be changed' (1 Cor. 15.51). The experience of the camps is an eschatological anticipation, an apocalypse in history. If he does not die, physically or morally, from the experience, man comes out renewed. He learns gentleness and understanding; he learns to measure his own weakness and so to understand that of others. He becomes strong, calm and detached. Freed from all future, he is left with his personal ontology, not so much the end he pursues but the means he uses to get there and the spirit inspiring those means. In *Gulag*, Solzhenitsyn unravels in one phrase the controversy aroused in the West by the passage in *One Day in the Life of Ivan Denisovich* where Ivan gives himself up joyfully to the building of a wall, his camp 'general work': 'You need that wall like you need a hole in the head, nor do you believe it is going to bring closer the happy future of the people, but, pitiful, tattered slave that you are, you smile at this creation of your own hands' (GA 2, p. 592).

Stripped to the bare essentials of a slave existence, man, renewed, rediscovers his freedom: 'What does not exist — not even God can take away. And this is a basic freedom' (*ibid.*, p. 589). That freedom cold become an empty stagnation (which perhaps threatens the camp officials), if it did not receive its content — an infinite content — from the deposit of communion, and for some, from the experience of communion itself. For, 'even if you haven't come to love your neighbours in the Christian sense, you are at least learning to love those close to you' (*ibid.*, p. 653). In Part I, chapter 5, Solzhenitsyn has a marvellous reflection of this grace of friendship in the midst of suffering, which is why the chapter is entitled, 'First Cell, First Love'. For several weeks the prisoner has been kept at the mercy of his interrogators, and locked up alone, till his reason begins to totter and suicide seems the best course. Then, suddenly, he is thrown into his first cell. There are others there, and their welcome, and their brotherhood. 'Now for the first time you were about to see people who were not your enemies . . .' (GA 1, p. 183). 'And those three lifted heads, those three unshaven, crumpled pale faces, seemed to me so human, so dear, that I stood there, hugging my mattress, and smiled with happiness' (*ibid.*, p. 185). And there one learns again the value of words, of human conversation; one finds oneself able to aspire to hitherto unimagined thoughts; one re-discovers charity.

Materialism — incessantly presented to the Soviet people as the truth of science — is here definitively set aside. At the Ekibastuz camp, Solzhenitsyn meets a religious poet, philosopher and theologian, Anatole Silin, who points out to him that the materialists' question, 'How can spirit engender matter?' should be turned upside down: how can the higher grow out of the lower, how can matter produce spirit? That, surely, is the far greater miracle?

The camps are full of poets and philosophers, thinking with an intelligence sharpened by suffering. At Ekibastuz there is also Arnold Rappoport, a real Renaissance man, interested in everything, a scientist who has written a treatise on love between man and woman.

No erotic fantasy born of frustration, this, Solzhenitsyn notes, but true chastity, an integration of *eros* in understanding and fidelity, with the stunning conclusion that, 'Love, as much as science or art, is a way of *knowing* the world'.

The restoration of a true hierarchy of being is not an idealist speculation, but an experience attested by the improbable, even impossible from a materialist point of view, cures effected in the camps. Solzhenitsyn cured himself of cancer through sheer strength of mind, and one of his companions, Dimitri Panin, the model for Sologdin in *The First Circle*, tells how he cured himself of pernicious dysentery: left alone to die, he meditated intensely on the Our Father, and life was restored to him. *The Gulag Archipelago* gives numerous instances of the influence of soul over body. There is the case of Grigory Grigoryev: 'because of the astounding influence on his body of his bright and spotless human spirit . . . the organism of Grigory Ivanovich . . . grew stronger in camp; his early rheumatism of the joints disappeared completely, and he became particularly healthy after the typhus from which he recovered: in winter he went out in cotton sacks, making holes in them for his head and his arms — and he did not catch cold!' (GA 2, pp. 607-8).

Undoubtedly Solzhenitsyn the émigré has been exploited by the most reactionary forces in the West. He does not really understand the West. He sees it as a non-Russia which preserves adequately or inadequately certain major legal freedoms. Therefore it is a place of refuge from which to exert pressure on the fate of Russia. One can take refuge in Zürich, like Lenin, to try to cure what Lenin did; to remake what he unmade: the national and spiritual continuity of Russia. The West has escaped the major totalitarianism of our century which, Solzhenitsyn reminds us, has taken more than sixty million victims, quite apart from the eastern European countries delivered up to Stalin in 1944-5. The West remains however unaware, still tempted by the 'spirit of Munich'. The West slumbers in riches. It ignores the threat and enjoys its freedom instead of establishing and defending it.

But does Solzhenitsyn quite understand the West? Perhaps he does not really want it to be the contrary of the Soviet Union, but constituted in its image, with an ideology and a common direction like the USSR? He visits the United States to find such an ideology and impulse, hoping to spark them into action to avoid disaster. But is the secret dynamics of the West ideological? Is it even uniform? Is the

United States the heart of the West or merely one aspect of the West? Is not the greatness of the United States the continually renewed capacity for self-criticism? When Solzhenitsyn in Spain, instead of saying that the Franco dictatorship was relatively minor in comparison with Stalin's, praises it for the triumph of 'Christian order', surely he is wrong and risks alienating the most worthwhile opinion? Christianity, in western history, is not order but ferment. Young westerners who are attracted by Marxism are not drawn because of their comfort but because they are looking for meaning and community — for communion — without seeing that Marxism is itself part of the system that they are rejecting, of the system which subjects man to insane consumption or to the hysteria of the mythic revolution, because there is no answer to death and ultimate nothingness. Solzhenitsyn does not seem to understand that the revolt of a section of western youth does not mean complicity with Soviet totalitarianism, but the eventual dislocation of a purely humanist culture which tried to get rid of God and death.

That is why the writer does see properly, and returns to the deep current of his work, when he questions the very foundations of that culture: its rejection for at least two centuries of the spiritual, to such an extent that Marxism, as Sartre has noted, constitutes its insurpassable horizon. But there is no question of returning to a Christian form of order. Here I prefer Berdyaev, whose acquaintance with the great western Quest was somewhat different, and for whom its essential movement posed the ultimate questions, from the death of God to the death of man, or his resurrection in the full Chalcedonian affirmation of the God-man. Berdyaev sees the great researchers into humanity as concentrating on antitheism because of the degeneration of a pietistic and moralizing Christianity which conceived God as against man, and not as the revelation of man. Perhaps these philosophies will find their place, once exorcised, in an authentic divine-humanism.

As with the Dostoevsky of *A Writer's Diary*, it seems to me that Solzhenitsyn's true message has less to do with his political pronouncements as an exile, than with the light which shines from his work as a whole. It is of that illumination that we should ask him to speak to us, while explaining to him what is essentially, today, the tragedy of the West — a West which is not non-Russia but includes Russia and needs Russia's spiritual witness.

The left-wing intellectuals of the West accuse Solzhenitsyn of sympathy for Nazism. In fact he shows that Communist totalitarianism has been bigger and more destructive than Nazism, and that it was the matrix of all the totalitarianisms of the century. The constant comparison between Nazism and Soviet Communism, often unfavourable to the latter, shocks the westerners who have seen Nazism as what Hegel called 'absolute concrete evil'. But that insistence re-establishes the truth. It definitively destroys the psychological process by which the Communist movement, immediately after the Second World War, both highlighted the Nazi concentration camps and tried to make everyone forget, or rather make unthinkable, the Stalinist camps. The 'liberation' of Europe meant an equal or worse slavery for the eastern half of the continent, which was shamefully abandoned by the West.

Solzhenitsyn has been accused of nostalgia for the past. But he has searched his country's past for the roots of present dislocations of the twentieth century, recalling the great schism of the 'Raskolniki' of the seventeenth century and later, and the responsibility of the Russian Church, which subjected those 'Old Believers' to a merciless inquisition (*Letter to the Synod of the Russian Orthodox Church in Exile*). Solzhenitsyn shows that the maxim 'only the end counts' was not invented by Soviet Marxism but already existed in the military expansionism of the Russian Empire and in many of the aspects of the rise of the bourgeoisie and capitalism in nineteenth-century Russia. As for Tsarism, Solzhenitsyn's viewpoint, already suggested in *August 1914*, is clearly set out in the *Archipelago*, where he evokes Nicholas II's inertia and total incomprehension of his time. Solzhenitsyn is no Russian monarchist when he criticizes Nicholas for having persisted in seeing Russia as his personal domain, where he could raise taxes and mobilize soldiers to make war against his Hohenzollern brother. Solzhenitsyn insists that at the end of the twentieth century one cannot live in the imaginary world in which the last Tsar perished.

Solzhenitsyn has also been accused of nationalism. But in the *Archipelago* and the *Letter to the Rulers of the Soviet Union*, he hopes that freedom will be restored to all nationalities whose apparent federalism puts them under Russian tutelage. He includes the Ukraine among those territories. It is all the more painful for him in that he feels both Ukrainian and Russian. But in the camps he discovered how different the Ukrainians felt. He points out that Russia will show that it is a great nation not by the size of its territory or the number of the people under its yoke, but by the greatness of its actions.

He has also been accused of wanting war, especially the cold war. But he reminds us that he has never resisted outside his spirit. All he asks from Soviet dissidents in their own country, from western leaders in their relations with the Soviet Union, is strength of spirit, a rejection of lies, and care not only for commercial benefits but for the signs of the Spirit. He insists that no one could sensibly find nuclear destruction desirable. There is no need of nuclear armaments. Any war situation only justifies and reinforces internal tyranny.

The *Letter to the Rulers of the Soviet Union* has been misunderstood. Solzhenitsyn states that the two major threats for Russia at the end of the twentieth century are a war of 'religion', inexplicable as such, with China, and ecological disaster. He recommends the 'disestablishment' of Marxism to defuse the controversy with China and because Marxism, like capitalism, conceives of no other relation with nature than domination and exploitation. Marxism in Russia today is extended and articulated by means of a gigantic official propaganda apparatus, and is financed by all taxpayers. He asks Russian Marxism (if it is not already dead) to show its vitality by forgoing that state aid. Its supporters alone should support it. The kind of secularization is necessary that Christian ideology underwent in the Europe of the Enlightenment.

The abandonment of ideocracy and of expensive efforts to export revolution to the four corners of the globe, and of an excessive armaments policy, would allow a reassessment of the vast North-Eastern territory; Russia could become an open world. In the pioneer regions it could establish communities with a human dimension where the economy would respect the environment.

This return to the interior in space should be accompanied by a return to the interior of the soul. The disestablishment of Marxism would allow freedom to explore the spiritual domain. Solzhenitsyn asks for no privileges for Christianity, even though he sets all his hopes (for Russia and the world) on a firm Christian renewal. But that would be meaningful only in freedom. The Churches and religion in the USSR must be allowed to organize themselves as they wish, to develop their worship and teaching and spread unconstrainedly. Only a spiritual renewal would enable the real problems of Soviet society (such as the situation of women and the demoralization of young people) to be solved.

For Solzhenitsyn, this development, for the present at any rate, can continue only within the authoritarian structures which still exist in Russia. The social can only crystallize the cultural. We have to ensure the chances of a new civilization which could gradually develop new forms of societies. Until then, we have to persuade the present ruling class to take up its responsibilities, not in terms of a dead ideology, but in accordance with people as they are and the land as it is. Authoritarianism has to be combatted at all levels by a return to the original structure of 'soviets', of councils, of partial self-control. These 'councils' will gain freedom from the Party's tutelage, and new élites will be born in a free cultural environment, to be continually renewed. These élites will gradually assume political responsibility.

Solzhenitsyn's conception of society is Slavophile and Orthodox. It makes the social relative to the spiritual; it emphasizes conviviality and communitarianism — an ecclesiology of communion. It rejects the utopian dream of integral conviviality, and prefers a tension with the inevitable vertical structures (themselves relativized at the highest level by a duality of élites founded on freedom of spirit and a relationship with nature which is not only one of domination but one of respect and spiritualization).

I think, on reading certain passages in Book Five of the *Archipelago* on the revolt of the *zeks*, that Solzhenitsyn sees the rise and multiplication of soviets in the spring and summer of 1917 as a positive creation of the Russian people which would have been fruitful in another context. In describing the major varieties of spiritual resistance in the camps, Solzhenitsyn says that it would only be right to include the life of an exemplary socialist (his personal qualities, and the assurance of his convictions) and something of the trials he has suffered.

Solzhenitsyn is not to be classified rigorously. We must listen through and perhaps even beyond him, to the really profound note in his work, which is the joint theme of death and resurrection.

Paris, Sunday May 2nd 1976, the Feast of the Apostle Thomas

*What I should like to do is make sure the
flickering candle of our soul stays alight till
it reaches one more witness. The essential thing
is that it should not be snuffed out in our
century, in this century of steel and the atom,
this cosmic, energetic, cybernetic century of ours . . .
And then, in the twenty-first century, let men do
what they will with it.*

(Alex, in *Candle in the Wind*).

DATE DUE

GAYLORD · · PRINTED IN U.S.A.